ORGANIZING FOR SUSTAINABILITY

ORGANIZING FOR SUSTAINABLE EFFECTIVENESS

Series Editors: Susan Albers Mohrman,
                Abraham B. (Rami) Shani,
                Peter Docherty,
                Christopher G. Worley

ORGANIZING FOR SUSTAINABLE EFFECTIVENESS
VOLUME 1

ORGANIZING FOR SUSTAINABILITY

EDITED BY

SUSAN ALBERS MOHRMAN

Center for Effective Organizations,
Marshall School of Business,
University of Southern California,
Los Angeles, CA, USA

ABRAHAM B. (RAMI) SHANI

California Polytechnic State University,
San Luis Obispo, CA, USA and
Politecnico di Milano, Milan, Italy

United Kingdom – North America – Japan
India – Malaysia – China

Emerald Group Publishing Limited
Howard House, Wagon Lane, Bingley BD16 1WA, UK

First edition 2011

Copyright © 2011 Emerald Group Publishing Limited

Reprints and permission service
Contact: booksandseries@emeraldinsight.com

British Library Cataloguing in Publication Data
A catalogue record for this book is available from the British Library

ISBN: 978-0-85724-557-1
ISSN: 2045-0605 (Series)

Emerald Group Publishing
Limited, Howard House,
Environmental Management
System has been certified by
ISOQAR to ISO 14001:2004
standards

Awarded in recognition of
Emerald's production
department's adherence to
quality systems and processes
when preparing scholarly
journals for print

INVESTOR IN PEOPLE

CONTENTS

LIST OF CONTRIBUTORS

Hilary Bradbury-Huang	Management Division of Oregon Health & Science University (OHSU), Portland, OR, USA
Peter Docherty	Centre for Healthcare Improvement and the Division of Quality Sciences, Institute for Technology Organization and Economics, Chalmers University of Technology, Gothenburg, Sweden
Ann E. Feyerherm	Graziadio School of Business and Management, Pepperdine University, Irvine, CA, USA
Svante Lifvergren	Skaraborg Hospital Group, Skövde, Sweden
Philip Mirvis	Boston College, Boston, MA, USA
Susan Albers Mohrman	Center for Effective Organizations, Marshall School of Business, University of Southern California, Los Angeles, CA, USA
Sally Breyley Parker	Currere, Inc., Cleveland, OH, USA
Jan Green Rebstock	Port of Los Angeles, San Pedro, CA, USA; School of Policy, Planning and Development, University of Southern California, Los Angeles, CA, USA
Abraham B. (Rami) Shani	Orfalea College of Business, California Polytechnic State University, San Luis Obispo, CA, USA; Politecnico di Milano, Milan, Italy

Christopher G. Worley   Center for Effective Organizations,
Marshall School of Business, University
of Southern California and Pepperdine
University, Los Angeles, CA, USA

INTRODUCTION TO THE SERIES "ORGANIZING FOR SUSTAINABLE EFFECTIVENESS"

Welcome to the first volume of the series "Organizing for Sustainable Effectiveness." The series provides a platform for scholars and practitioners to share new research-based insights about the organizing imperatives associated with achieving sustainable economic, environmental, and social effectiveness. The series will explore and illuminate the development of sustainable systems, with a special focus on reporting theoretically informed, empirically based, and rigorously created knowledge to guide purposeful design approaches. The intent is to provide actionable knowledge about the processes, organization and work designs, system regulation, and continuous learning approaches that enable simultaneous focus on and advancing of economic, social, and environmental outcomes through time.

There has been a recent burgeoning of interest by commercial and civil organizations, among citizens, in many companies, industries, regions, countries, and communities, and from governments in building new approaches to address the complex problems that threaten humanity and the earth. These include challenges associated with climate change; environmental degradation; population growth and global economic growth and the associated resource shortages and competition; demographic shifts in both developed and developing nations that threaten the capability of nation states to deliver important infrastructure and services; social and economic inequities and unrest; and changes in expectations and aspirations around the globe that are putting an ever-increasing demand on the limited resources of the earth. Accelerated generation of knowledge to address these challenges is badly needed.

These pressing global issues are being addressed by academics and organizations who have taken the broad lens of social responsibility and the more specific focus on environmental sustainability. The argument has been advanced that with the proper leadership, focus, and investment, organizations can introduce practices that positively impact their "footprint" not only by reducing carbon emissions, but more broadly by decreasing negative and increasing positive impact on the social and economic challenges being faced by humanity. Yet these practices are not widespread, and there is evidence of considerable slip back during times of economic pressure, such as during the 2008–2009 global recession.

There is concern that the focus on social and environmental responsibility by management in many cases is largely motivated by concerns of image and public relations, so-called "greening," instead of becoming embedded in the values, business models, and organizing approaches of the company. Even the most robust case studies of companies that are becoming well known for social responsibility often boil down to the implementation of particular initiatives rather than a corporation-wide commitment to fundamental changes in the organization's capabilities with respect to "triple bottom line" outcomes for the company and its many stakeholders.

This book series will highlight research and practice aimed at understanding how organizations, individually and in partnership with others can develop a continuous, unfaltering focus on sustainable functioning. The series is predicated on a belief that the earth and the global economy, and society are approaching key limits that require change in how we function. It will examine how current organizing approaches and assumptions need to change given the expanded purposes of acting responsibly toward all stakeholders, and contributing to a world that is sustainable through time. We believe the needed change is fundamental and goes beyond the imperative for every organization to get its own house in order. It includes changes in the relationships among various stakeholders and blurring of the boundaries between organizations and other elements of the environment in which they operate. It entails the creation of shared leadership to unleash the ideas, energies, and commitment of diverse and often geographically dispersed stakeholders. Solving the problems of sustainable effectiveness requires a greatly increased capacity to innovate and change, to redesign organizational systems and processes, and to develop new competencies and capabilities.

Underpinning the research that will be highlighted in this book series is the view that we are striving to achieve sustainable effectiveness in complex, interdependent systems populated by a wide variety of independent actors – people, governments, NGOs, and organizations – each with its own purposes. Behavior is difficult to predict, change is relentless, and our actions have both intended and unintended impacts on the markets, societies, communities, and ecosystems in which we operate and upon which we depend for their own survival. To thrive in such complexity, we both compete and collaborate to secure the resources we need to accomplish our purposes. We form and structure relationships with other actors to combine mutual resources and coordinate actions in a way that enables them to more efficiently and effectively accomplish their different or similar purposes. Our strategies and the relationships we form will define the changing contours of the world in which we live, and contribute to its sustainability as well as to our own within it.

Achieving sustainable effectiveness is only possible if we accept and internalize our responsibility for our impacts on the ecosystems in which we exist. Our health through time depends on the health of the ecosystem itself. The important problems being faced by humanity cannot be addressed within the confines of single organizations – and organizations cannot be sustainable if they accomplish short-term gain while weakening the capacity of the system from which they draw their sustenance. Organizations can only be sustainable if they learn new ways of operating where they contribute to the current and future effectiveness of the larger systems of which they are part. This fact requires new ways of examining organizations, new models of organizational effectiveness, and new capabilities among the various actors in the ecosystem.

We cannot fully understand models of sustainable performance by focusing on single organizations and conceiving of them solely as resource-acquiring and wealth-accruing input/output systems. Although clearly each organization has to get its house in order to be sustainable, it will do this by arriving at new understandings of its purposes. In addition, it will learn to interrelate in new ways with customers, communities, regulators, suppliers, employees, and even competitors that enable the ecosystem to be healthy. Building a sustainable world will require the transformation of whole industries, regions, global supply chains, and communities to achieve the highly interdependent economic, social, and environmental outcomes necessary for humankind to prosper through time. This is a tall order for humanity, given centuries of organizing for local optimization and a global economy that has been guided by the pursuit of wealth, often at the expense of social and ecological concerns.

Human presence is differentiated from the natural environment by our ability to learn and invent. In generating knowledge about how to organize for sustainability, we therefore have to look at the ways we establish purpose, learn, and invent solutions. How individuals, organizations, groups of organizations, networks, and communities are learning to operate in a sustainable manner will be a major focus of the book series. Our intent is to yield knowledge to fuel learning systems that rapidly disseminate knowledge that yields, protects, and preserves the variety of solutions and responses required for the ongoing evolution of societies and ecosystems.

The books in this series will be the product of the rapidly expanding global community of scholars and practitioners deeply concerned about the challenges facing humanity, and interested in collaborating to accelerate knowledge generation and dissemination. Urgent challenges face humanity if we are to sustain ourselves given the rate of growth of the global population and economy, and to use the incredible profusion of new scientific and technical knowledge to create a sustainable future. Many organizations have already embarked on change processes designed to become more sustainably effective. It is imperative that we learn from them and accelerate the generation of knowledge about how to organize for sustainable effectiveness that can inform the transitions that are required.

The path to a sustainable future is a journey full of uncertainty. It will involve contesting values and interests, require fundamental transformations in the assumptions and purposes underpinning economic, political, and social activities, and demand a new relationship between humanity and the natural environment. This is perilous territory in which we must apply standards of rigor and vigilance to make sure that we contribute to a well-grounded knowledge base rather than prescriptions based on hope and enthusiasm alone. Our intent is to bring to this series a variety of perspectives, disciplines, and cultures. Through the dialogue among many communities of practice we hope to link many theories, preferences, values, and aspirations for the future in a robust learning system that combines the knowledge of theory and practice to address fundamental problems. We are grateful to Emerald Group Publishing for providing the opportunity to build a series in which we and our many colleagues in academia and practice can not only understand and chronicle the journey, but most importantly can generate knowledge to guide it.

Susan Albers Mohrman
Abraham B. (Rami) Shani
Peter Docherty
Christopher G. Worley
Editors

We dedicate this volume to Peter Docherty, a friend and scholar. Peter brings joy, laughter, and wisdom to us all.

ACKNOWLEDGMENTS

ACKNOWLEDGMENTS

Producing a book like this one requires the help of many talented individuals. The idea emerged from a working conference on Organizing for Sustainable Effectiveness in October 2008, hosted by the Center for Effective Organizations (CEO) and the Center for Sustainable Cities at the University of Southern California. We would like to acknowledge the academic and practitioner participants who came to that conference to share experiences and learn. They got us interested and excited enough about the potential of organizing for sustainable effectiveness that we and our series co-editors, Peter Docherty and Christopher Worley, developed a vision of a community of inquiry that would learn together through a series of conferences, action research projects, and books. Arienne McCracken does a beautiful job of managing this program, and we are extremely grateful to be working with such a gifted colleague and indispensable team member.

We learned a tremendous amount working with the chapter authors, each of whom came with different perspectives but equally great concern for rigor and richness in describing and analyzing the cases. It was obvious that they felt strongly about sustainability and, as you will see, produced first-rate chapters. We especially appreciate the practitioners who care deeply enough about creating a sustainable world to share their experiences and open up their organization to scrutiny. Several of these practitioners helped author the chapters, but many others gave hours of time talking with us, sharing documents, and connecting us to others in the system who could be key informants about what went on.

Special thanks go to the director of the Center for Effective Organizations, Edward E. Lawler III, for having founded CEO, a research center dedicated to increasing the effectiveness of organizations, for employees, customers, society, and shareholders. It is a very special center that supports collaborative research with companies and other stakeholders, and provides a home to researchers who want to advance theory and practice. The dean of the Marshall School of Business at USC, James Ellis, is totally supportive of that vision. The dean of the Orfalea College of Business, California Polytechnic State University, Dave Christy, is supportive of the vision of collaborative research, as are professors Emilio Bartezzaghi, Cristina Masella, Emanuele Lettieri, and Raffaella Cagliano at the Politecnico di Milano, Milan, Italy.

We are deeply indebted to Chris Hart, Kim Foster, and Emerald Group Publishing for seeing the promise of the series and providing guidance and support. We look forward to working with them, and with many scholars and practitioners, in producing and disseminating useful knowledge about Organizing for Sustainable Effectiveness in the volumes to come.

Last but definitely not least, we would like to thank our families, who have been supportive and loving through the many unrealistic deadlines and concentrated work that has been required to get this ambitious program off the ground. Thanks especially to our wonderful grandchildren, Ava, Madi, and Mia, who make us know that it's really important to worry about a sustainable future.

CHAPTER 1

ORGANIZING FOR SUSTAINABLE EFFECTIVENESS: TAKING STOCK AND MOVING FORWARD

Susan Albers Mohrman and
Abraham B. (Rami) Shani

ABSTRACT

The large number of publications about sustainability and sustainable development that have been published during the past decade has dealt largely with the science of sustainability, the content of sustainability initiatives, and increasingly with the need to more closely link the economic, environmental, and social purposes and operating logic of the firm. Recent literature stresses the inherent social nature of the challenges to aggressively moving to more sustainable ways of operating for the well-being of our planet, society, economy, organizations, and humans. Despite rich case examples, guidance on how to organize to achieve the triple bottom line is limited. We take stock of the current state of knowledge, using an adaptive complex system perspective to articulate the challenges of organizing for sustainable effectiveness. Most of the global economy and the knowledge upon which it is predicated carry a logic of resource abundance even in the face of increasing competition for scarce resources, and a singular focus on economic outcomes. We argue that the development of new capabilities to address triple bottom line sustainability requires a

Organizing for Sustainability
Organizing for Sustainable Effectiveness, Volume 1, 1–40
ISSN: 2045-0605/doi:10.1108/S2045-0605(2011)0000001006

change in that logic and requires new rules of interaction, new organizational and interorganizational designs, and new ways of learning. The premise is that systems can build on their inherent capabilities to learn and to act collectively in order to adapt. We argue that by working together to collaboratively explore how to organize for sustainability, academics and practitioners can accelerate knowledge generation and progress. This chapter provides the theoretical framing context for the chapters to come.

Keywords: Sustainability; sustainable practice; sustainable effectiveness; new capability development; complex adaptive system; designing for sustainable effectiveness; learning mechanisms and processes; collaborative research; knowledge generation

In the twenty-first century, organizing for sustainable effectiveness has become increasingly challenging and fraught with uncertainty. The requirements of the global economy and the escalating population are approaching the "carrying capacity" of the earth on which we live, while the global economy has seen rapidly developing economies in many nations, increased affluence, and aspirations, expectations, and means for material comfort. Near and longer term impacts of the global economy are widely believed to demand adaptive and mitigative measures to avoid or ameliorate ecological, social, and economic disruption. Globalization has also been accompanied by a growing and highly visible division between the haves and have-nots within and between countries, along with increased potential for social unrest. Aging and stable or declining populations in developed nations and youthful, growing populations in poor nations portend certain but not fully understood tensions and discontinuities in the global economy that supports us all.

Burgeoning complexity related to global interconnectedness and rapid change yields organizational, societal, ecological, and economic landscapes that are difficult to predict and navigate, and impossible to control. Individuals, organizations, families, communities, and governments deal with only one certainty: that the actions they take and the decisions they make today must prepare them for an uncertain future. Achieving sustainable effectiveness requires agility informed by frameworks of thought and action in which actors see themselves as contributing to, operating within, and dependent on the larger systems of which they are part, and take future scenarios into account while acting in the present. Sustainable effectiveness of each actor depends on the overall sustainability of complex ecosystems – of the natural environments, markets, and societies that define the contexts in which we function.

A large literature has been generated about sustainability, and many organizations, governments, communities, and citizens have focused on it. Yet, given how quickly the limits of the current models of the global economy are being approached, we must accelerate the rate at which we learn to operate differently. In this first volume of the Emerald series *Organizing for Sustainable Effectiveness*, our goal is to learn from some of the pioneers articulating these challenges and organizing to address them.

There is an urgent need to grow the knowledge bases to guide the transition. For this reason, each chapter in this volume is crafted to bring together the knowledge of practice and theory. The chapters are based on rich empirical data about particular cases in which organizations are, individually or collectively, working to build a more sustainable future. The authors of these chapters also bring theoretical knowledge to bear on these case examples. In so doing, they test the applicability of the formal knowledge base about management and organizations, while refining, modifying, and extending it to increase its usefulness in addressing the challenges of organizing for sustainable effectiveness. By combining knowledge from multiple stake-holders and multiple disciplines, it is the intention of the authors in this book to contribute to the broader learning discourse through which practical organizing solutions are designed and research-based guidance is provided.

In this introduction, we describe and frame the sustainability challenges being faced by humanity using a complex adaptive systems perspective (Holland, 1995, 1998), and we draw from the literature to examine how the topic of sustainable effectiveness has been approached and what has been learned to date. We focus particularly on the issues of purpose and capabilities development. A capabilities development perspective leads us to suggest that organization design and learning processes are critical to building a sustainable world.

SUSTAINABILITY: THE CHALLENGES OF SURVIVAL IN A COMPLEX SYSTEM

A fundamental predicament for each of us as individuals and organizations trying to prosper in this new millennium is that the contexts around us are changing, in ways that are uncertain and at a speed that is both dizzyingly quick and frustratingly slow. We are, we believe, resourceful and competent, and ready and eager to adapt, *if* we know the new rules of the game, and to what we need to adapt. If we could just get environmental regulations defined, we could adjust our operations accordingly. If we know that consumers are willing to pay for "green" products, we can change out our technology and redesign our products. If we could reduce the uncertainty about our healthcare coverage, we could plan for our future. If we could get a commitment to preserve jobs at home, we could work hard, contribute to the organization we work for, save money, and prepare to be self-sufficient in the future. Yet, the reality is that our health, effectiveness, and perhaps even our survival depend on adapting to a relentless and continuous reconfiguration of the world we have known. In this section, we frame the challenges and use the key tenets of complex adaptive systems to understand how sustainable practices may be created. We argue that the transition to a sustainable global economy can be best accomplished by the advancing of practice and theory, and by the collaborative creation of knowledge.

The Macro Challenges to Sustainable Development

Sustainable development has been defined as meeting "the needs of the present without compromising the ability of future generations to meet their own needs" (Brundtland, 1987). In reality, the future is here. Our current ways of operating are not doing a very good job of meeting the needs of many in the current generation. Today, nine out of ten children under the age of 15 live in developing countries, and 70% of the world's population growth is in countries with average per capita income of under $3,855, increasingly in urbanized areas with extreme poverty and social unrest (Goldstone, 2010). The parts of the world most vulnerable in the face of environmental change have the least resources for adaptation and mitigation, and experience the most severe social impacts (Martens & Ting Chang, 2010). Many of these nations are at the same time experiencing explosive economic development and wealth creation, yet struggling to put in place the infrastructure to address the social and environmental outcomes of that growth. In developed nations as well, governments and populations deal with the social and economic impacts of work and of industries moving around the world. Communities and the individuals within them are faced with unreliable economic bases and with the relentless pressures for lean and often virtual operations and competitiveness with the associated social costs resulting from increased work intensity and insecurity (Docherty, Forslin, & Shani, 2002; Docherty, Kira, & Shani, 2008a). Even in developed nations, the disparity between the haves, with the resources to adapt, and the have-nots, who are most negatively impacted by the externalities, has grown immensely in the last decades (Hart & Christensen, 2002; Brown, 2008).

Advances in global transportation and information technology have enabled global economic connectedness, knowledge exchange, and rapid economic development that have carried with them immeasurable benefits for a large segment of humanity. These forces have also made very apparent our dependence on and vulnerability in the face of macro-level factors that create the context in which we live. Scientists have long pointed out that the natural ecosystems of earth are fundamentally threatened by the patterns of human activity associated with economic growth that disregards the costs of the impacts on the natural environment, treating these as externalities (Stead & Stead, 2009). Many management scholars and organizational leaders have now become concerned that current patterns of economic activity and the ways of life associated with them are unsustainable, and that the time has come, and indeed is short, to build new approaches that enhance rather than deplete the global ecological and social systems in which we exist. In 1997, during the height of unprecedented global economic growth and the building of unprecedented wealth and prosperity, Stuart Hart (1997), among others, pointed out that we face a pressing challenge to develop a sustainable global economy – one that the planet is capable of supporting.

The challenges we face are multifaceted and intertwined. Successfully addressing them entails intentionally altering the patterns of interaction and activities in our complex system in which all of our activities have economic, societal, and environmental impacts. This reality is captured by Elkington's (1997) notion of the "triple bottom line," a management and accounting framework entailing commitment to and measurement of outcomes in all three of these dimensions. The inevitable interplay among economy, environment, and society occurs at all systems levels. The sustainability challenge must be confronted by the nation states that comprise the global whole; by corporations and industries within and across nations, NGOs, and local governments and agencies, large and small, that operate within and across these nation states; and by the citizens, employees, consumers, factories, shops, networks, families, communities, and regions whose behavior and activities comprise the reality we confront.

The forecast is stark, and is no doubt so alarming that it is dismissed by many: If the whole world were to consume natural resources and generate CO_2 at the current European rate, we would need three planets to support us – or five planets if we consumed and polluted at the level of United States (WWF, 2010). This projection is based on the rate of growth of the earth's population (estimated to reach 9.4 billion by 2050), and the increase in the numbers of the middle class with associated material expectations and means. The footprint can be roughly calculated using Ehrich and Ehrich's (1990) formula: Population × Affluence (measured by GDP) × Technological Efficiency. This dire forecast addresses only the resource limits element of the current trajectory of growth, with its obvious implications for competition, collaboration, and the limits to the growth of the global economy. Associated stressors come from the environmental and social impacts of such population and economic growth.

Environmental impacts include climate change and its potentially devastating impact on the economic and physical health and well-being of entire regions and populations, as well as the direct social and ecological impacts of waste, toxicity, and pollution. The biodiversity that is needed for resilient ecosystems is rapidly declining (United Nations Environment Programme, 2007). The pervasive reach but uneven impact of globalization has drawn attention to the associated issues of social justice. Developed nations have exported many of their uncomfortable externalities to emerging economies, including jobs that could not command a living wage in the developed world, and the pollution and toxicity associated with dirty industry. Yet the rapid ascendance of large developing economies such as China and India that will soon surpass developed nations in many measures of economic leadership are rapidly conferring greater power on these nations. Demographic patterns of rapid and often destabilizing population growth in poor nations increase the urgency of bringing these parts of the world into the global economy (Hart, 1997; Goldstone, 2010; Prahalad, 2004). In voice and action, developing and poor nations are demanding a rebalancing of relationships and economic frameworks that may radically reconfigure the patterns of activity, growth, and prosperity in the global economy.

Modernity and global connectedness have yielded macro-level benefits and threats to the population's material, health, and financial well-being. Modern transportation has given us easy access to markets and goods, including fresh foods from around the world, while at the same time resulting in the spewing of greenhouse gases into the atmosphere, and leading to the homogenization of goods and services that threatens cultural diversity. Medical technology has yielded significant advances in treating and preventing disease, and great leaps in life expectancy. Yet even in developed economies, the combination of a growing population, greater costs, and greater longevity have carried with them the associated threats of insufficient healthcare resources to address routine healthcare, let alone to deal with pandemics and global surge of chronic disease, much of which relates to affluence, urbanity, and modern lifestyles.

The global financial system, enabled by advanced information technology, mobility, and the opening of global markets, has provided great opportunities for economic growth, high standards of living, and wealth creation. Yet sophisticated modeling and simulation capabilities have contributed to the proliferation of innovative approaches to creating concentrated wealth based on poorly understood and fundamentally unsound tools and products. The 2008 recession, triggered by defaults on derivative papers, demonstrates that while these created immense wealth for some, they were also capable of seemingly instantaneously throwing the financial "order" into disarray through a complex causal chain that triggered a global recession, wreaking havoc on the financial well-being of citizens throughout the world. Even micro-lending, a financing approach for which Muhammad Yunus received the 2006 Nobel Prize for Peace, that makes small amounts of money available to individuals in poor communities to start up small businesses and build local economies, has almost ground to a halt in some parts of India. Large banks got into the action and started charging interest of up to 50%, and a social and political outcry has resulted as people are increasingly defaulting on their loans and losing their livelihood (Anonymous, 2010). These examples demonstrate the close connection between economic and social dynamics, as financial practices and bubbles grow based on socially constructed understandings and trust, and can collapse just as readily when those understandings and that trust change.

How do we deal with this level of complexity and uncertainty? We tend to rely on what we know and what has worked in the past, and to bring to these issues our cognitive biases and tried and tested heuristics that allowed us to succeed in a simpler world (Hoffman, 2010). We may assume that there will be technological fixes that will allow us to solve these problems and continue with our way of life. We may believe that protectionism – or alternatively, truly open and free trade – will enable us to thrive. We may believe that these problems are developing slowly and unlikely to affect us. We may see them as someone solve problems, or at least someone else's to solve, and believe that our responsibility is simply to be part of successful enterprises that provide jobs and wealth to ourselves and others. In other words, we may believe that we need to get better at what we already know how to do in order to be effective in a world where the context is changing dramatically.

Yet a close examination of the elements of this transitional period shows how fundamental and discontinuous it is, largely because we are facing a world characterized by scarcity. A number of leaders of major global corporations have recognized this new reality, and are actively leading their corporations to change the way they operate. For example, Jeff Immelt, chairman and chief executive officer of General Electric Corporation, believes that the next decades will be about technologies and economies to address issues of scarcity (Mirvis, Googins, & Kinnicutt, 2010). Patrick Cescau, group chief executive officer of Unilever, believes that companies need to plan for a future "where resources are under threat and externalities need to be paid for" (2008, p. 14). And there are many others who are starkly defining the challenge and setting out to find a viable path forward. There is an urgent need to find solutions and models of growth that do not accelerate the looming crises in resources and associated environmental and social damage. We need to find new ways of functioning, new models for managing and organizing, and new ways for the various actors in the complex global economic system to interrelate that enable sustainable development.

The macro threats to our sustainability are overwhelming to most of us, and many of us would like to limit our responsibility and accountability for dealing with them, and especially our liability for our contribution to the problems. For decades we have seen these issues as governments' problems to solve. Yet a global pattern of rising public deficits and reduced public spending means that companies and individuals can no longer expect the polity to pay for their externalities. Some predict that governments will assume a new role in convening others to find solutions (Googins, Mirvis, & Rochlin, 2007) and will look to businesses and the nonprofit sector to work together to achieve economic, environmental, and societal objectives. Even the regulatory role of government is weakened, as fewer, larger firms operate across many borders, yielding a globally integrated economy while global society is politically divided and unable to deal with issues that are inherently global in scope (Sachs, 2008). No one sector and certainly no single organization can solve these problems or create a sustainable future. So it is up to each of us, as agents operating in a complex global system, to individually and collectively find ways to operate and organize that contribute positively to a sustainable future.

Evolution of Sustainable Practice in a Complex System

The important problems facing mankind cannot be solved within the confines of single organizations or entities. Viewing today's complex, highly interdependent world and the more local ecosystems within it as complex adaptive systems provides conceptual leverage on the seemingly intractable problems embedded in current operating principles. It also disabuses us of the notion that top-down and/or governmental control mechanisms can generate the kinds of changes in behavior, patterns of economic and societal activity, and socially and environmentally responsible goals and outcomes that are needed. Yet it offers the hope that actors in this complex space can find ways of interrelating to one another that will yield more sustainable outcomes and impacts.

Complex adaptive systems are composed of many interactive agents, each with its own strategy for adapting to the environment and pursuing its goals (Axelrod & Cohen, 1997). These agents are of multiple types and at multiple levels of aggregation – individuals, companies and other organizations, industries, factories, alliances, governmental entities, and so forth. They act independently and interdependently – collaboratively and competitively – to secure the resources they need to pursue their purposes. Their actions have intended and unintended impacts on the markets, societies, communities, and natural environments in which they operate and on which they depend for their own survival.

The properties of the larger system emerge as a result of the actions and interactions of the various agents who comprise the system. These emergent properties – which would include levels, patterns, and types of social or environmental health or degradation – are not simple aggregations of the impact of individual agents. Nor are impacts of the actions of the agents within the complex system linear. Emergent properties reflect complex, dynamic interactions resulting in outcomes that cannot be fully planned or anticipated. For example, the intended and unintended impact of industry collaborations to create shared measures and standards for environmental or social sustainability may include a focus on incremental increases in outcomes that result in progress in targeted areas. But such collective action by an industry may also stifle true discontinuous innovation because the political processes of collaboration may yield conservative and easily accomplished outcomes that do not spur fundamental innovation. Effort to reduce toxins in the environment by encouraging organic farming by offering higher prices for products from organically farmed crops may inadvertently raise the costs of production in a manner that makes a region vulnerable if the price of organic crops declines because of increasing global supply.

Within earth's vast, complex system are communities – sets of coevolving populations of agents that are tied together by common orientations, dependence on common resources, and interdependence of flows of activities and outcomes. These communities may be geographically defined, or defined by a set of interrelated activities around the globe such as industries and supply chains. The various populations of agents who form a community require resources in order to prosper, and seek them out by inhabiting niches or parts of the ecosystem where they believe they can gain access to them (Hannan & Freeman, 1977). Organizations move their activity to parts of the world that are rich in the resources they require – natural resources and social resources such as skilled or cheap labor, raw materials, and markets. They may set up relationships with other entities who bring synergies and scale or access that give them an advantage with respect to achieving an ongoing flow of the resources they need for success. For example, Western oil companies set up joint ventures with local government-owned oil companies in developing nations to ensure access to reserves. Retail coffee companies may set up preferred purchasing arrangements and invest in local rural communities to ensure a flow of fair-trade coffee beans. In the process, the various members of the community may develop new capabilities, and they contribute to changing patterns of activities, network relationships, and outcomes in the overall ecosystem.

Organizations have been described as learning and changing through coevolutionary relationships with their environment – through relationships that are interdependent, mutually causal, and iterative (Stead & Stead, 2009), such that changes in the macro environment emerge in mutual interaction with change in its component inhabitants. There is an ongoing need for adaptation. Drawing on institutional theory, Hoffman (1999) talks about organizational fields, in which organizations evolve in concert with the demands and institutional forces in their environments. Environmentalism has become increasingly deeply embedded in the chemical industry, for example, as companies have found increasingly sustainable ways to operate. Initiated by Du Pont, the industry has collaboratively participated in the Responsible Care initiative (Hart & Milstein, 1999) through which standards have been set and knowledge shared. The environment has responded with greater and greater demands for environmental responsibility, as stakeholders have become increasingly aware of the negative consequences of chemicals and have come to believe that these are not necessary or tolerable (Hoffman, 1999). Companies such as DuPont have established new ways to relate to their various stakeholders, and in so doing have adopted strategies to meet financial, environmental, and social expectations. For example, research and development is focusing on the use of bio-based feedstock rather than fossil fuels in creating new materials (Hoffman, 2010).

A key to understanding the emergence of system level properties is to discover the mechanisms that guide the interactions among the agents within it, and in its various subpopulations and niches (Holland, 1995; Monge & Contractor, 2003). "Rules" have developed in complex systems. They characterize the system's interactions as each agent pursues adaptation through experience, mimicry, and learning (Holland, 1995). "Move work to low-cost regions" is a rule that has characterized many industries in the global economy. "Seek to avoid paying the cost of and having liability for externalities" is another. Rules such as these have underpinned global capitalism, and have contributed to the operating characteristics and outcomes, both positive and negative, of the global economy.

The hope for developing a sustainable global economy is that new meta rules – such as "take actions that build long-term sustainability" – could come to guide actions and interactions. Unlike natural ecosystems, the strategies of actors in socially fashioned systems are based on purposes, interpretation, and anticipation of possible futures (Leydesdorff, 2001). Agents in a social system are able to engage in intentional adaptive strategizing (Knight, 2002), borrowing of ideas (Campbell, 1960), repurposing, and learning that guide their adaptation to a changing environment and contribute to its evolution. This capability for intentional, purpose-related activity provides the possibility that new patterns of interaction can be purposefully established to alter the overall outcomes of the system and its actors. For example, Beghelli, a highly successful Italian lighting firm, has purposefully decided to stay operationally rooted in the Emilia Romagna region of Italy, and to develop the local knowledge and resources it needs rather than moving operations to low-cost locations (Del Bosco, 2010). Walmart is increasing its dependence on local food, to reduce the need to transport food around the earth and the associated greenhouse gas emissions. And there are many other organizations making decisions based on principles of sustainability.

The patterns of interaction that characterize today's global economy have evolved during a period of ecological munificence, when mankind could continue to seek and find new frontiers of economic and natural resource abundance. Ecological niches evolve and go through life cycles, characterized by changing patterns of interaction among their inhabitants and changes in the abundance of needed resources (Astley, 1985). New niches tend to be characterized by few actors pursuing many resources. But as the number of actors grows and the niche becomes overpopulated for the resources it provides, competition increases and actors form various kinds of alliances and symbiotic relationships to ensure a resource stream. Communities emerge to coordinate the assemblage, pursuit, securing, and distribution of resources.

During the industrial and postindustrial eras, we have had an era of rapid growth of population and several centuries of exploration and global economic and societal expansion to access what seemed to be an endless supply of resources. If our population, our governments, and our corporations step up to the challenge that we are moving toward a future where the demands for resources may surpass the carrying capacity of the earth, it can be hoped, and possibly predicted: (1) that organizations may come to believe that it is necessary to repurpose themselves to preserve resources in order to secure a sustainable future; and (2) that they will interrelate symbiotically and collaboratively with other agents in their environment to adapt to the changing environmental context and create a sustainable future.

Although top-down and hierarchical direction are insufficient to change a complex system, such systems can be highly responsive to seemingly small inputs that create amplifying effects (Axelrod & Cohen, 1997), and to discontinuous innovations that provide models or open up possibilities for action by many elements of the larger system. Requiring company transparency around measures of key indicators of environmental and social impact might be one such intervention that would have ripple effects throughout the system as companies have to worry not only about measuring and reporting, but also about improving in order to satisfy the many stakeholders that are now serving in watchdog roles. Capping carbon emissions and setting up a market for carbon credits stimulates far-reaching change efforts by companies to derive financial advantage. The bottom of the pyramid templates and examples described by Prahalad (2004) offer new approaches to doing business in emerging markets in a locally appropriate manner and lay out frameworks that have achieved broad dissemination and impact. This perspective has fundamentally altered some basic assumptions and strategies of global firms. Backwards innovation results from designing products for poor communities and introducing them back into developed nations, turning on end the assumption that innovation inevitably is a linear progression in the direction of increasing sophistication and functionality of product (Prahalad, 2004). By describing a different way to interact with poor communities and a different economic model for doing so, Prahalad and others have catalyzed the emergence of new rules of commercial interaction among the companies, governments, and populations in these communities.

It has been argued that complex activities are inevitably self-organizing (Fukuyama, 1999), and that they cannot be fully externally or hierarchically controlled. In fact, governments and hierarchies rely on the various agents in their domains to find solutions to the problems of complexity. Order arises from local interactions of actors even if those actors are not aware of how their actions contribute to the larger order (Holland, 1995, 1998). New rules of interaction emerge as organizations try out new behaviors, experience success, and incorporate the knowledge they gain and the new behaviors into their routines. The literature points to four conditions for self-organizing systems (Monge & Contractor, 2003, pp. 95–97). First, self-organization happens when a system is not in equilibrium and the agents in the system seek to adapt to change, a condition that currently characterizes our global economy. The other three conditions relate to knowledge and learning capability. Are the components of the system self-generative – that is, can they self-create and renew? Does knowledge flow between components, and result in greater capability and the creation of new knowledge? And, is there a "requisite variety" of knowledge (Ashby, 1956, p. 64) to address the problems of interest? Achieving sustainability will only happen if we can accelerate self-organization toward that purpose. The last three conditions provide guidance as to the kinds of rules of interaction that must come to be prevalent in our industries and societies to establish an accelerated cycle of generation and adoption of sustainable practice.

Many organizations, governments, NGOs, and other entities are engaged in learning about how best to operate and interrelate to contribute to a sustainable future. It is only through changes in how we behave that new rules of interaction will emerge to underpin a sustainable global economy and societies. Organizations and societies that are pioneering approaches to adapt to the new world of resource shortages are inventing and learning on behalf of the rest of us. We need to learn from their efforts and broadly disseminate knowledge to enable self-organization and to accelerate the transition to a sustainable future (Mohrman & Worley, 2010).

There will not be one best approach to achieve sustainability, but rather principles that guide behavior and lead to many models of sustainable effectiveness. Healthy systems require diversity. Different organizations face different sustainability challenges and opportunities to impact on the sustainability of their contexts. Manufacturing firms are substantially altering their carbon footprints by creating closed loop product life cycles in which only heat and biodegradable wastes are returned to the environment. Product innovation firms are inventing new green materials and products that vastly reduce the amount of energy required to build and operate infrastructural capabilities. Local firms, governments, NGOs, and citizens may band together and create synergies that allow a region to become economically self-sufficient, green, and socially sustainable (Worley & Breyley Parker, 2011). Previously unconnected elements of a regional healthcare system may find synergies and integrate processes to yield higher quality healthcare delivery and improved outcomes, while reducing the resources consumed and the footprint generated.

The problems that must be solved emerge and change through time and differ for actors in different niches. Diverse models of operations and approaches to creating a sustainable future are required to create and maintain the requisite variety to match the diversity of agents, cultures, communities, and niches, and to fuel ongoing evolution of practice in the uncertain environments we face.

Companies and other organizations are key actors shaping the changes in the environmental and social contexts that we all inhabit. Through innovation, strategies, business and operating models, and through the way they organize and the relationships they set up with other stakeholders, companies profoundly impact the contexts in which they operate, and in turn are constrained and enabled by those contexts. We need to generate and share knowledge about innovations, new business models, new patterns of interaction among the various components of the ecosystem, new organizational forms, new forms of governance, incentives, and regulatory elements that will constitute sustainable systems and accelerate the transitions that are required.

Evolution of Theory for a Sustainable Economy

Our theories of organizing coevolve with the societies, economies, and ecologies that are the focus of our knowledge creation activities. The social sciences examine human artifacts – the political and economic systems, organizations, communities, and societies that humanity has created as people have pursued survival and other purposes. The variety and forms of these artifacts and their operating characteristics have changed through time, as new problems have been solved in order to accomplish changing purposes. Theories have evolved to keep pace with this change, although practice has tended to precede advances in theory (Pfeffer, 2007; Mohrman & Lawler, 2011). This lagging role of academic research and theory development has meant that academic research focuses on the past and has not been very useful to practitioners charged with creating the future.

Changes in organizing models are emerging as organizations become aware of the limits of current approaches, and their threats to a sustainable future. Academic research can help accelerate the transition only if academics collaborate with practitioners to understand these new approaches, and more importantly, to provide a knowledge base to guide them rather than simply understand them after the fact (Mohrman & Lawler, 2011; Mohrman & Mohrman, 2011).

To meet this challenge, academic frameworks must be tested against the new reality and altered as needed to provide more powerful understandings of current dynamics shaping our world. The social sciences developed during the height of the industrial era that entailed scientific and organizational breakthroughs to harness seemingly unlimited resources. Economists have studied and modeled the dynamics of economies where each individual and organization pursued its own interests, as the infrastructure for a global economy emerged that enables commerce and the movement of wealth around the world. Management and organizational scholars have studied organizational forms that developed over time to increase efficiency, growth, reach, and exploitative capacity of that economy and to address human needs and purposes. Political scientists have studied the role of the nation state in the regulation of economic activity and the distribution of its benefit, the changing bases of power and legitimacy, and the breakdowns that have occurred within and between populations and governments as various actors position themselves for benefit. Sociologists have studied groups and social interactions, and the relationship between those with and without power as societies have unfolded. The perspectives of each of these disciplines are potentially useful but each may need to adjust its assumptions rapidly to fit with the changing realities faced by the individuals, organizations, societies, economies, and polities that it studies.

Early work on sustainability issues has focused largely on the "green" arena, and has been the purview of the hard sciences and engineering. Knowledge of the physical and natural ecological limits of growth has motivated significant attention to understand, prognosticate, and generate technologies for mitigation of and adaptation to the negative impacts of man's behavior on the natural environment. There are many initiatives, regulations, plans, and projects to increase sustainability, coming from businesses, governments, NGOs, and communities. These include recycling programs, energy efficiency and other carbon reduction schemes, the adoption of alternative energy sources, water preservation and toxicity remediation, resource replenishment and conservation, zero waste and closed cycle product and service provision that return only heat and biodegradable waste to the environment. These approaches in many cases have achieved measurable impacts on environmental indicators. Yet we still face the challenge of scaling them up for global impact amidst a burgeoning population and global economy. It is indisputable that science and technological advances are needed, but we also face the challenge of building new organizing approaches that incorporate attention to the environmental and social impacts of human activity into the operating values and logic of organization and communities. The transition challenge is fundamentally a social one – of repurposing and behavioral change (Hoffman, 2010), and of implementing scientific and technological advances in practice (Ting Chang, Martens, & Amelung, 2010).

Theories are needed to understand and help deal with the changes in practice required to be sustainable in a global economy of scarcity, uncertainty, and constraint. Current economic theories have not taken into account the cost of natural resources or of other externalities. Current concepts of liability and accountability do not fit with the complex system interdependencies and the nonlinear cause and effect that cuts across political boundaries (Ting Chang et al., 2010). Fewer and bigger firms whose activities (and associated externalities) cut across political boundaries have decreased the ability of nation states to regulate negative external costs and have undermined the conditions for efficient market allocation. Political divisions between nation states lead to contention over the rules of global commerce and the distribution of benefit that make it difficult to make progress on truly global issues and call out for new conceptualizations of system governance and emergence. Micro-economically based decision frameworks are overwhelmed by the uncertainty of inputs, changing expectations of stakeholders regarding outputs, and geopolitical, macro-economic, and technological forces that are not controllable. Geographically dispersed organizations find their effectiveness threatened by a myriad of diverse local forces and their opportunities dependent on finding many different context-specific ways of operating while at the same time trying to derive the benefits of scale and scope. Issues of centralization and decentralization of decision making now have geopolitical and socioeconomic ramifications and implications for the survival of the ecosystem.

To contribute knowledge useful in crafting a sustainable future, the purposes of research and theory must change. Positivistic social sciences grew up to understand and explain the unfolding of institutions, economic systems, and individual and collective behavior – not to influence it. In taking an arm's-length view and examining collective patterns, we explain the past, but do not predict or enable future effectiveness. As the urgency increases to find solutions to the problems humanity faces, the purposes of theory-based investigation are being questioned. For management and organizational research, for example, Sumantra Ghoshal (2005) advocated a fundamental change in purpose when he stated that researchers in business schools should be creating knowledge that makes the world a better place. He pointed out that values are inherent in all theory and research, and he decried not only prevailing, supposedly "objective" methodologies but also the prevailing economics-centric theoretical base underpinning much organizational research. In his view, the emphasis on short-term shareholder value and the basic assumptions that economic self-interest should drive organizational activities result in minimal attention being paid to other human values. These would include the values of preserving sustainable natural environments and building sustainable societies.

The world we all live in is being shaped by the way organizations decide to operate and interact with other entities in their chosen niches. Modern history has been characterized by a continual emergence of new organizational forms. Methodologies that assume stability are not appropriate (Starkey, Hatcheul, & Tempest, 2009); theory must be applied and generated to enable and learn from new ways of organizing to achieve human purpose. Knowledge relevant to sustainable effectiveness will come from focusing on the outliers – those organizations that are ahead of others in finding organizing approaches that address the opportunities and challenges inherent in achieving a sustainable way of operating. Synthetic, design-oriented approaches rather than analytic approaches are required to yield knowledge that contributes to solutions relevant to the problems organizations face (Simon, 1969; Avenier, 2010; Mohrman, Mohrman, & Tenkasi, 1997; Van Aken, 2005; Romme, 2003). Organizations must be examined in relationship to the contexts in which they are situated, and approached through interdisciplinary, multi-method, and collaborative methodologies that can capture the complexity of the phenomena, the approaches being taken, and the multiple purposes of the various actors (Mohrman & Lawler, 2011).

ORGANIZING FOR SUSTAINABLE EFFECTIVENESS: VALUES AND PURPOSE

As mentioned above, the ability of humans to plan and to act collectively to design artifacts and create contexts in which they can survive and achieve purposes differentiates social systems from natural systems. Humans can change behavior and thus alter the attributes of and the rules in play in their systems. Humanity has gone through different eras in which the natural environment was first respected as the embodiment of gods, and more recently viewed as the source of resources to be exploited to support the worldly purposes of people. Attitudes toward and the treatment of natural resources have coevolved with the development of technology that has enabled the exploitation of natural resources and cultures reflecting this perspective. Most recently, advances in information, communication, and computational technology have enabled global reach and integration – with economic growth based on access to and exploitation of both natural and human resources around the globe.

If indeed we are approaching the limits of an economy and global societies based on unbridled exploitation of natural and human resources, we can expect that new conceptualizations of nature and new patterns of economic and social behavior will emerge to adapt to this new reality. Patterns of behavior in a complex system depend on the level of resource munificence, and changes in the latter lead to new patterns of interaction, both collaborative and competitive (Astley, 1985). New rules emerge that are based on and shape these changing collaborative and competitive patterns.

The weight of responsibility for the viability of our systems is on humans, and the characteristics of the emerging system will depend on our ingenuity and the choices we make. Our choices derive from our purposes. The study of sustainable organizing must start by examining purpose. Organizations that are leading the way toward establishing a sustainable way of operating are repurposing themselves (Googins et al., 2007). Purpose expands beyond the narrow focus on exploiting resources to make quarterly profit for shareholders to include a broader scope of outcomes and stakeholders and a future-oriented time horizon. Expanded purposes incorporate systemic outcomes and are appropriate in a world in which environmental, social, and economic dynamics, costs, and benefits cannot be disentangled. They rest on the understanding that a sustainable company and organization requires resources, healthy environments, and healthy communities in which to operate now and in the future, and that stewardship of a corporation requires stewardship of the earth and its societies.

Many organizations have long had philanthropy programs, and have contributed financial and human resources to various causes in the communities in which they operate. In the past, such philanthropic activity has largely been tangential to the strategy, operations, and purposes of the organization. Many organizations have not leveraged financial or knowledge resources to build sustainable capabilities of individuals and communities, but have simply given handouts that may in fact have perpetuated the dependency of recipients. Philanthropy has been used to establish a positive reputation in the community as a socially responsible company, and to convey legitimacy and secure a "license" to operate.

Leaders and members in many organizations have come to appreciate that their activities positively and negatively impact well-being and sustainability in the broader environment and have ramifications for the current generation and for the kind of world in which their children and grandchildren will live. At the very least, some are realizing that the current patterns of global activity are accompanied by problems that they have a stake in and a responsibility to help solve. Often under the designation of Corporate Social Responsibility (CSR), attention to these broader purposes is starting to be seen not as philanthropy, but rather as core to the purpose of the firm and intertwined with its strategy and sustainable effectiveness (Arnold, 2010). To make a difference, this shift in purpose must be accompanied by an attendant shift in the values that shape behavior.

Value has been used in two ways in the sustainability literature. One use relates to the mission of the firm and the value that it intends to deliver to its various stakeholders (e.g., Louche, Idowu, & Filho, 2010a). A second use of value refers to the values – cultural norms and personal beliefs – that guide behaviors (e.g., Mirvis et al., 2010). This second use also relates to the ethical foundations of the firm. The two conceptualizations of value are in fact integral in shaping practice (Laszlo, 2008). We discuss these two aspects of value next, starting with the value the firm intends to deliver to stakeholders, and then discussing several values that are enabling the shift to sustainable functioning.

Value to Stakeholders

Working to achieve sustainable effectiveness involves an expansion of the stakeholder set to which an organization intends to contribute value. Value comes to be defined as contribution to the sustainable well-being of societal stakeholders – all those who are impacted by the activities of the organization – including but not limited to the traditional focus on shareholders (e.g., Maas & Boons, 2010). Accepting responsibility to deliver stakeholder value indicates a shift from seeing activity designed to contribute to the environment or to society as a cost, to seeing it as part of the value that the firm yields (Figge & Hahn, 2005). For example, rather than seeing pollution mitigation as a cost of doing business, it is seen as value contributed that creates healthy communities in which to operate. This is a stark departure from the traditional concern that applying shareholder resources to societal issues represents a moral hazard.

The "sweet spot" for the organization is when delivering societal and environmental value aligns with the financial imperatives of the firm to deliver value to owners, such as in instances when customers are demanding and willing to pay more for fair-trade products or products that are completely recyclable. The development of innovative products, such as small and efficient generators with a much broader market potential in emerging markets aligns customer interests in lower cost and lower polluting infrastructure with the company's interests in building growth markets for its products. Such a convergence also is present when adopting sustainable practices, such as lower energy consumption, results in lower costs.

Adding a time element to the measurement of value results in greater potential convergence between investing in social and environmental outcomes and sustainable economic returns for the firm. For example, the investment by firms operating in developing nations in mitigation techniques that result in healthy water supplies for communities helps assure viable communities and markets in which to operate into the future, healthy employees and families, and good reputation that diminishes the likelihood of a sudden political backlash against the company. Similarly, firms that are focusing on creating work systems that promote the health and development of employees and provide them a platform for contributing to the well-being of their families and communities are simultaneously developing their own performance capabilities and delivering social value well beyond gainful employment.

The organization may articulate a mission that includes the delivery of value to shareholders, employees, society, and the environment. Products, services, and operations may be examined to ensure that they enhance rather than deplete well-being. Unilever's Vitality Mission is an example: "To add vitality to life by meeting everyday needs for nutrition, hygiene and personal care brands that help people feel good, look good, and get more out of life" (Mirvis et al., 2010, p. 318). This mission implies an umbrella commitment to operate in a manner that contributes positively to the health and well-being of consumers throughout the life cycle of products. At Unilever and many other companies, philanthropy has also been reshaped to be synergistic with the mission of the organization, by aligning it with the organization's strategy and by getting employees engaged in mission-related community service. This leverages the human and social capital of the organization and its knowledge assets to optimize the value delivered in all three domains. IBM's emphasis on "innovation that matters" has led to a socio-commercial strategy that uses its commercial, environmental, and social capabilities to build a "smart world" in key areas like education, community development, and infrastructure planning (Mirvis et al., 2010, p. 319). Community service activities allow IBMers to apply their expertise in these areas to help solve real world problems such as improving the communication and coordination capabilities of aid workers and governments in disaster settings.

Valuing Collaboration

Repurposing the organization to simultaneously address economic, social, and environmental outcomes leads to the blurring of many boundaries, both internal and external, as organizations adopt the orientation that "we're in this together" and can have greater impact collectively than we can individually on the sustainability of the world in which we operate. Collaboration is enabled by the emergence of new rules of transparency, knowledge sharing, and mutual problem-solving. Building a closed loop supply chain, for example, requires cross-functional integration within and across organizations. Solving complex problems such as fostering human rights along a supply chain requires shifting connections among the elements of the ecosystem, including new forms of collaboration with an expanded set of stakeholders. One company alone, no matter how much investment it is willing to make, cannot build a reliable global supply chain for organic, fair-trade cotton without partnering with many "on the ground" agencies, NGOs, community groups, educators, and farmer representatives (Worley, Feyerherm, & Knudsen, 2010). New ways of organizing reflect the new reality that it is no longer possible to draw a boundary around the operations of the corporation and say "for this we are solely responsible to our shareholders."

The value placed on organizational control and optimization by functions within an organization or by a single organization operating to maximize its return underpins much economic and administrative dogma and practice. It does not fit a world where organizations are subject to many forces that they cannot fully anticipate and definitely cannot fully control. Collective action, mutual adjustment, and multiple interventions are required. As one example, social unrest in developing nations may threaten the stability of the very growth markets that corporations have been entering and expanding. Any one company can work to build socially responsible operations in such markets, but avoiding social unrest is not simply the aggregate of the social responsibility policies of many companies. Corporations contributing to the sustainability of emerging markets are moving from a compliance to a development orientation. They are partnering with each other and collaborating with NGOs and local governments and community leaders in order to secure the knowledge, experience, and legitimacy to bring behavior into alignment with formal policies in their plants, and to start to impact local norms, capabilities, and prevailing attitudes toward workers. The Gap's collaboration with their vendors, SAI and other NGOs, local governments, and other clothing manufacturers using the same vendor plants is a case in point (Worley et al., 2010). This collaborative approach is aimed at developing local capabilities and influencing norms and regulations to sustain human rights in the plants, and to contribute to viable and secure communities, stable governments, and social justice. The Gap has also learned that collaboration along the supply chain requires new ways of collaborating and integrating work across the various functions within the company.

Valuing the Health of the Whole System

The change in values from the emphasis on unilateral control to system-wide sustainability is perhaps most exemplified when responsibility to nontraditional stakeholders becomes formalized in new forms of governance. These recognize the insufficiency of our current delineations of companies with their hierarchical control and nations with their powers to centrally impact commerce, health and safety, and social development within a country. New network forms of governance have been emerging, including industry specific and multi-sectoral collabora-tives and global compacts. The rule of interaction that guides them is to collaborate to foster system-wide health and sustainability, and their legitimacy stems from agreement among the members (see Worley & Breyley Parker, 2011).

These forms of self-organization are relatively new to corporations, and carry with them levels of risk and transparency that have not been common and in fact fly in the face of many of the operating values of traditional corporations such as secrecy, control, and proprietary ownership of assets. Companies are coming together in voluntary collectives such as signing on to the Universal Declaration of Human Rights, and becoming signatories to the Global Compact, and to the Millennium Development goals that emphasize and formalize business's role in promoting human rights, and agree to transparent reporting. Nations are meeting to generate and try to agree to global standards to halt global warming. Companies such as Xerox, DuPont, and Bosch are sharing sustainability related technical knowledge through the establishment of eco-patent commons through which they forfeit intellectual property rights in order to provide public access to environmentally friendly technologies. Companies work with NGOs and others who speak for the health of the earth and its oceans and atmospheres, such as World Wildlife Fund (WWF) and the Nature Conservancy, to create transparent and collaborative approaches to advance environmental interests while maintaining the ability to achieve business goals. For example, Coca-Cola Company and WWF have spearheaded the formation of a multi-sector, multi-stakeholder alliance to address water insecurity around the world. In some cases companies are catalyzing the establishment of NGOs and/or industry consortia to create an industry wide, multi-stakeholder capacity, with clear agreed-upon standards. Unilever's collaboration with WWF in establishing the Maritime Stewardship Council to provide third party leadership and industry collaboration to establish sustainable seafood chains is one example (Googins et al., 2007, p. 54). In the same vein, Nike has joined with other shoe and apparel makers in groups such as Fair Labor Association and Ethical Trading Initiative to ensure broad based buy-in to and compliance with labor and trading codes (Epstein, 2008).

Valuing Involvement

Behavior change to achieve sustainability is required at all system levels and among the varied agents in a system. For example, product Design for the Environment (DFE) is only possible if consumers are willing to buy products designed in this manner and carry out their part in the recycling, disassembly, and reuse cycle. Nike, Gap, and many others are finding ways to involve customers in environmental campaigns and in so doing raising awareness and influencing how citizens think about the environment. Social impact is a socially constructed phenomenon. Companies such as DuPont that set up community input meetings or such as IBM that sets up electronic "jams" for customers to give input find that taking the perspectives of those who are impacted by the company's decisions into account enhances the company's ability to contribute social value and achieve economic outcomes.

A company's individual employees daily make decisions that impact the environment, their jobs, their volunteer work, and their personal lives. Innovative ideas often come from the periphery of an organization and from work units deep within an organization that are confronting the day-to-day challenges of sustainable functioning and seeing the opportunities to improve work processes and product DFE and for safety (Schroeder & Robinson, 2010). Self-organization at all levels in an organization influences the economic and social outcomes of work, as individuals and teams are able to develop and use capabilities to do work better and deliver more value (Kira & van Eijnatten, 2008). Sustainable effectiveness demands a high involvement, high performance workplace (Russo, 2010; Schroeder & Robinson, 2010) in which employees are treated as stakeholders of the corporation and engaged in socially responsible jobs (Googins et al., 2007).

Valuing Diversity

As we have seen, some common patterns are starting evolve to govern complex system interactions in response to the challenges of achieving a sustainable future. Purposes are expanding, and new forms of collaboration and governance are emerging. These patterns are emerging from the self-organizing processes of various agents individually and collectively, and are embodied in quite different artifacts and processes designed to fit the particular configuration of different ecosystems. Indeed, ensuring diversity is necessary for a sustainable future. Just as biodiversity is the foundation for the health and adaptation of natural ecosystems (Stead & Stead, 2009), cultural and social system diversity underpin social system resilience. It is only through trying out and embedding many approaches that any organization, community, region, or the global system as a whole can recalibrate and refashion its activities to achieve positive cycles of renewal.

The elements of any natural ecosystem depend on each other to preserve the strength of the system. Certainly no single organization or consortium of organizations can address all the interacting elements that are currently cycling toward non-sustainability in our manmade systems. For example, carbon caps and trading systems may support deceleration of the growth of emissions in developed nations, but a different approach based on discontinuous technological innovation may be required to prevent disastrous increase in carbon emissions that is resulting from the immense growth in population and emerging markets. Both these approaches and many more will be required if the earth is to achieve the 2°C limit on global warming that most scientists feel is required to prevent calamitous impact, and that has been agreed to in principle by many nations at the 2010 United Nations sponsored meetings on climate change negotiations in Cancun. Protecting and stimulating diversity is a key rule that must govern our transition to a sustainable future.

The intertwined issues of sustainability transcend many different regions, nations, cultures, ethnicities, and even species. Given the unpredictability and nonlinearity of cause and impact in a complex system, organizations cannot expect to find a sustainable solution with every initiative and direction they take. The interdependencies in today's world are such that we must consider the health of the earth as a whole, while working to build resilient local communities and niches and preserving and growing the diversity that will enable ongoing evolution.

Ethical Underpinnings

Instrumental and pragmatic arguments are necessary but insufficient catalysts for the transition to a sustainable future that entails a fundamental shift in the purposes and the values that have guided behavior in the past. Much of the literature on sustainability stresses the need to align sustainability and corporate responsibility initiatives and strategies with business strategy (e.g., Googins et al., 2007; Epstein, 2008; Galbreath & Benjamin, 2010), and to focus on opportunities to reduce cost or to create growth through the development of innovative products and services that sell into a burgeoning market created by the need to be environmentally sustainable (Hockerts & Morsing, 2007). These approaches in effect reduce the tension between the elements of the triple bottom line by aligning the environmental and social with the economic purposes of the firm. Yet they also may lead to incrementalism in the changes that are made (Louche, Idowu, & Filho, 2010b), and may give the impression that it is possible to pick and choose when to act in a sustainably effective manner and to do it within a business-as-usual framework.

The transition to sustainable functioning can and perhaps must be predicated on an ethical foundation to guide the transition that is independent of instrumental motivations. Acceptance of the responsibility to be stewards of the earth to ensure not only our own health and well-being but that of others on this earth and of our descendants is fundamentally based on values. Many organizations touted as leading the way to a more sustainable future have built on their historically core values relating to community, humanity, and ecology. A recommitment to these values in the context of today's reality provides both the touchstone and the North Star during this period of transition – and enables the alignment of far-flung and diverse activity. This is true in large corporations with global reach and significant scale and impact, such as Unilever, UPS, Levi-Strauss, and Nokia (Googins et al., 2007), and in small entrepreneurial mission driven organizations that are growing and prospering by building and being part of niches that strive to operate with sustainable principles (Russo, 2010). Core values underpin the leadership role these companies are playing in addressing the increasingly obvious unsustainable patterns that currently characterize the global economy. They trigger a set of instrumental and pragmatic decisions about how to fulfill the obligation to posterity. There will inevitably be many decisions where delivering environmental and social value adds cost without offsetting benefits. Core values enable people in the firm to resolve tough trade-offs by "doing the right thing" – and to make more nuanced decisions about how to increase their commitment in the full triple bottom line.

The values shift described above is clearly not a phenomenon for corporations alone. Economic systems are anchored in the moral and normative fabric of society (Habermas, 1971). Future-oriented stewardship will only become pervasive if the various agents in the complex system place a value on sustainability. These include corporations, individual citizens, households, communities, churches, governments, NGOs, and broad social networks that exist independently of any formal entities and that may be fueled by the ready communication capabilities in today's world. The reality is that for many elements of society at large, becoming sustainable poses a distinct challenge to prevailing values-in-use, even when the espoused values are in alignment with that goal. The values that have driven the consumption culture and the rapidly growing global economy have coevolved with cultural patterns of behavior and with the evolution of industries, communities, governments, and societies.

Many of the proposed solutions to the dislocations and disruptions that have accompanied globalization rely on increasing consumption and growth in order to feed the engine of prosperity and to expand the beneficiaries of the capitalist economy. Governments face being voted or forced out of power if they are perceived as not doing what is necessary to meet their citizens' expectations of continued or increased affluence. They stimulate spending and consumption in order to put people to work and to get the tax dollars to provide infrastructure, social services, and security for their populations. Simultaneously, they struggle to avoid large government deficits and struggle to get the political will to establish, fund, and uphold sustainable policies. In global economic meetings nations prod each other to stimulate consumption to keep the global economic engine going and to avoid deep and prolonged recession or worse, with its attendant social suffering. In an entirely different set of meetings nations negotiate to try to get agreement to take global action with respect to the environment. Meanwhile, the global population grows daily. The challenge is to find ways to extend the benefits of global economic activity more broadly while not overtaxing the earth to a point of no return. This will occur not through government decisions, but through the decisions on the ground, made by all the different elements of the system.

In recent history we have looked to governments to be the stewards of the future and to deliver prosperity today without putting too much strain on the businesses that fund government and provide growth and income to the population. Through policy and regulation, governments are in a unique position to intervene into the ecosystem to promote sustainable behaviors; however, complex systems cannot be controlled centrally. And, governments, like corporations, are often paralyzed by a value-based dissention about spending today's resources to invest in tomorrow's healthy world. Businesses are the key engines of economic activity and prosperity, and must be the key agents in the self-organizing processes that will result in a sustainable global economic system. The earth relies upon them to take a leadership role in this transformation, and to do it quickly.

ORGANIZING FOR SUSTAINABLE EFFECTIVENESS: BUILDING CAPABILITIES

Over time organizations are generating a variety of responses to adapt to the challenges humanity faces. Optimistically, the simultaneous introduction of many innovative approaches will fuel adaptive cycles that result in the rise of new patterns of behavior, more self-renewing organizational forms, and more robust ecosystems. Will this happen fast enough and in a manner that preserves the potential, diversity, prosperity, and cultural richness of mankind? One of the premises of this book series on "organizing for sustainability" is that we can build on our inherent capacities to learn and to act collectively. We can detect and disseminate successful approaches, discover and articulate the "rules" that can underpin sustainable ecosystems, design new approaches, and in this way accelerate the transition to a sustainable future.

Even if we describe and give examples of the high level operating rules of an ideal world in which the various actors in the ecosystem work collaboratively to develop a sustainable system, the required transition is immense. Acknowledging the risk inherent in business as usual, and accepting the responsibility to contribute to the long-term health of the societies and natural environments in which we operate represent fundamental shifts. Even then, many new capabilities will have to be developed by the various actors in the system in order for a new meta rule to guide the interactions in the system: "Operate in a sustainably effective manner."

Among the dynamic capacities organizations will need to develop are: (1) managing ecologically and socially efficient supply chains; (2) advancing science and technology and developing and disseminating innovations that radically decrease the negative impact of our global economy on the natural environment; (3) continuous improvement and learning to increase economic, environmental, and societal outcomes; and (4) collaboration in order to do the first three.

The prevailing short-term logic has evolved through time. It is reflected in organizations' internal processes, organizational frameworks, communication channels, and problem-solving approaches (Henderson & Clark, 1990), and in their patterns of interaction with the various elements of the environment. The development of new capabilities to address triple bottom line outcomes will require the implementation of new rules of interaction and new organizational and interorganizational designs to support a new logic.

The Challenge of Organization Design for Sustainability

Conceptualizing the transition to sustainable functioning as a design challenge provides change leverage complementary to the mission and values perspective. Organizational design involves the purposeful configuration of the organization's structures and processes to accomplish its purposes and strategies. Redesign to accomplish new purposes occurs intentionally over time and requires continuity and shared focus to allow capabilities to grow and become embedded in the way the firm operates and performs (Dosi, Nelson, & Winter, 2000). Such change is not a series of bolted on one-shot initiatives led by temporary task teams whose work is separate from the business units of the organization. Social and environmental responsibility must be integrated into business decision making of organizations to support the growth, innovation, cost reduction, and differentiation required for economic viability (Epstein, 2008; Maas & Boons, 2010).

We can conceptualize the design challenge using the organization design framework articulated by Jay Galbraith (1994) that specifies that an organization can best achieve its strategy if the various designable elements of an organization fit with it and with each other. Among the organizational design elements that have to be addressed to achieve sustainable effectiveness are the specification and design of the *work processes* that are core to enact the strategy to deliver triple bottom line value. Closed loop manufacturing processes and product DFE are two examples. Core *structural units and dynamic lateral structures and processes* must be designed to carry out these effectively, to link to other stakeholders in the ecosystem, and to enable focus on local diversity and global concerns. Structures and processes are designed to enable integration across functions to enable life-cycle product and service sustainability. Because systemic interdependencies coexist with local performance, effective use of a wide variety of empowered cross-functional and cross-organizational councils, dynamic networks, partnerships, and focused project teams is required.

Robust *management processes* enable these structural and work process elements to accomplish sustainability purposes. These include processes for establishing strategies and aligning goals, direction, and accountabilities throughout the organization. Robust future-oriented environmental scanning processes are integral to the establishment of sustainability strategies (Stead & Stead, 2009; Epstein, 2008). Shell's scenario planning that examines the trajectories of various market forces, community interests, and national, cultural, and political trends is one example. Nokia's "World Map" is another. Organizations will have to find ways to analyze highly intertwined institutional settings in order to plan effectively (e.g., Oikonomou, 2010).

Organizations accustomed to using financial accounting metrics as the touchstone for alignment and performance management processes struggle with establishing and getting agreement to *substantive metrics for measuring environmental and social impact*. A number of measures being broadly used across organizations, such as ISO 14000 and GRI measure processes rather than performance and impact (Epstein, 2008). Some progress has been made in measuring environmental impact and relating it to the firm's economic outcomes through the application of various activity-based accounting approaches, life-cycle costing, and full cost approaches. Little progress has been made in establishing standards for measurement that capture social value. Unilever's Overall Business Impact Assessment (OBIA) is one example tying together impact in all three domains of the triple bottom line (Taylor & Postelwaite, 1996, cited by Maas & Boons, 2010).

New decision making routines are necessary to ensure that the key principles of sustainable effectiveness are followed. These include data-based decision frameworks that are sensitive to the expanded set of purposes, and clarification of decision rights and involvement processes. These are essential to the management of uncertainty and risk, adherence to the values of collaboration, involvement, and diversity, and to the acceleration of change (see, e.g., a decision framework provided by Epstein, 2008). Multidirectional communication and reporting processes and transparency norms underpin the establishment of trust and legitimacy required to support effective collaboration and involvement, and the sharing and leveraging of knowledge.

The design of *reward systems* and of *people processes* for sustainable effectiveness are particularly challenging organizing features because people are the carriers of purpose and values, and they determine how sustainably an organization operates through their day-to-day actions and decisions. Entrepreneurial mission driven organizations attract and select employees with values and purposes consistent with CSR (Russo, 2010). Consistency and authenticity with respect to these values is part of the organization's social contract with them, and failure to deliver on them will undermine the founding values of the company. Organizations transitioning to become sustainably effective are faced with the challenge of establishing and developing new employee understandings of purpose and mission. In these, the people practices of the organization are an indicator to employees of the credibility of this undertaking.

Employees increasingly expect socially responsible jobs and work, including opportunities to grow and develop and to contribute to the environment and further social justice. The fairness of the distribution of opportunities to learn, develop, and contribute, and of outcomes within the firm are indicators of the same social justice issues as the firm's impact on the external distribution of benefit societally and globally. The social sustainability within the firm, including its approaches to ameliorate negative consequences of the intensity of work in many sectors of today's global economy, is an important element of the firm's overall contribution of social value (Docherty et al., 2002; Docherty, Kira, & Shani, 2008b). Internal people practices consistent with the values of collaboration, involvement, and diversity provide a foundation for the broader application of these values that are core to sustainable effectiveness in the complex ecosystem.

We know from earlier movements to establish high involvement/high performance systems based on the broad distribution of resources, responsibility, and benefits, that such transitions rely heavily on people throughout the organization learning a new way to operate and on the organization using a participative process to put in place the design features to support it (Mohrman & Cummings, 1989; Pasmore, 1988). Strong leaders can create a context with clear strategies, mission, and values, but putting in place the work systems to make these a reality can only occur through widespread self-organization (Mohrman, 1998) and learning.

The Learning Challenge

There are many examples where significant progress is being made. Yet even in the most advanced companies, progress is partial and targeted, and, in a sense, we are all struggling to get beyond the low-hanging fruit and deal with the magnitude of the change that is required. The scale-up issues are formidable. Organizations and collectives of organizations have to become learning systems, as the changes will come from within through self-organizing processes. Rapid dissemination of knowledge is of paramount importance, as actors in a complex system adapt not only through experience-based learning and innovation but also by mimicry. Even the implementation of new technologies entails significant learning in the context where they are being implemented.

Existing models of learning and change that rely on linear progressions of unfreezing, changing, and refreezing do not fit the realities of today's global economy. The increasing economic pressures being experienced by organizations around the world while facing the challenges of the triple bottom line suggest that learning must be continuous and fundamental. It must take place at all levels in the organization: the individual, collective, and organizational levels, and indeed, beyond that – among organizations in networks, coalitions, and systems (Pawlowsky, 2001). At the individual level, it may involve acquiring new knowledge and skills, but definitely involves thinking through one's assumptions, attitudes, beliefs, and values. In this context, Schön (1983) sees learning as a process of reviewing theories-in-use in the light of unexpected events and unexpected discrepancies in the details of a problem situation. Docherty et al. (2008b) maintain that it is especially useful in the context of sustainable development to regard learning as a social event, as changes implied in sustainable development require joint action by many actors. Double-loop or second-order learning questions the assumptions behind how things are or how they are done (Argyris & Schön, 1978). Such learning is particularly relevant – even imperative – for a shift toward sustainable effectiveness, which requires important shifts in values. Learning for sustainability requires thinking about why certain decisions are being taken and about alternatives.

System (and individual) transformation can be triggered by a variety of events that occur in the "contextual mess" of the system (Ackoff, 1981). Environmental forces or events may trigger realizations, insights, or goals that precipitate alternative thinking, actions, and new behaviors. Isabella (1992) argues further that these forces and events challenge managers to manage into the future as well as in the present. The system's leaders must address the day-to-day operational changes in response to triggering events, while at the same time considering the events and their impact as possible new windows of opportunities for future growth and development.

Due to their magnitude and potential system impact, triggering events set in motion a series of mental shifts as individuals try to understand and redefine the situation. They challenge current thinking, practices, and routines, and evoke conscious thought on the part of the system's members about possible new ways of organizing. They often stir up feelings and emotions that affect how people relate to each other and lead to openness to changes that might be implemented. At the most basic level, triggering events create a dynamic that brings organizational members' mindsets into the arena of transformation.

The changes required to achieve a sustainable way of functioning fit into a category described by Ackerman (1986) as transformational because the new state is usually unknown until it begins to take shape, and most of the thinking, practices, and processes are yet to emerge (Jick, 1992). CEOs that have led their companies through transformation toward a more sustainable system have claimed that such transformational change requires to a certain degree a "leap of faith" (i.e., Cox, 2008).

A system developing a radical reconceptualization to become a sustainable organization will change its vision and mission, and its design. It will have to attend to two kinds of learning processes: the learning that must take place during the transformation process and the learning that must then take place in the "transformed" organization (Useem & Kochan, 1992). The capacity to learn (and at times to learn fast) is crucial in systems transformation (Argyris & Schön, 1978; Boud, Cressey, & Docherty, 2006; Edmondson, 2008). Developing the appropriate learning mechanisms and processes is key to successful transformation (Schein, 1993; Mitki, Shani, & Stjernberg, 2008). There is a need not only to design the new organization, but also make design choices about the nature of the learning mechanisms and processes (Shani & Docherty, 2008).

Learning mechanisms are structures and processes that are devoted to the facilitation of understanding and action (Lipshitz, Popper, & Oz , 1996; Popper & Lipshitz, 1998). During the transformation process, experimentation with alternative ways of organizing to promote sustainability are developed and tested. For instance, meeting practices and collaborative spaces may be developed to allow stakeholders to seek solutions for sustainability (e.g., Bradbury-Huang, 2010). While emergent, the capability to learn can be designed and managed rather than left to evolve through the normal activities of the system. Cognitive, structural, and procedural mechanisms can enable learning (Shani & Docherty, 2003). Cognitive mechanisms provide language, concepts, symbols, models, theories and values of thinking, reasoning, and understanding; structural mechanisms provide organizational, technical, and physical infrastructures such as communication channels, databanks, and databases, learning specific structures; and procedural mechanisms concern the rules, routines, methods, and tools that have been institutionalized in the organization to promote and support learning. Systems are likely to develop a tapestry of learning mechanisms that fit well within their culture and context as they proceed through the transformation process – toward sustainable effectiveness. Skaraborg's regional healthcare coalition is one example of a tapestry of learning mechanisms that resulted in the development and implementation of a sustainability strategy for higher quality of healthcare delivery (Lifvergren, Docherty, & Shani, 2011).

The intentional design of learning mechanisms increases the likelihood that core learning processes such as experiential learning and the development of tacit knowledge, the building of communities of practice, and the fostering of creativity will occur. Learning mechanisms can be purposefully put in place to increase the likelihood that members throughout the organization will contribute to the emergence of new, more sustainable approaches to doing work and making decisions.

ORGANIZATION OF THE VOLUME

This volume focuses on rich case examples where organizations and networks of organizations have set out to become more sustainable. It examines how they have developed new capabilities to attend to the triple focus on economy, environment, and society. We can learn from these empirical examples of the kind of practical approaches that are effective in becoming more sustainable. The intent is that we can go even further, and develop generalizable theory-based principles that can contribute to the design of sustainable organizations and accelerate the transformation process that is required. Each chapter is anchored in a solid theoretical point of departure that illuminates our understanding of the case, as well as explores the power of that theory in guiding responses to the challenges and solutions to the challenges we face. We start with cases that are centered on the activities of a focal organization and proceed to initiatives that are inherently multi-organizational and multi-stakeholder in nature.

Chapter 2, by Philip Mirvis, examines Unilever's ten-year transformation to build corporate responsibility and sustainable operations into its entire value stream. Referencing complex adaptive systems, Mirvis uses the case example to address the theoretical and practical questions about the role of top-down versus communal leadership, the importance of mission versus vision, and the relevance of emotive and psycho-spiritual versus more programmatic interventions.

In Chapter 3, Christopher Worley examines the Gap Corporation's journey to become more sustainable. It began with the development of collaborative approaches to improve human rights in its global supply chain. This experience triggered a broader reevaluation of how Gap does business that has led to an examination of internal processes and structures. Worley and Feyerherm explore the case through the lens of institutionalization theory.

In Chapter 4, Svante Lifvergren, Peter Docherty, and Abraham (Rami) Shani highlight the establishment of a development coalition between the three main types of healthcare providers in the Swedish healthcare value chain. The purpose is to achieve greater integration of their activities to provide higher quality of healthcare, greater personnel satisfaction, and a better use of the system's social, economic, and material resources in the West Skaraborg Healthcare System. Building on participation theories that have been particularly influential in shaping expectations and approaches in Sweden, it closely examines the approaches used to create a system capable of regenerating from within.

In Chapter 5, Ann Feyerherm and Sally Breyley Parker illustrate how the Cleveland Municipal Housing Authority built on their learnings from a public–private energy partnership with Siemens to build collaboration as a core methodology to increase the sustainability of the public housing system. The authors focus particularly on new leadership approaches that emerged to involve a broad variety of stakeholders in working toward social, economic, and ecological sustainability.

In Chapter 6, Jan Green Rebstock and Hilary Bradbury-Huang describe a complex, ongoing, multi-year, multi-sectoral initiative that has fundamentally changed the capabilities of the Port of Los Angeles to address what had previously been treated as environmental and social externalities from the Port's operation. The authors depict the complex force field stemming from the sheer number and diversity of stakeholders whose activities intersect at the Port. They use systems theory and learning theory to analyze the approaches that were taken to respond to a governmental mandate for change in social and ecological outcomes. The initiative involved the collaborative generation of knowledge and tools, and the creation of agreement without hierarchical authority about initiatives that have led to significant improvement at the Port and in its surrounding communities.

In Chapter 7, Christopher Worley and Sally Breyley Parker describe the unfolding of the Cuyahoga Valley Initiative (CVI) – A coordinating organization set up by the Cuyahoga County Planning Commission in Northeast Ohio to address the sustainability of a region defined by the river that runs through it. Because of the myriad of agencies, governments, NGOs, and companies that comprise this region, CRVO is, by necessity, a voluntary organization. Its challenge has been to bring together scores of organizations, both public and private, to achieve synergy and maximum impact from what started out as uncoordinated efforts to revitalize and introduce sustainability to a deteriorating region of the United States. The authors apply transorganizational development theory to understand how CRVO has unfolded and point out what we can learn from this example about this form of organization.

In Chapter 8, Rami Shani and Sue Mohrman draw learning from the collection of cases, particularly with respect to the challenges of capability development for sustainable effectiveness. We also chart an agenda for future research about Organizing for Sustainable Effectiveness, and offer a challenge to academics and practitioners alike to collaborate in the acceleration of progress in this area.

This volume, like the volumes to come, ensures that academic work captures and provides value to the real work of creating a sustainable world. This real work occurs in practice, as members of organizations and society come together to craft new approaches. The work that appears in this volume confirms that there is no shortage of ideas, activities, and energy around the importance of sustainability. Progress is being made company-by-company, situation-by-situation, as early adopters use their ingenuity and resources to find ways to make a difference. It is also clear that even the early adopters have a long way to go, and that we all have to learn together.

REFERENCES

Ackerman, L. (1986). Development, transition or transformation: The question of change in organizations. *Organization Development Practitioner*, 1–8.

Ackoff, R. L. (1981). *Creating the corporate future*. New York: Wiley.

van Aken, J. E. (2005). Management research as a design science: Articulating the research products of mode 2 knowledge production in management. *British Journal of Management, 16*, 19–36.

Anonymous. (2010). Asia: Under water; Banyan. *The Economist, 297*(8712), 56.

Argyris, C., & Schön, D. (1978). *Organizational learning: A theory of action perspective.* Reading, MA: Addison-Wesley.

Arnold, M. F. (2010). Competitive advantage from CSR programmes. In: C. Louche, S. L. Idowu & W. L. Filho (Eds), *Innovative CSR: From risk management to value creation* (pp. 102–130). Sheffield, UK: Greenleaf Press.

Ashby, W. R. (1956). *An introduction to cybernetics.* New York: Wiley.

Astley, W. G. (1985). The two ecologies: Population and community perspectives on organizational evolution. *Administrative Science Quarterly, 30*, 224–241.

Avenier, M.-J. (2010). Construction and use of generic knowledge in organization science viewed as a science of the artificial. *Organization Studies, 31*(9&10), 1229–1256.

Axelrod, R., & Cohen, E. (1997). *The complexity of cooperation: Agent-based models of competition and collaboration.* Princeton, NJ: Princeton University Press.

Boud, D., Cressey, P., & Docherty, P. (Eds). (2006). *Productive reflection at work: Learning for changing organizations.* London: Routledge.

Bradbury-Huang, H. (2010). Sustainability by collaboration: The SEER case. *Organizational Dynamics, 39*(4), 335–344.

Brown, L. (2008). *Plan B 3.0: Mobilizing to save civilization.* New York: W.W. Norton and Company.

Brundtland, G. (1987). *Our Common Future: The World Commission on Environment and Development.* Oxford: Oxford Press.

Campbell, D. T. (1960). Blind variation and selective retention in creative thought as in other knowledge processes. *Psychological Review, 67*, 380–400.

Cescau, P. J. (2008). Foreword. In: C. Laszlo (Ed.), *Sustainable value: How the world's leading companies are doing well by doing good.* Stanford, CA: Stanford University Press.

Cox, K. (2008). Organizational visions of sustainability. In: P. Docherty, M. Kira & A. B. Shani (Eds), *Creating sustainable work systems: Developing social sustainability* (2nd ed.). London: Routledge.

Del Bosco, B. (2010). A strategic approach to CSR: The case of Beghelli. In: C. Louche, S.O. Idowli & W. L. Filho (Eds), *Innovative CSR.* Sheffield, UK: Greenleaf Publishing.

Docherty, P., Forslin, J., & Shani, A. B. (2002). *Creating sustainable work systems: Emerging perspectives and practices.* London: Routledge.

Docherty, P., Kira, M., & Shani, A. B. (2008a). *Creating sustainable work systems: Developing social sustainability* (2nd ed.). London: Routledge.

Docherty, P., Kira, M., & Shani, A. B. (2008b). Organizational development for social sustainability in work systems. In: W. A. Pasmore, A. B. Shani & R. W. Woodman (Eds), *Research in organizational change and development* (Vol. 18, pp. 77–144). London: Emerald.

Dosi, G., Nelson, R. R., & Winter, S. G. (Eds). (2000). *The nature and dynamics of organizational capabilities.* New York: Oxford University Press.

Edmondson, A. C. (2008). The competitive imperative of learning. *Harvard Business Review* (July–August), 60–67.

Ehrich, P. R., & Ehrich, A. H. (1990). *The population explosion.* New York: Simon and Schuster.

Elkington, J. (1997). *Cannibals with forks.* Oxford, UK: Capstone Publishing Limited.

Epstein, M. J. (2008). *Making sustainability work: Best practices in managing and measuring corporate social, environmental, and economic impacts.* San Francisco: Greenleaf and Berrett-Koehler.

Figge, F., & Hahn, T. (2005). The cost of sustainability capital and the creation of sustainable value by companies. *Journal of Industrial Ecology, 9*(4), 47–58.

Fukuyama, F. (1999). *The great disruption: Human nature and the reconstitution of social order.* New York: Free Press.

Galbraith, J. R. (1994). *Designing organizations: An executive briefing on strategy, structure and process.* San Francisco: Jossey-Bass.

Galbreath, J., & Benjamin, K. (2010). An action-based approach to linking CSR to strategy: Framework and cases. In: C. Louche, S. O. Idowu & W. L. Filho (Eds), *Innovative CSR: From risk management to value creation* (pp. 12–37). Sheffield, UK: Greenleaf Press.

Ghoshal, S. (2005). Bad management theories are destroying good management practices. *Academy of Management Learning and Education, 4*, 75–91.

Goldstone, J. A. (2010). The new population bomb: The four megatrends that will change the world. *Foreign Affairs, 89*(1), 31–43.

Googins, B. K., Mirvis, P. H., & Rochlin, S. A. (2007). *Beyond good company: Next generation corporate citizenship.* New York: Palgrave MacMillan.

Habermas, J. (1971). *Knowledge and human interests.* Boston: Beacon Press.

Hannan, M. T., & Freeman, J. (1977). The population ecology of organizations. *American Journal of Sociology, 82*, 929–984.

Hart, C. L., & Milstein, M. B. (1999). Global sustainability and the creative destruction of industries. *Sloan Management Review, 41*(1), 23–33.

Hart, S. L. (1997). Beyond greening: Strategies for a sustainable world. *Harvard Business Review* (January–February), 66–76.

Hart, S. L., & Christensen, C. M. (2002). The great leap: Driving innovation from the base of the pyramid. *Sloan Management Review, 44*(1), 51–56.

Henderson, R. M., & Clark, K. B. (1990). Architectural innovation: The reconfiguration of existing product technologies and the failure of established firms. *Administrative Science Quarterly, 35*, 9–30.

Hockerts, K., & Morsing, M. (2007). *A literature review on corporate responsibility in the innovation process.* Copenhagen: Copenhagen Business School.

Hoffman, A. J. (1999). Institutional evolution and change: Environmentalism and the U.S. chemical industry. *Academy of Management Journal, 42*(4), 351–371.

Hoffman, A. J. (2010). Climate change as a cultural and behavioral issue: Addressing barriers and implementing solutions. *Organizational Dynamics, 39*(4), 295–305.

Holland, J. H. (1995). *Hidden order: How adaptation builds complexity.* Reading, MA: Helix Books.

Holland, J. H. (1998). *Emergence: From chaos to order.* Reading, MA: Perseus Books.

Isabella, L. A. (1992). Managing the challenge of trigger events: The mindsets governing adaptation to change. In: T. D. Jick (Ed.), *Managing change* (pp. 18–29). Burr Ridge, IL: Irwin.

Jick, T. D. (1992). *Managing change.* Burr Ridge, IL: Irwin.

Kira, M., & van Eijnatten, F. M. (2008). Sustained by work: Individual and social sustainability in work organizations. In: P. Docherty, M. Kira & A. B. Shani (Eds), *Creating sustainable work systems: Developing social sustainability* (2nd ed., pp. 233–246). London: Routledge.

Knight, L. (2002). Network learning: Exploring learning by interorganizational networks. *Human Relations, 55*(4), 427–454.

Laszlo, C. (2008). *Sustainable value: How the world's leading companies are doing well by doing good.* Stanford, CA: Stanford University Press.

Leydesdorff, L. (2001). *A sociological theory of communication: The self-organization of the knowledge-based society.* Parkland, FL: Universal Publishers.

Lifvergren, S., Docherty, P., & Shani, A. B. (2011). Towards a sustainable healthcare system: Transformation through participation. In: S. A. Mohrman & A. B. Shani (Eds), *Organizing for sustainability.* Bingley, UK.

Lipshitz, R., Popper, M., & Oz, S. (1996). Building the learning organization: The design and implementation of organizational learning mechanisms. *Journal of Applied Behavioral Science, 32*(3), 292–305.

Louche, C., Idowu, S. O., & Filho, W. L. (2010a). *Innovative CSR: From risk management to value creation.* Sheffield, UK: Greenleaf Press.

Louche, C., Idowu, S. O., & Filho, W. L. (2010b). Innovation in corporate responsibility: How innovative is it?. In: C. Louche, S. O. Idowu & W. L. Filho (Eds), *Innovative CSR: From risk management to value creation* (pp. 285–304). Sheffield, UK: Greenleaf Press.

Maas, K., & Boons, F. (2010). CSR as a strategic activity: Value creation, redistribution and integration. In: P. Martens & C. Ting Chang (Eds), *The social and behavioural aspects of climate change: Linking vulnerability, adaptation and mitigation* (pp. 154–172). Sheffield: Greenleaf Publishing.

Martens, P., & Ting Chang, C. (2010). *The social and behavioural aspects of climate change: Linking vulnerability, adaptation and mitigation.* Sheffield: Greenleaf Publishing.

Mirvis, P., Googins, B., & Kinnicutt, S. (2010). Vision, mission, values: Guideposts to sustainability. *Organizational Dynamics, 39*(4), 316–324.

Mitki, Y., Shani, A. B., & Stjernberg, T. (2008). Leadership, development and learning mechanisms: System transformation as a balancing act. *Leadership & Organization Development Journal, 29*(1), 68–84.

Mohrman, S. A. (1998). Top management viewed from below: A learning perspective on transformation. In: J. A. Conger, G. M. Spreitzer & E. E. Lawler (Eds), *The leader's change handbook: An essential guide to setting direction and taking action* (pp. 271–300). San Francisco: Jossey-Bass.

Mohrman, S. A., & Cummings, T. G. (1989). *Self-designing organizations: Learning how to create high performance.* Reading, MA: Addison-Wesley.

Mohrman, S. A., & Lawler, E. E., III. (2011). Research for theory and practice: Framing the challenge. In: S. A. Mohrman & E. E. Lawler, III (Eds), *Useful research: Advancing theory and practice* (pp. 9–33). San Francisco: Berrett-Koehler.

Mohrman, S. A., & Mohrman, A. M., Jr. (2011). Collaborative organization design research at the Center for Effective Organizations. In: S. A. Mohrman & E. E. Lawler, III (Eds), *Useful research: Advancing theory and practice* (pp. 57–79). San Francisco: Berrett-Koehler.

Mohrman, S. A., Mohrman, A. M., Jr., & Tenkasi, R. V. (1997). The discipline of organization design. In: C. L. Cooper & S. E. Jackson (Eds), *Creating tomorrow's organizations* (pp. 191–206). Chichester: Wiley.

Mohrman, S. A., & Worley, C. G. (2010). The organizational sustainability journey: Introduction to the special issue. *Organizational Dynamics, 39*(4), 289–294.

Monge, P. R., & Contractor, N. S. (2003). *Theories of communication networks.* Oxford: Oxford University Press.

Oikonomou, V. (2010). Interactions between white certificates for energy efficiency and other energy and climate policy instruments. In: P. Martens & C. Ting Chang (Eds), *The social and behavioural aspects of climate change: Linking vulnerability, adaptation and mitigation* (pp. 177–201). Sheffield: Greenleaf Publishing.

Pasmore, W. A. (1988). *Designing effective organizations: The socio-technical systems perspective.* New York: Wiley.

Pawlowsky, P. (2001). The treatment of organizational learning in management science. In: A.B. Antal, M. Dierkes, J. Child & I. Nonaka (Eds), *Handbook of organizational learning and knowledge* (pp. 61–88). New York: Oxford University Press.

Pfeffer, J. (2007). A modest proposal: How we might change the process and product of managerial research. *Academy of Management, 50*(6), 1334.

Popper, M., & Lipshitz, R. (1998). Organizational learning mechanisms: A structural and cultural approach to organizational learning. *Journal of Applied Behavioral Science, 34*(23), 161–179.

Prahalad, C. K. (2004). *The fortune at the bottom of the pyramid.* New York: Prentice-Hall.

Romme, A. G. L. (2003). Making a difference: Organization as design. *Organization Science, 14*, 559–573.

Russo, M. V. (2010). *Companies on a mission: Entrepreneurial strategies for growing sustainably, responsibly, and profitably.* Stanford, CA: Stanford Business Books.

Sachs, J. (2008). *Common wealth: Economics for a crowded planet.* New York: Penguin Press.

Schein, H. (1993). How can organizations learn faster: The problem of entering the green room. *Sloan Management Review, 34*(2), 85–92.

Schön, D. A. (1983). *The reflective practitioner.* New York: Basic Books.

Schroeder, D. E., & Robinson, A. G. (2010). Creating sustainable competitive advantage through green excellence. *Organization Dynamics, 39*(4), 345–352.

Shani, A. B., & Docherty, P. (2003). *Learning by design: Building sustainable organizations.* Oxford: Blackwell Publishing.

Shani, A. B., & Docherty, P. (2008). Learning by design: Key mechanisms in organization development. In: T. Cummings (Ed.), *Handbook of organization development* (pp. 499–500). Thousand Oaks, CA: Sage.

Simon, H. A. (1969). *The sciences of the artificial.* Cambridge, MA: MIT Press.

Starkey, K., Hatcheul, A., & Tempest, S. (2009). Management research and the new logics of discovery and engagement. *Journal of Management Studies, 46*(3), 547–558.

Stead, J. G., & Stead, W. E. (2009). *Management for a small planet* (3rd ed.). Armonk, NY: M.E. Sharpe.

Taylor, A.P., & Postelwaite, D. (1996). Overall business impact assessment (OBIA). Paper presented at the 4th LCA Case Studies Symposium: SETAC-Europe, Brussels, December 3, 1996, pp. 181–187.

Ting Chang, C., Martens, P., & Amelung, B. (2010). Conclusion. In: P. Martens & C. Ting Chang (Eds), *The social and behavioural aspects of climate change* (pp. 288–296). Sheffield, UK: Greenleaf Publishing.

United Nations Environmental Programme. (2007). *Global Environmental Outlook.*

Useem, M., & Kochan, T. (1992). Creating the learning organization. In: T. Kochan & M. Useem (Eds), *Transforming organizations* (pp. 391–406). New York: Oxford University Press.

Worley, C. G., & Breyley Parker, S. (2011). Building multi-stakeholder sustainability networks: The Cuyahoga Valley Initiative. In: S. A. Mohrman & A. B. Shani (Eds), *Organizing for sustainability*. Bingley, UK.

Worley, C. G., Feyerherm, A. E., & Knudsen, D. (2010). Building a collaboration capability for sustainability: How Gap Inc., is creating and leveraging a strategic asset. *Organizational Dynamics*, *39*(4), 325–334.

WWF. (2010). Building a one planet future. Available at www.wwf.org.uk/what_we_do/about_us/building_a_one_planet_future.cfm. Retrieved on January 28, 2011.

CHAPTER 2

UNILEVER'S DRIVE FOR SUSTAINABILITY AND CSR – CHANGING THE GAME

Philip Mirvis

ABSTRACT

This chapter examines Unilever's transformation in sustainability and corporate social responsibility (CSR) over the past decade. It tracks the author's involvement with an internal team that studied Unilever's world "outside in" and "inside out" through the engagement of over 100 organizational leaders to awaken the company for change. The case reports how Unilever embraced a "vitality mission" to align its strategies and organization around sustainability and CSR and infuse social and environmental content into its corporate and product brands. Among the innovations described are certification of the sources of sustainable fish and tea, Dove's inner-beauty campaign, and several "bottom of the pyramid" efforts. Particular attention is given to the makeover of its high-growth Asian business. The transformation is examined as a "catalytic" approach to change and discussed with reference to theories of complex adaptive systems. This raises theoretical questions about the role of top-down versus more communal leadership, the importance of mission versus vision in guiding change, and the relevance of emotive and

Organizing for Sustainability
Organizing for Sustainable Effectiveness, Volume 1, 41–72
ISSN: 2045-0605/doi:10.1108/S2045-0605(2011)0000001007

*psycho-spiritual versus more programmatic interventions in the rear-
chitecture of an organization as it progresses on sustainability and CSR.*

Keywords: CSR; vitality; sustainability; catalytic change; complex
adaptive systems

By almost any criterion or measure, Unilever qualifies as a socially
responsible company. Its consumers, over 2 billion per day worldwide, know
the roughly €40 billion global company with operations in one hundred
companies, through its home-and-personal care brands such as Dove,
Lifebuoy, Sunsilk, and Vaseline, or when sipping Lipton teas, spreading
Hellman's mayonnaise, or preparing Knorr foods. Unilever is also well
known for its historic concern for employees and communities, for its
environmental practices, and for its efforts to promote human welfare in
developing countries.

Activists praise the firm for its sustainable sourcing of raw materials from
farms and fisheries and for its partnerships with groups ranging from
UNICEF to the World Wildlife Fund. Unilever has been the "food
industry" category leader for twelve years running in the DJSI, is part of the
FTSE4Good Index, and has been listed among the 100 Most Sustainable
Corporations at the World Economic Forum in Davos, Switzerland. This
chapter reports why and how this company, acknowledged as a global
leader, made wholesale changes in its approach to sustainability and
corporate social responsibility (CSR) in the past decade.

Six years ago, Unilever worked with the author and internal specialists to
scan its world and reconsider is role in society. Over two hundred executives
discussed and analyzed trends toward fair trade products, problems of
obesity and malnutrition germane to food-and-beverage businesses, the
company's impact on air-and-water, and so on. This stimulated heated
debate about the moral responsibilities of corporations versus the moral
hazard posed by using shareholders' monies to address the world's
problems. Then one executive made this comment about Unilever's game-
change in this arena: "It's who we are. And the way we do business .... It's
in our genes."

THEORETICAL FRAMING

Shortly before this effort began, Mirvis and Googins (2006) had developed a
model of the "stages" of corporate responsibility (encompassing both the

social and environmental aspects of sustainability). What does it mean that a company is at a "stage" with respect to sustainability and CSR? The general idea, found in the study of maturing children, groups, and systems of all types, including business organizations, is that there are distinct patterns of activity at different points of development. Typically, these activities become more complex and sophisticated as development progresses and therefore capacities to respond to environmental challenges increase in kind.

Piaget's (1969) developmental theory, for example, has children progress through stages that entail more complex thinking and finer judgments about how to negotiate the social world outside of themselves. Similarly, groups mature along a developmental path as they confront emotional and task challenges that require more socially sensitive interaction and sophisticated problem solving (Wheelan, 2004).

Greiner (1972), in his groundbreaking study, found that companies also develop more complex ways of doing things at different stages of growth. They must, over time, find direction after their creative start-up phase, develop an infrastructure and systems to take on more responsibilities, and then "work through" the challenges of over-control and red-tape through coordination and later collaboration across work units and levels.

Likewise, our model has companies develop progressively more sophisticated ways of operating with respect to sustainability and CSR. The stages of development posited – from an elementary to an increasingly more engaged, innovative, integrated and, at its most creative edge, a game-changing approach to sustainability and CSR – emerge from continuous interaction between a firm and its environment that stimulates organizational learning. At each stage, a company's engagement with societal issues is progressively more open and its dealings with stakeholders are more interactive and mutual. In the same way, how companies think about sustainability and CSR becomes more complex, and the organizational structures, processes, and systems used to manage corporate responsibilities are more sophisticated and aligned with the everyday business.

This model treats the development of sustainability and CSR in companies as a stage-by-stage process whereby a combination of internal capabilities applied to social and environmental challenges propels development forward in a more or less normative path. These challenges initially center on a firm's *credibility* as a responsible company, then on its *capacities* to meet stakeholder expectations, followed by efforts to create *coherence* among its many activities, and finally, on the extent of its *commitment* to operate as a global corporate citizen (cf., Schwab, 2008). In developmental logic, companies have to "work through" these matters to progress on CSR and sustainability.

Or do they? And in the same way? It is important to qualify that in development models of this type, as opposed to biological or lifecycle frameworks, movement along a single development path is not fixed nor is attaining a penultimate "end state" a logical or inevitable conclusion (Van de Ven & Poole, 1995). This means that the arc and pace of sustainability and CSR development within any particular firm can vary depending on conditions in its operating environment, its own internal makeup and culture, and how intentional and intensive it is about developing its sustainability and CSR profile.

Four Developmental Trajectories

Mirvis (2008a), illustrating these points, has identified four trajectories to the development of social and environmental responsibility in companies. A small and select set of firms, for one, seem to be "born" to sustainability and CSR. Studies of Ben & Jerry's, along with the Body Shop, Esprit, Smith & Hawken, Patagonia, and so on, suggest that firms founded on principles of corporate responsibility make it central to their business models and integral to their organization and culture from the get-go (Mirvis, 1994). A second route toward sustainability and CSR stems from crisis. The Shell Group's response to socio-environmental calamities in the mid-1990s illustrates movement from crisis-management to a makeover of policies and practices and ultimately of company values and culture (Mirvis, 2000). Complementary studies of Nike and Chiquita show a similar progression (Zadek, 2004; Kramer & Kania, 2006).

The third trajectory, the most common one, has companies advance their sustainability and CSR agenda through a process of planned change across the stages of development. This typically involves some form of diagnosis of a situation, identification of performance gaps or problems and possible solutions, and development of action strategies and their attendant goals, followed by the implementation of proposed changes in an organization.

Reading through the case material that follows, it might seem as though Unilever adopted this process in embarking on its journey. But actually the company took a "step-change" as it progressed – in effect moving from stage 3 (innovative) to stage 5 (transformative) on the developmental continuum. This approach to development of sustainability and CSR involves "game-changing" as it engages the whole business, and often the corporate brand; and it involves a complete makeover of the responsibility profile of a company (Googins, Mirvis, & Rochlin, 2007).

To an extent, differences in the developmental pacing between the third and fourth trajectories are akin to those between change management and what scholars term "transformational" change (cf., Bartunek & Louis, 1988). Blumenthal and Haspeslagh (1994) provide a colloquial distinction between the two, noting that transformational interventions are typically "bigger, deeper, and wider." The chapter next describes the transformational activities at Unilever some of which are big, deep, and wide and some of which are more modest and subtle. This sets the stage for a subsequent discussion of some theoretical and practical questions about organizational transformation applied to sustainability and CSR.

UNILEVER'S TRANSFORMATION STORY

Unilever's corporate history begins in the 1880s with William Hesketh Lever who, along with his brother James, launched the world's first branded and packaged laundry soap, called Sunlight. The Lever brothers had a sense of justice about inequities in Britain and had been schooled in Disraeli's writings that described the difference between rich and poor in England as "two nations between whom there is no contact and no sympathy; we are as ignorant of each other's feelings as if we were dwellers in different zones or different planets." William was determined, early in his business career, to make personal washing soap available and affordable to the working class who had never had access to quality hygiene products. Lifebuoy was the Lever's soap bar.

Like other leading Victorian industrialists, William was also committed to "prosperity sharing" with his workers. Biographers report that the squalor of the slums in which most workers lived appalled him (Jones, 2005). Thus he decided to buy a site on the banks of the Mersey River, opposite Liverpool, construct a factory, build twenty-eight cottages, and create Port Sunlight, a company village offering housing at reasonable rents. The company village included a school for workers' children as well as lodging and education in cooking, sewing, and shorthand for the large number of women he employed.

Lever introduced the then-unheard-of eight-hour workday at the factory and gave sickness benefits, holiday pay, and pensions for both male and female employees. The company also extended its paternalistic policies to workers in India and South Africa in the first decades of the twentieth century. In 1929, the company merged with the Margarine Unie, headquartered in the Netherlands, to become Unilever. Over the next decades, it expanded its scale through a series of acquisitions and introduced hundreds of new brands. The challenge confronting the company at the time of our study was, as one executive put it, "to take Lever's heritage and move it into the new world."

In early-2005, when we launched our research, Unilever, like other companies based in the United Kingdom and continental Europe, had been under the full lash of shareholder capitalism for just over a decade. The company had undergone several restructurings involving extensive delayering and downsizing and was "cutting the tail" by slimming its product portfolio to global brands and a few national gems. A leading player in the home-and-personal care markets, it was ready to reach this scale in the foods-and-beverage business with the acquisition of U.S.-based Best Foods (home to brands like Wishbone salad dressings), Slim-Fast, and Ben & Jerry's. To refit the firm to emerging standards, the company abandoned its division into English and Dutch companies, consolidated governance into one Board of Directors, and appointed a single CEO: Patrick Cescau.

Cescau, who rose through the ranks through several businesses and a stint as chief financial officer, had a mandate to improve the balance sheet and move Unilever forward on a path of profitable growth. Frankly, sustainability and CSR, long-standing interests of his twin predecessors, were not big items on his agenda. Nevertheless, Cescau knew that Unilever was under pressure, like other European companies, to expand and integrate its social and environmental reporting. He was also aware that Procter & Gamble, a major American competitor, had regained its competitive edge and was becoming more innovative in sustainability and CSR. Nestlé, long a bête noire for pushing infant formula as an alternative to far healthier breast-feeding in developing countries, had also begun to make sensible moves in this arena. It seemed timely, then, for the new CEO to sponsor a full-scale assessment of corporate responsibility in Unilever that would look at the current reality, review competitors' and global best practices, and consider what, if any, changes in approach might be needed.

A GLOBAL SCAN

Louis "Tex" Gunning, then a Unilever business group president in Asia, headed the study team. The author joined as a "research arm" to support Unilever's Santiago Gowland, Lettemieke Mulder, Paulus Verschuren, and other social and environmental specialists. Over the course of one month, this team, racing from executive offices to videoconferences, interviewed nearly all of Unilever's top executives, many of its business leaders and marketers around the world, and staff specialists in finance, human resources, logistics, and such, plus outside experts advising the company and members of the Board of Directors. We also benchmarked the practices of other firms in Unilever's industries, examined best practices, and added findings from surveys of business leaders, consumers, and CSR experts.

One of the inputs into the analysis was the aforementioned model of the stages of development of corporate responsibility in companies. On these counts, the Unilever team saw the company at an innovative stage but needing to be "in a different place with consumers and employees." To simplify the framework and translate it into practical constructs, the study team constructed a three-stage version – dubbed a reactive, proactive, and transformative approach to sustainability and CSR (see Fig. 1). This frame was a point of discussion within the study team and the broader CSR/ sustainability community, with executive interviewees, and later with Cescau and the Unilever Board of Directors. A brief look at the study findings shows what was behind Unilever's decisions to opt for a transformative approach to sustainability and CSR; ultimately, they went for game-changing because, as one executive explained it: "We have no choice given our business."

Outside In

Many of the themes raised in the scan of Unilever's world – such as increased scrutiny of corporations, NGO activism, global warming, rich–poor gaps, new consumer trends, and myriad threats to a firm's "license to operate" – are familiar to any global business. Two were specifically material to Unilever. The first concerned its access to and use of natural resources. As an example, over two-thirds of the company's raw materials come from agriculture. At a 4 percent growth rate, that would mean the company would use, over five years, 20 percent more raw material. That would translate, in turn, into 20 percent more pesticides on farms, 20 percent more packaging and associated waste and litter, 20 percent more water needed to grow crops, and 20 percent more water used by consumers to cook, wash, or clean with company products. The issues? Most of the company's growth was projected to be from developing and emerging (D&E) markets in Asia, Africa, and South America where there are growing

	Re-Active	Pro-Active	Transformative
Purpose and Role of Business	• Numbers driven • Economic role	• Market driven • Responsible economic development	• Mission driven • Business for society
Responsible to:	• Shareholders	• Shareholders & constituents	• All stakeholders & society
Leadership Role	• Aware • Invisible	• Understands • Supportive	• Owns • Champions
Issues Management	• Competent • Loose initiatives	• Responsive • Programme	• Self-defined/leading • Strategies
Strategic Intent	• No reputation damage	• Build positive reputation	• Part of who and how we are • See the growth opportunity
Organisation for Sustainability/CSR	• Functional • Low level staff	• Functional and cross functional • Some senior management	• Board representation • Embedded in business

Fig. 1. From Re-Active to Pro-Active to Transformative – The Choices.

water shortages and serious concerns over water contamination, plus the environmental costs associated with transport, waste, and the like.

A second set of threats involves consumption. Obesity, as one example, is widespread in the United States and Europe and growing in India, China, and elsewhere. As a result, type II diabetes is projected to reach pandemic proportions – from roughly 180 million cases today to 370 million by 2030. At the same time, public attitudes have shifted dramatically about the "causes" of obesity. An analysis of New York Times articles on obesity found that in 1990 some 84 percent of the stories stressed that obesity was caused by individual eating-and-exercise habits and only 14 percent attributed causation to the environment. Some thirteen years later, by comparison, personal causes were emphasized in 54 percent of the articles while 46 percent cited environmental causes – a threefold increase (Lawrence, 2004–2005).

The chief culprits – processed- and fast-food companies and soft-drink makers – have been targeted as proffering what some term the "new tobacco." Needless to say, this technically termed problem of "over-nutrition" was very relevant for a food purveyor like Unilever. It applies to everything from ingredients and their processing to advertising and promotions. And then there were problems of "under-nutrition" in poor parts of India, Southeast Asia, and Africa, where fortified and affordable foods could be a godsend.

But there were also opportunities ahead for Unilever. Particularly in the West, but growing worldwide, there is a move toward healthy and sustainable consumption. This is reflected in preferences for organic foods and clothing (a market growing 20 percent annually), for fair trade coffee and chocolate (over 70 percent annually), and for local sourcing of agricultural produce. There is also a trend toward "ethical" consumerism, as evidenced by an increase in cause-related products, as well as interest, among at least half of the world's consumers, in a brand's connection to social responsibility (Kleanthous & Peck, 2006).

Inside Out

The research team found that the company had a plethora of sustainability and CSR initiatives but no consistent strategic thrust behind them. "Too many unaligned programs and messages," reported one leader. "CSR has not been 'interiorized' in the company," said another. This is common to many companies like Unilever who have "islands of excellence" but not much pulling them together. Thus many spoke of the need for a "common denominator" or a "framework" to integrate things, and urged: "We need everybody thinking about this."

When it comes to tackling some of the biggest risks facing companies – and societies – Unilever has been a recognized leader. In the areas of sustainable agriculture, water, and fishing, for example, the firm was the founding force or a leading member of global, multi-company forums that develop policies, share best practices, or monitor results in these natural resource areas. In addition, it participated in partnerships, alongside other firms, government agencies, and NGOs concerned with social issues involving nutrition, health, hygiene, dental care, and the plight of the poor.

However, as progressive as these efforts might have been, they were not connected to the commercial side of the business at the time of the study. No one had set goals on sustainable sourcing for major brands, for instance, and business leaders had not considered carefully whether their social and environmental interests had any marketing relevance or might differentiate products for consumers. The message, said one: "We need a change from 'corporate initiatives' to 'business initiatives.'" Unilever's top leaders saw it as their responsibility to reposition the company in society. They recognized that there were serious challenges to face and big opportunities to consider; and it was agreed that "now was the time" to focus on sustainability and CSR. They noted, too, that employees, worn out from constant restructuring, were hungry for more meaning and inspiration in their work – something that a fresh social and environmental agenda might provide.

STRATEGIC INTENT

Under the stewardship of marketing executive Clive Butler, Unilever had developed a new corporate brand identity that would integrate its home-and-personal-care and food-and-beverage businesses beneath a corporate umbrella. The new corporate mission was: "To add vitality to life by meeting everyday needs for nutrition, hygiene, and personal care brands that help people feel good, look good, and get more out of life." In recognition of Unilever's historic commitment to and contemporary strengths in its relationships to society, it was proposed that the company reinvent its sustainability and CSR thrusts through its new vitality mission – in messaging and deeds. In a contentious move, the decision was made to put Unilever's new logo on product packaging, and let consumers know the corporation behind the brands they selected in the marketplace.

The study team found great interest throughout Unilever in the new brand identity but a lot of uncertainty about what it might mean for corporate conduct. "It's like a bar of soap," said one, "Difficult to grasp." Yet several argued that corporate responsibility was integral to the company's vitality mission. As one put it, "CSR becomes relevant through the vitality mission; and vitality becomes more exciting with the CSR thrust."

Thus the study team made two major proposals: (1) integrate sustainability and CSR into the company under the vitality mission and (2) align business strategies and brands with a more expansive corporate commitment to add vitality to society. To buttress this latter proposal, benchmark data were supportive: Unilever's competitors Danone and Kraft were repositioning their product brands in this space and key customers, such as Carrefour, Marks & Spencer, Tesco, and even Walmart were tracking and responding to new consumer trends. Most compelling were voices within Unilever calling for transformation, a sampling of which appears in Fig. 2.

The leader of the study team, Tex Gunning delivered these proposals in a brief, passionate presentation to Cescau who greeted it with a combination of skepticism and interest. Following a series of charged executive meetings, Cescau and his team determined that Vitality would be the theme to

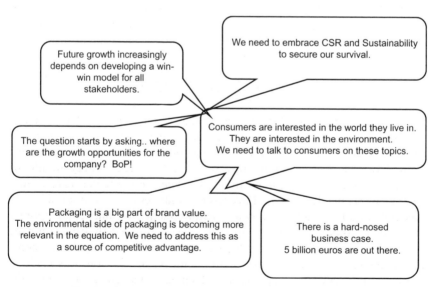

Fig. 2. Executive Voices for Transformation in Unilever.

integrate sustainability and CSR into the company, and that "values-led" brands would help drive business strategy.

BRINGING VITALITY TO THE MARKETPLACE

One of the first orders of business was to be more proactive on issues around nutrition. The company had previously introduced a margarine aimed at reducing cholesterol. But with its vitality mission, nearly twenty thousand recipes were put through a nutrition profile model and subsequently reformulated to reduce trans fat, saturated fats, sugar, and salts – amounting to over thirty thousand tons worth in three years, according to the latest company reports. In addition, Unilever began to put a "Healthy Choices" logo on products to help consumers identify foods that have limited amounts of these ingredients.

On the market face of sustainability, Unilever's fish products began to display a certification from the Marine Stewardship Council, co-founded by Unilever and the World Wildlife Fund, which assures consumers that the fish comes from sustainable fisheries; and the company asked the Rainforest Alliance to certify the sustainability of its tea plantations and products.

On the growth side, Unilever, like nearly all consumer goods companies, has found its markets saturated in the United States and Europe. The lion's share of its future growth comes from D&E markets. (Indeed, Unilever's sales in the D&E world overtook those from developed markets in 2010.) Unilever's prior commitments to sustainability and CSR in those markets had given it what might be called a "license to grow." The intent going forward was to use these to both unlock markets and serve pressing human needs in D&E markets – a "win–win" value proposition.

BoP

C. K. Prahalad (2005), whose case studies and book *The Fortune at the Bottom of the Pyramid* drew extensively on Unilever's pathbreaking "BoP" efforts. Its strategies include the sale of iodized salt in India and parts of Africa, which addresses a dietary deficiency common among the poor, and a campaign for hand washing in India, where its Lifebuoy soap aims to reduce diarrheal disease. In each instance, the company devised new local supply chains to make products more affordable and developed distribution channels that turned underprivileged women into village-level entrepreneurs.

In the case of hand washing, for instance, Unilever launched its Swasthya Chetna, or Health Awakening, campaign that has sent health education teams to thousands of schools and communities, many in remote areas, to teach children about germs and the importance of hand washing. The health teams also give every child a height and weight checkup and invite mothers to health education workshops. Under the vitality mission, this overall socio-commercial thrust was accelerated and spread under the vitality mission throughout Asia and globally to Africa, Latin America, and the Middle East.

Global Brands

Meanwhile, Unilever began looking to add social and health content to growing numbers of global brands. On the beverage side, the company introduced new tea products that feature their antioxidant benefits and at the same time dramatically reduced the sugar content of iced tea. It also has on offer a new smoothie beverage made from concentrated vegetables and fruit juices. And on the food side, in partnership with UNICEF, Gunning helped to launch a "kid's nutrition" campaign that includes research into the impact of saturated fats on children's physical and mental performance, conferences on improving youth eating patterns and preferences, and development of healthy breakfast foods aimed at fortifying the diet of poor kids.

Perhaps the most visible of the Vitality initiatives in modern trade has been the Dove soap "inner-beauty" campaign that is, according to one Unilever leader, a "dislocating idea." Company research found that just 12 percent of women are very satisfied with their physical attractiveness; 68 percent strongly agree that the media sets an unrealistic standard of beauty; and 75 percent wish the media did a better job of portraying the diversity of women's physical attractiveness, including size and shape, across all ages. Dove's public message about inner beauty has been conveyed through advertisements showing "real women have curves" and a film that shows how fashion model images are distorted to conform to an idealized but unattainable type. It is carried to schools around the world in a complementary program to promote young women's self-esteem.

TRANSFORMATION FOR GROWTH: A NEW S-CURVE

Fig. 3 presents the logic and flow of the sustainability and CSR self-study and its conclusion in a transformational commitment at Unilever. Following Cescau's decision to go for transformation and the Unilever Board's

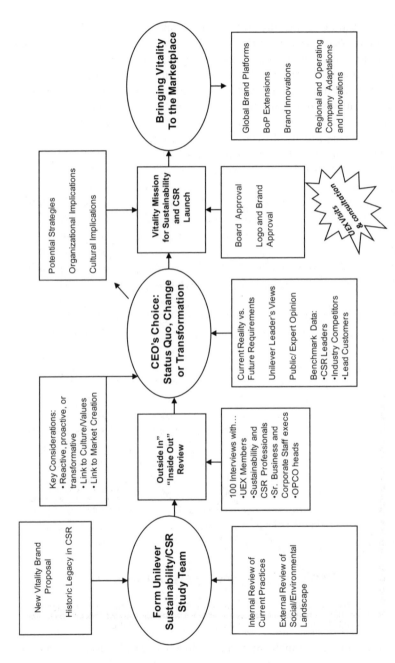

Fig. 3. Unilever's Sustainability and CSR Self-Study Process.

concurrence, Gunning and the study team members, in consultation again throughout Unilever, began to detail potential action strategies for brands and the company's value chain, including its community outreach and communications. In turn, Cescau and the other members of Unilever's executive board fanned out across the globe to meet with national operating company executives and marketers as well as global and local customers.

The vitality mission was heralded as Unilever's new growth platform. An evocative slide (see Fig. 4) illustrated how the company had moved from its entrepreneurial history of *value creation* through new product and market development (1925–1985) to an emphasis on *value extraction* via product promotion and cost cutting (1985–2005) as the primacy of shareholder returns came to define core strategies. In S-curve logic, business growth was peaking and would soon head south; and it was observed that the culture was becoming marked by conformity and risk-aversion. The new vitality mission offered the prospects of future growth, organizational excitement, and with the company's advance in the D&E world, the prospect of adding diversity to the culture and sparking "alchemy" in its approach to the marketplace.

Summarizing his views on what game-changing through sustainability and CSR meant to Unilever, Cescau has this to say, "Companies that

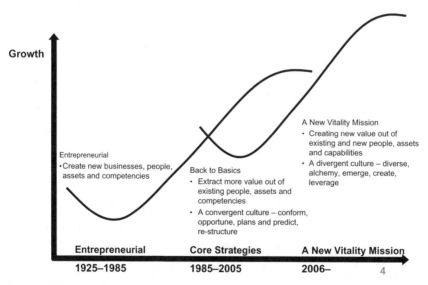

Fig. 4.   What can the Vitality Mission, Sustainability, and CSR Mean for Unilever?

succeed will serve the whole pyramid – with consumers at every economic
level ... Social responsibility is not just about sustainable development
and building reputation. It's also about growing markets and fueling
innovation."

REFLECTIONS ON "GAME-CHANGING" CHANGE

What's involved in "changing the game" with sustainability and CSR?
Analyzing Unilever's progress on its agenda, Keys, Malnight, and van der
Graaf (2009) come to some sensible conclusions about "making the most"
of corporate social responsibility: concentrate your efforts, understand the
short- and longer-term benefits, and find the right partners with whom to
work. However these kinds of lessons apply to almost any company and
nearly every social and environmental strategy. Digging deeper into the
change process in Unilever shows many elements in the transformational
recipe: diagnose the current state, engage internal and external stakeholders,
create a guiding coalition, envision a desired future, empower others to act
on that vision, and so on (cf., Kotter, 1996). But what if anything is
distinctive about the transformational process in this case and how might
the practices apply to the development of sustainability and CSR in other
firms? Start with a foundational question: Was this transformation planned
or emergent?

Planned Change

Many models for advancing corporate responsibility advocate a planned
approach that begins by assessing a company's risks and opportunities on
the social, ethical, and environmental front (Dunphy, Griffiths, & Benn,
2003; Werther & Chandler, 2005). These models then have firms develop a
comprehensive, strategic, and long-term plan for moving ahead on
sustainability and CSR. It is often executed from the top-down in a formal
change program.

There is much to recommend this approach. First, leadership by
and going-in support from the top of the organization can focus attention
on and lessen resistance to needed changes in priorities, structures,
and behavior. Second, a comprehensive and planned approach builds
momentum for change and promotes coordinated movement on multiple
fronts. Third, a strategic perspective adds commercial relevance and

potential rewards for line managers who might otherwise not see the importance of moving forward on sustainability and CSR in light of other concerns.

What are the problems with this planned change model? First, in many companies, absent a crisis, top management may not initially regard sustainability and CSR as strategic requirements nor spend the time, energy, or political capital in leading system-wide change in this arena. Second, corporate staff units, who would be called upon to integrate or align their efforts, often don't see the necessity or value of working together, particularly as they are often stretched by their own agendas and competing for scarce resources. Finally, many line managers, suffering from chronic "change fatigue," are not apt to give even a top-down model their full support.

More broadly there are questions as to whether, even in the best of circumstances, a makeover of corporate responsibility in a company can be effectively managed through a strategic program led from the top-down. In many respects, the issues around sustainability and CSR fit into the class of situations that Emery and Trist (1965) call "meta-problems" where understandings of risks, cause–effects, and benefits are not agreed upon and even validity of information and how best to interpret it are open to question.

The Catalytic Approach

In such cases, studies find that corporate actions are better guided by what Isenberg (1987) terms "strategic opportunism" and undertaken through what Quinn (1980) describes as "the simultaneous incremental process of strategy formulation and implementation" (p. 145). This general approach to navigating an unpredictable situation also goes by the names of emergent strategy (Mintzberg, 1978). This means that even as managers move toward a desired direction, their plans, actions, and near-term goals continually shift depending on the situation at hand. Obviously this puts a premium on their capacities to flexibly adapt and creatively respond to changing circumstances. This combination of opportunism, strategy-in-action, and emergence constitutes a "catalytic" approach to change (Mirvis & Manga, 2010).

There is a long literature on patterns of change that categorizes activities temporally in terms of steps (Greiner, 1967) or spatially with reference to pathways (Beer & Nohria, 2000). Tichy and Devanna (1986), for example, characterize transformation as a "three act drama" involving awakening, visioning, and rearchitecting an enterprise. Certainly that general framing fits the Unilever case. But Turner (1957) classifies transformation as a universal drama (in theater and societies) that takes the form of an upheaval, then conflict and reordering, and finally reintegration. In the Unilever case, take note, there was no burning platform, no contentious infighting, and certainly no master plan to reorder and restructure the organization. On the contrary, the sense of the study team and many in the organization was that we were making it up as we went along.

The field of complexity science is concerned with the study of emergent phenomena – behaviors and patterns – that occur at the multiple levels of systems. What is key in the context of change theory is these emerge from nonlinear interactions among complex systems that veer between equilibrium and randomness (Kauffman, 1996; Dooley, 2004). It is at this "edge of chaos" that living systems are most dynamic and, in effect, organically change. Such systems are characterized as "complex adaptive systems" (CAS) – a term coined by theorists at the Sante Fe Institute.

CAS theory offers some familiar and some fresh perspectives on the process of change. How does the transformational drama look when examined through a CAS lens?

AWAKENING AN ORGANIZATION: ALARMS OR ALCHEMY?

Many of the CAS concepts match up with notions of change familiar to theorists and practitioners. For instance, Prigogine's (1984) work in chemistry highlights the importance of disequilibria in a system because it "dissipates" structure in order that the system might recreate itself in a new form. The analog in change management is to "unfreeze" a system through new inputs. Certainly there was unfreezing in this case as executives undertook their analyses of Unilever's world inside-out and outside-in.

However, many of the best known corporate transformations in areas of sustainability and CSR seem to start with and depend on transformational leaders – whether fiery founders like Anita Roddick at the Body Shop or makeover artists like Jeff Immelt at General Electric and Ray Anderson at Interface Carpets. What fascinates in this case is that Unilever's Cescau showed few characteristics of a transformational leader and provided scant hands-on leadership during Unilever's journey forward. Instead, he simply set it in motion by authorizing a study, giving his imprimatur to the conclusions, and providing legitimacy through the authority of his office.

Can transformation occur without top-down leadership and an "upheaval" to get things started? In an analysis of traditional writings about leadership, Rost (1991) summarizes a main conclusion: "Leadership is great men and women with certain preferred traits influencing followers to do what the leaders wish in order to achieve group/organizational goals ... defined as some kind of higher level excellence" (p. 180). A more critical reading finds that the literature is marked by a Western cultural (chiefly Anglo-American) bias; a self-interested and traditionally male-oriented point of view on leadership itself; a modernist, linear, structural-functionalist view of organizations; and a hierarchical, power-based view of the exercise of corporate leadership. Thus leadership models applied to the traditional paradigm of corporate responsibility tend to focus narrowly on the individual leader, achieving corporate goals, and overcoming "resistance to change."

Leading Toward Chaos

CAS theory, by comparison, turns attention away from single leaders and toward what Wheatley (1992) terms "the participative nature of the universe." Gunning was, by temperament and training, a communally oriented executive, deeply versed in the emotive and psycho-spiritual aspects of leadership, and taken to building cross-functional, multidisciplinary brand innovation and business teams (Mirvis & Ayas, 2008). With Cescau's backing, he engaged hundreds of Unilever's executives in a participatory process and brought "a whole system in the room." Ironically, as "everyone got to thinking about it," this yielded multiple and often competing, understandings of sustainability and CSR, and many and varied different ideas on how Unilever should respond to the challenges. In its essence, bringing the whole system into the room creates a microcosm of organization dynamics that helps to identify system dynamics in "real time" and becomes a "practice field" in which to experiment with new ways of working together collaboratively (cf., Weisbord, 1992).

In the stage model of corporate responsibility, the developmental challenge posed in this stage is integrate heretofore differentiated perceptions and activities. Now many companies do so with by establishing coordinative structures, reporting frameworks, and the like to pull things together. At Unilever, the opening act was to further complicate things by "informing" the system with data about the world outside and within the company, to dialogue deeply about its meaning, and, in so doing, to "contextualize" the company's attention. This process, to use adaptive system language, created a new informational and relational "field" within the organization (McTaggart, 2002) – one more open to the advance sustainability and CSR.

What about a burning platform? Think here, instead, about the "chaos" created by some many perspectives about the situation at hand and some many inputs on what to do. A chemical process that both breaks down existing elements and recombines them in new forms involves catalysis. In organizations, new knowledge has catalytic potential: it can simultaneously disconfirm old understandings and point to new directions. New relationships can also be catalytic: they can disrupt existing structural configurations and establish new ones. Suddenly marketers were talking to business leaders, HR was talking to the supply chain, and everyone was talking about sustainability and CSR.

In this CAS frame, Cescau, as CEO, and Gunning, heading the study team, sharpened the system's attention on sustainability and CSR, brought the company into and through a punctuated bout of chaos, and set the field for new thinking to emerge as people spoke of their understandings of the changing world around them and of the need for their company to be in a different place with its consumers and employees. Based on their approach, consider these questions for further theorizing about change in this area: Does this form of transformation mean that corporate leaders should operate more like alchemists than alarmists? And should leaders be less concerned about shaping their company's destiny and more about contextualizing it through information and dialogue?

NAMING THE NEW: VISION, VALUES, OR MISSION?

Most every article on advancing sustainability and CSR in companies stresses the importance of building a "business case." This means calibrating the potential risks and benefits of new initiatives for, say, company reputation, employee recruiting and retention, and cost savings or revenue enhancements, factoring in the expected time frame for return, and ensuring the investments deliver value to society as well as to the business.

Yet in building a business case firms often take a fragmented look at their overall corporate strategy and can miss the real benefits and impact that comes from first asking more fundamental questions, such as: "Who are we?" "How do we want to do business in society?" "What do we want to offer consumers and the public?" These questions evoke reconsideration of a company's core purpose and its corporate brand promise (Hatch & Schultz, 2008). Answering them helped Unilever to get out of chaos and into a "different place" with consumers and employees.

Who We Are

Experts on transformational change emphasize the importance of vision for guiding change and of values for keeping people enlisted and engaged (Senge, 1990). That said, while vision (what we want to achieve) and values (how we achieve them) are important, particular attention in the case of sustainability and CSR should be given to mission (an organization's answer to why we exist). There is always a need to confront tensions between the "old" and "new" way when making change. In periods of high instability, complex systems hit a "bifurcation point" or "fork in the road" at which energies for change either dissipate in ways that allow an old "attractor" to reassert itself or a new one to shift the system into a new form (Quinn & Cameron, 1988). This underscores the importance of a identifying a new or "strange" attractor in change management. Wheatley, among others, suggests that the equivalent to an attractor in human systems is "meaning." Thus one hypothesis is that Unilever's vitality mission served that attractor function in this case.

Mission speaks to the identity of a firm and what it seeks to contribute to society. Here's another theoretical (and researchable) question to reflect on: Could it be that an ennobling mission (more so than vision and values) affords authenticity and legitimacy to the development of sustainability and CSR in firms? What made Unilever's vitality mission especially compelling is that it drew a connection between the founder's ideals and the firm's renewed purpose to serve society through its products and people.

Why does mission matter? PepsiCo has committed itself to "performance with purpose" by "investing in a healthier future for people and our planet." Nestlé, in turn, is moving – in spirit and in its portfolio – from being an agro-food to a nutrition, health, and wellness brand. Its thrust was built on a foundation of compliance, moved to social and environmental sustainability, to a new platform of "creating shared value." Yet while both companies have made notable strides on sustainability and CSR, they have no founding heritage or legacy in these spaces. Perhaps this is one reason that they lag behind Unilever in Newsweek's (2010) green ranking of global companies and engender a great deal more criticism from consumers, CSR activists, and bloggers who see much of what they do as greenwashing.

Finally, the joining of the corporate brand with sustainability and CSR symbolizes a commitment to all stakeholders of the company – internal and external (McElhaney, 2008). Fulfilling a corporate brand promise creates a "virtuous cycle" whereby a stronger brand produces a better image of the company, and a better reputation in the eyes of the public yields effects back on employee attitudes and organizational identity. This, in turn, licenses employees to engage with other stakeholders both inside and outside the firm in activities in which they are invested as citizens of the planet. This has the potential to unleash tremendous motivation to use the resources of the firm to contribute more fully to society and can often create new sources of revenue for the company in the process (Hatch & Mirvis, 2010). Consider how Unilever unleashed its people as the transformation "rolled out" to the businesses and regions.

REARCHITECTING: ENGINEERING OR AUTOPOIESES?

Oddly, scholars of transformational change treat the rearchitecting and rebuilding of an organization rather matter-of-factly (Abrahamson, 2004). It is as though, once the new has been defined, getting there can be engineered through traditional change management techniques – analyses, plans, goals, and so forth. CAS theorists like Maturana and Varela (1987) and Jantsch (1980) have identified the property of self-reference in systems whereby small changes feed back on themselves and reverberate through the larger system. The dynamic, called autopoieses or self-organization, involves a series of nonlinear interactions that set the path by which a system evolves. There are a finite set of "possible" paths that systems follow depending on their complexity, feedback loops, energy flows, and the like. To see this process in action, consider how Unilever Asia enacted the vitality mission.

Prior to embarking on its game-changing agenda, Unilever was operating thousands of sustainability and CSR initiatives and programs around the globe and, as one put it, had a "thousand flowers blooming." The vitality mission may have aligned them conceptually, but it did not, of itself, activate or educate staff throughout Unilever, break down silos, promote cross-functional and cross-national collaboration, or stimulate break-through innovation. The rearchitecting called for coordinated movement in four areas: (1) management and staff activation; (2) translating the mission into the organization and practices; (3) product content and branding; and (4) customer, employee, and community engagement. Consider each of them in Unilever Asia.

- *Management and Staff Activation.* Leading the Asian business, Tex Gunning created a Pan-Asian community of leaders and led upward of 250 of them on periodic journeys throughout the region to explore economic, social, and environmental conditions and to "raise consciousness" about the world around them and consider their individual and collective mission (Mirvis, 2008b). The regional effort inspired the managers to conclude that rather than serving stockholders, or even stakeholders, their vitality mission was to "serve the world." Said one Asian leader, "Connecting with poverty in India reminds us that we need to build our business success by taking on social responsibilities – to help to protect the environment, to relieve poverty.... At the same time these actions will help our business grow."
- *Mission into Organization.* The Asian team went through a rigorous process of translating the vitality mission into brand platforms, market strategies, organizational models, and partnerships. A starting point was to connect senior leaders of seventeen national companies in the Asia Pacific region – which had previously operated independently – and to include the next layers of country marketers, supply chain managers, and corporate staff in setting strategy and reviewing performance for the whole of the regional business. The Asian leaders spent many months in varied forums sharing market information, consumer insights, and competitive analyses to develop a holistic picture of the region and to decide where to use local products and processes and where to reach across country lines. The sustainability and CSR challenges, less clear and more daunting, were to go through their own "outside in" and "inside out" analyses to determine how to connect their business to the interests of the markets *and* the societies in which they were doing business.
- *Product Content and Branding.* Ultimately, all of Unilever's product brands were put through economic, social, and environmental screens. This led to jettisoning some profitable brands that ran counter to their mission (because of ingredients or disposal issues), improving the chemical content of home-and-personal care products, and enhancing the nutritional value of most foods. In turn, social content was added to brand through innovations in fair trade and cause-related marketing

Fig. 5. Integrating Economic, Social, and Environmental Strategies in Unilever Asia.

(see Fig. 5). As an example, the company relaunched its Omo soap powder through a "dirt is good" campaign that promoted outdoor play among Southeast Asian schoolchildren by emphasizing its health benefits, building playgrounds, and educating mothers in how physical fitness complements academic success (a prime preoccupation in Asia families). And, of course, its Omo washing powder would clean children's mud-stained clothes! In turn, various national operating companies focused their attentions on cleaning up polluted rivers – where poorer mothers would wash their clothes.
• *Employee and Customer Engagement.* Finally, Unilever's Asian leaders took thousands of their staff on local mind-opening and heart-rending journeys, and worked with retailers, customers, and communities in a variety of social campaigns. In a journey to Sri Lanka, where many Asian leaders and the Indonesian staff went to offer service following the devastating tsunami, the sense of collective purpose was palpable. The volunteers spent several days cleaning up debris in schools and public buildings, helping local merchants to assess inventory and connect with suppliers, playing with children, and talking deeply with Sri Lankans, individually and in large gatherings. What did this soulful work teach the volunteers? "We listened to the fears and hopes of the mothers, fathers, and children left behind in this beautiful but devastated country. We shed tears of pain, hope, and love," recalled one leader. "We shed even more tears when we realized that by simply sharing our spirit with them we

made an incredible difference not only to their lives but also to our own. It continues to surprise me how care and service for others helps me discover my own love."

This four-dimensional effort was complex, feedback rich, and energizing – hardly the mechanical approach to "refreezing" or "institutionalization" found in the change management literature (cf., Zaltman & Duncan, 1977). The effort brought alignment to Unilever's game-changing in Asia and unleashed innovation throughout the region. Another question to consider from this case is to what extent the communal, emotional, even "soulful" aspects of the rearchitecting in Asia were crucial to its success. The change management literature gives pro forma attention to participation, activation, and emotional engagement of people through the change process. Many who frame change through CAS, however, speak of the importance of deep dialogue (Bohm, 1989), inner work (Senge, 2004), and surrender to the unfolding universe (Scharmer, 2009). Unilever's Asian journeys speak to the importance of these practices. In principle, evidence-based knowledge about environmental and social conditions can be gleaned from texts, documentary films, and conversations in any forum. But the experience of *being there physically* and *seeing first hand* adds texture to this knowledge and yields memories that increase mindfulness about the larger world (Wuthnow, 1991). Listen to one of Asian leaders on his mindfulness: "The core insight about great leadership comes down to service. Somehow it humanizes us. One of our problems, especially as we advance in positions of leadership, is that our egos get bigger and bigger, we suppress our human sides, and we don't listen to people – employees, customers, and others – whose needs should shape our business agenda. Face-to-face with great need, a leader is compelled to listen to the one in need."

CONTINUITY AND DISCONTINUITY

A few years after the transformation was launched, Gunning left Unilever (2007) and Cescau later retired (2008). Nevertheless, the transformation has continued on the global and local level. On the environmental front, for example, the company has significantly improved the eco-efficiency of its network of factories: CO_2 from energy has gone down by 40%, water use by 65%, and total waste by 73% per ton of production compared to a base of fifteen years ago. Roughly 15% of its tea and palm oil products are certified to be sustainably sourced and the company has opted to emphasize fair trade in its new product offerings.

Unilever has also tried to put an economic value on its engagement with society. It partnered with Oxfam to study the impact of its operations and products on Indonesia (Clay, 2005). The study looked at direct economic impacts via wages and taxes and throughout the value chain from suppliers to distributors to consumers. The total value generated in Indonesia over the five years of the study was conservatively estimated at US$633 million. Of this, Unilever Indonesia earned about US$212 million and the remaining US$421 million was distributed among other actors in the chain. A more in-depth study of microeconomic effects addressed Unilever's economic role in reducing poverty among the nation's agricultural workers and shopkeepers. Since that study, Unilever has conducted similar investigations of its impact in Vietnam and South Africa.

Finally, on the commercial front, Santiago Gowland translated the vitality mission into a brand imprint program that enables product brand managers to explore opportunities to innovate and improve their brands

Fig. 6. Unilever's Vitality Wheel.

in three ways: (1) boosting people's personal vitality and well-being, (2) addressing social issues, and (3) reducing environmental impacts (see Fig. 6). Metrics today cover greenhouse gas emissions, water use, waste, and sustainable sourcing and all Unilever brands are scored on these dimensions.

Balancing Acts

None of the foregoing, however, should imply that Unilever's transformation was seamless or that conflicts and tradeoffs were absent. Brown and Eisenhardt's (1998) studies of complexity in strategy highlight complex balancing acts, wherein managers have to, for example, balance past precedents versus future needs or movement toward intended directions versus available opportunities. In the case of sustainability and CSR, Mirvis and Manga (2010) find that managers have to balance corporate interests against those of line managers, trade off the benefits of conforming to external standards versus developing ones unique to their own businesses, and help their companies navigate through risks versus opportunities of taking a bolder stance on social issues.

Not all of Unilever's balancing acts have been successful. Take, for example, the Dove soap "inner-beauty" campaign. While this is a powerful message for women, Unilever also sells Axe deodorants and soaps aimed at young men. Advertisements for this product line emphasize how Axe products generate sex appeal and lead women, all portrayed as young, thin, and very attractive, to wantonly pursue men. Here the company is speaking out of both sides of its mouth and seemingly undermining its CSR message. Some argue, of course, that vitality for young men equals sex appeal, but the imagery associated with and product promotion of Axe versus Dove couldn't be more contradictory.

Furthermore, its acquisition of Ben & Jerry's has not been seamless. Massive layoffs at the company, the separation of the factory from reporting relationships to company management, and some ham-handed efforts to reduce the costs of ingredients had a telling effect on the acquired company's morale and customer satisfaction. It took the appointment of a new CEO, unaffiliated with Ben & Jerry's and Unilever, to fix product products and revitalize the ice cream maker's fun-and-funky culture (Mirvis, 2008c). This involved improvisation, time pacing, and what Brown and Eisenhardt term "co-adapting" among many interests.

A bold Step Forward

In late 2010, Unilever unveiled its Sustainable Living Plan whereby it intends to improve the health of 1 billion people, to buy 100% of its agricultural raw materials from sustainable sources, and to reduce the environmental impact of everything it sells by one-half, while doubling its revenues. The Unilever plan was announced with fanfare in London, New York, Rotterdam, and New Delhi by new CEO Paul Polman and it constitutes what Collins (1999) terms a "big hairy audacious goal (BHAG)." Interestingly, to achieve it the company will have to reach out to its consumers and activate them on sustainability and CSR. For instance, to reduce energy use associated with its soaps by half, Western consumers would have to cut their shower time by one minute. If 20 million consumers did so, the emissions reduced would be the equivalent of taking 110,000 cars off the road! Accordingly, Unilever has announced a "Turn off the tap" campaign for the United States in 2011.

RECONCEPTUALIZING TRANSFORMATION IN THE CASE OF SUSTAINABILITY AND CSR

Case studies of the transformations of Interface, General Electric, IBM, Novo Nordisk, and Levi Strauss & Co. find that each company considered carefully issues of sustainability and their responsibilities to society, involved outside experts, consulted multiple stakeholders, including critics, and involved their employees in self-study as they embarked on their transformational journeys (Mirvis, Googins, & Kinnicutt, 2010). Unilever, however, took the additional step of resurrecting its founding principles and adapting them to a new era. How important is legacy in this area?

GE referenced Thomas Watson in its recommitment to "do big things" and Levi Strauss could point to its founder who, after setting up his dry goods business in San Francisco in 1853, gave $5.00 to a local orphanage (the current equivalent of about $110), beginning a tradition of philanthropy and community service that continues today. One hypothesis is that this kind of back-to-the-future positioning can accelerate the pace of transformation and aid in authentic branding of new ventures. Interestingly, as Walmart embarked on its greening, there were early attempts to link it to founder Sam Walton's ideals and legacy. The connection, however, didn't ring true to employees, evoked an outcry in the blogosphere, and was soon dropped. The message here is that "saying it's so, don't necessarily make it so."

What is also notable is the extent to which Unilever's journey included so many "high touch" interventions – aimed at emotional engagement and consciousness raising, particularly in Asia. IBM, by comparison, used e-technology to engage employees – a values jam to redefine its core purpose and then innovation jams to develop and apply its smarter planet platform to megacities, environmental challenges, and poverty. Is this all about finding a culturally appropriate form of intervention to move a company forward on sustainability and CSR? Or are more emotive practices and sensibilities especially germane to the emergence of new forms of sustainability and CSR? (cf., Senge, Smith, Schley, Laur, & Kruschwitz, 2008).

The Sustainable Living Plan could be another game changer for Unilever going forward. Interestingly, however, with its BHAG and all the metrics, it seems to be primarily vision- and numbers-driven effort. Mirvis et al. (2010), looking over transformations on sustainability and CSR, conclude that a "combination of mission, vision, and values allows a company to triangulate its journey from three guideposts. Missing any one risks setting a company off course" (p. 322). A final question to consider then is whether a strong, hard number's driven vision will propel Unilever forward toward its ambitious aims; or might it work against some of its mission principles and humanistic values?

REFERENCES

Abrahamson, E. (2004). *Change without pain*. Boston: Harvard Business School Press.

Bartunek, J., & Louis, M. (1988). The interplay of organization development and organizational transformation. In: R. Woodman & W. Pasmore (Eds), *Research in organizational change and development* (Vol. 2). Greenwich, CT: JAI Press.

Beer, M., & Nohria, N. (2000). Cracking the code of change. *Harvard Business Review*, September.

Blumenthal, B., & Haspeslagh, P. (1994). Towards a definition of corporate transformation. *Sloan Management Review* (Spring), 101–106.

Bohm, D. (1989). *On dialogue*. David Bohm Seminars, Ojai, CA.

Brown, S. L., & Eisenhardt, K. M. (1998). *Competing on the edge: Strategy as structured chaos*. Boston: Harvard Business School Press.

Clay, J. (2005). *Exploring the links between international business and poverty reduction: A case study of Unilever in Indonesia*. Oxfam, GB, Novib Oxfam Netherlands, and Unilever.

Collins, J. (1999). Turning goals into results: The power of catalytic mechanisms. *Harvard Business Review* (July–August), 70–80.

Dooley, K. (2004). Complexity science models of organizational change. In: S. Poole & A. Van De Ven (Eds), *Handbook of organizational change and development* (pp. 354–373). Oxford: Oxford University Press.

Dunphy, D., Griffiths, A., & Benn, S. (2003). *Organisational change for corporate sustainability*. London: Routledge.

Emery, F. E., & Trist, E. L. (1965). The causal texture of organizational environments. *Human Relations, 18*, 21–32.

Googins, B., Mirvis, P. H., & Rochlin, S. (2007). *Beyond 'good company': Next generation corporate citizenship*. New York: Palgrave.

Greiner, L. (1967). Patterns of organization change. *Harvard Business Review* (May–June), 119–131.

Greiner, L. (1972). Evolution and revolution as organizations grow. *Harvard Business Review* (July–August), 37–46.

Hatch, M. J., & Mirvis, P. H. (2010). Designing a positive image: Corporate branding + CSR. In: T. Thatchenkery, D. Cooperrider, & M. Avital (Eds), *Positive design and appreciative construction: From sustainable development to sustainable value*, Advances in Appreciative Inquiry (Vol. 4). New York: Emerald.

Hatch, M. J., & Schultz, M. (2008). *Taking brand initiative: How companies can align strategy, culture, and identity through corporate branding*. San Francisco: Jossey-Bass.

Isenberg, D. J. (1987). The tactics of strategic opportunism. *Harvard Business Review, 65*, 92–97.

Jantsch, E. (1980). *The self-organizing universe*. Oxford: Pergamon.

Jones, G. (2005). *Renewing Unilever: Transformation and tradition*. Oxford: Oxford University Press.

Kauffman, S. (1996). *At home in the universe: The search for laws of complexity*. Harmondsworth: Penguin.

Keys, T., Malnight, T. W., & van der Graaf, K. (2009). Making the most of corporate responsibility. *McKinsey Quarterly* (December), 1–9.

Kleanthous, A., & Peck, J. (2006). *Let them eat cake*. World Wildlife Fund. WWF-UK.

Kotter, J. (1996). *Leading change*. Boston: Harvard Business School Press.

Kramer, M., & Kania, J. (2006). Changing the game. *Stanford Social Innovation Review* (Spring), 22–29.

Lawrence, R. G. (2004–2005). Framing obesity: The evolution of news discourse on a public health issue. The Joan Shorenstein Center on the Press, Politics, and Public Policy, Harvard University. Available at http://ksg.harvard.edu.

Maturana, H. R., & Varela, F. J. (1987). *The tree of knowledge*. Boston: Shambhala Publications.

McElhaney, K. A. (2008). *Just good business: The strategic guide to aligning corporate responsibility and brand*. San Francisco: Berrett-Koehler Publishers.

McTaggart, L. (2002). *The field: The quest for the secret force of the universe*. New York: HarperCollins.

Mintzberg, H. (1978). Patterns in strategy formation. *Management Science, 24*(9), 934–948.

Mirvis, P. H. (1994). Environmentalism in progressive businesses. *Journal of Organizational Change Management, 7*(4), 82–100.

Mirvis, P. H. (2000). Transformation at Shell: Commerce and citizenship. *Business and Society Review, 105*(1), 63–84.

Mirvis, P. H. (2008a). Development of corporate citizenship: Four trajectories. In: C. Cooper & R. Burke (Eds), *The peak performing organization*. London: Routledge.

Mirvis, P. H. (2008b). Executive development through consciousness raising experiences. *Academy of Management Learning & Education, 7*(2), 173–188.

Mirvis, P. H. (2008c). Can you buy CSR?. *California Management Review, 51*(1), 109–116.

Mirvis, P. H., & Ayas, K. (2008). Enhancing the psycho-spiritual development of leaders: Lessons from the leadership journeys in Asia. In: J. Gallos (Ed.), *Business leadership: A Jossey-Bass reader*. San Francisco: Jossey-Bass.

Mirvis, P. H., & Googins, B. (2006). Stages of corporate citizenship: A developmental framework. *California Management Review, 48*(2), 104–126.

Mirvis, P. H., Googins, B., & Kinnicutt, S. (2010). Vision, mission, values: Guideposts to sustainability. *Organization Dynamics, 39*, 316–324.

Mirvis, P. H., & Manga, J. (2010). Integrating corporate citizenship: Leading from the middle. In: N. Craig Smith, C. B. Bhattacharya, D. Vogel & D. Levine (Eds), *Global challenges in responsible business* (pp. 78–106). Cambridge: Cambridge University Press.

Newsweek. (2010). Green rankings: Global companies. Available at http://www.newsweek.com/2010/10/18/green-rankings-global-companies.html#

Piaget, J. (1969). *The psychology of the child*. New York: Wiley.

Prahalad, C. K. (2005). *The fortune at the bottom of the pyramid*. Upper Saddle River, NJ: Wharton School Publishing.

Prigogine, I. (1984). *Order out of chaos*. New York: Random House.

Quinn, B. (1980). *Strategies for change: Logical incrementalism*. Homewood, IL: Irwin.

Quinn, R. E., & Cameron, K. S. (Eds). (1988). *Paradox and transformation: Toward a theory of change in organization and management*. Cambridge, MA: Ballinger.

Rost, J. C. (1991). *Leadership for the twenty-first century*. Westport, CT: Praeger.

Scharmer, C. O. (2009). *Theory U: Leading from the future as it emerges*. San Francisco: Berrett-Koehler Publishers.

Schwab, K. S. (2008). Global corporate citizenship. *Foreign Affairs*, January.

Senge, P. M. (1990). *The fifth discipline: The art and practice of the learning organization*. New York: Doubleday/Currency.

Senge, P. (2004). *Presence: An exploration of profound change in people, organizations, and society*. New York: Currency.

Senge, P., Smith, B., Schley, B. S., Laur, S. J., & Kruschwitz, N. (2008). *The necessary revolution: How individuals and organizations are working together to create a sustainable world*. New York: Doubleday.

Tichy, N. M., & Devanna, M. A. (1986). *The transformational leader*. New York: Wiley.

Turner, V. (1957). *Schism and continuity*. Manchester: Manchester University Press.

Van de Ven, A. H., & Poole, M. S. (1995). Explaining development and change in organizations. *Academy of Management Review, 20*, 510–540.

Weisbord, M. (1992). *Discovering common ground*. San Francisco: Berrett-Koehler Publishers.

Werther, W. B., & Chandler, D. (2005). *Strategic corporate social responsibility: Stakeholders in a global environment*. Thousand Oaks, CA: Sage.

Wheatley, M. J. (1992). *Leadership and the new science: Learning about organization from an orderly universe*. San Francisco: Berrett-Koehler Publishers.

Wheelan, S. A. (2004). *Group processes: A developmental perspective*. Sydney: Allyn & Bacon.

Wuthnow, R. (1991). *Acts of compassion: Caring for others and helping ourselves.* Princeton, NJ:
     Princeton University Press.
Zadek, S. (2004). The path to corporate responsibility. *Harvard Business Review* (December),
     125–133.
Zaltman, G., & Duncan, R. (1977). *Strategies for change.* New York: Wiley.

CHAPTER 3

ON THE ROAD TO CORPORATE RESPONSIBILITY: THE INSTITUTIONALIZATION OF SUSTAINABILITY AT GAP, INC.

Christopher G. Worley

ABSTRACT

Purpose – *This chapter explores the use of evolutionary and institutionalization models to understand the progression of sustainability in organizations and their contribution to sustainable effectiveness. It describes the evolution of Gap, Inc.'s sustainability approach, its increasingly central role in the organization's strategy and design, and the methods it is using to institutionalize this critical change.*

Design – *The chapter describes alternative models of sustainability evolution and change institutionalization, and then applies the concepts in those models to understand Gap, Inc.'s sustainability journey.*

Findings – *The models of sustainability evolution and change institutionalization provide different but complimentary views on the extent to which sustainability is embedded in Gap, Inc.'s organization. These models can be a useful tool for assessing progress and recommending actions to increase the institutionalization of sustainability strategies and initiatives.*

Organizing for Sustainability
Organizing for Sustainable Effectiveness, Volume 1, 73–97
Copyright © 2011 by Emerald Group Publishing Limited
All rights of reproduction in any form reserved
ISSN: 2045-0605/doi:10.1108/S2045-0605(2011)0000001008

Originality and value – The findings of this chapter will help senior executives with responsibility for sustainability implementation. In addition to providing indicators for assessment of progress, findings of sustainability's institutionalization should prove helpful in predicting achievement of sustainable effectiveness.

Keywords: Institutionalization; sustainability; collaborative capability

Sustainability is an increasingly important organization concern and element of organization effectiveness (Worley & Lawler, 2010). But there is still a lot of unresolved debate over exactly what that means. Are the importance of sustainability and the definition of sustainable effectiveness a function of how many "green" initiatives the organization is implementing? Is it a function of how often it is mentioned in public speeches by executives or its prominence in mission and value statements? Is the importance of sustainability a function of how many resources the organization is devoting to it? All of these are, to some extent, indicators of how well sustainability has been internalized inside the organization and its slow but steady diffusion into our definitions of effectiveness.

The challenges associated with becoming a sustainably effective organization are only beginning to emerge, and the organizational requirements to support social, environmental, and financial outcomes is an active area of exploration and learning. But our experiences with other major organization changes, including six sigma, participative management, and reengineering, suggest that the number of black belts, employee engagement scores, and cycle time reduction are often inadequate measures of whether a strategy, capability, or organization change has become institutionalized. If sustainability is important, we would want to see sustainability and its structural and cultural corollaries become more central and embedded in the organization's operations, as taken for granted as financial performance. This article describes the evolution of Gap, Inc.'s sustainability approach, its increasingly central role in the organization's strategy and design, and the methods Gap, Inc. is using to institutionalize this critical change.

PERSPECTIVES ON THE INSTITUTIONALIZATION OF SUSTAINABILITY

Designing for sustainability is part strategy, part structure and process, and part culture. Case studies of the "usual suspects," such as Interface Carpet,

Patagonia, Unilever, Nike, and others, provide rich, qualitative, and empirical clues to the evolution and institutionalization of sustainability in organizations. The Interface story, for example, is intriguing because of its continuing commitment to sustainability in the face of severe cost cutting requirements. Environmental sustainability was part of their identity. However, there has been limited theoretical/conceptual work on the facets of institutionalization per se (Goodman & Dean, 1982) or how organizations evolve toward sustainable effectiveness (Mirvis & Googins, 2006; Werbach, 2009; Zadek, 2004; Amodeo, 2009). In this section, we review four such models, three specifically related to sustainability and one model of change institutionalization (Table 1).

Table 1. The Evolution and Institutionalization of Sustainability.

	Mirvis and Googins (2006)	Werbach (2008)	Zadek (2004)	Goodman and Dean (1982)
Primary phases	Elementary Engaged Innovative Integrative Transformative	Blind Aware Compliant Transparent	Defensive Compliant Managerial Strategic Civil	N/A
Key dimensions indicating persistence	Citizen concept Strategic intent Leadership Structure Issues management Stakeholder relationships Transparency	Role of the media/NGOs Transparency	Maturity of perspective	Knowledge Performance Preference Normative consensus Value consensus
Drivers of change	Challenges (credibility, capacity, coherence, commitment)	Strategy implementation	Market forces (social and organizational) Organizational learning	Congruence (market, strategic, organizational) Socialization Commitment Reward allocation Diffusion Sensing and calibration

Using data collected by Boston College's Center for Corporate Citizenship, Mirvis and Googins (2006) described a progression of "corporate citizenship." They suggested that firms could manifest five different stages – elementary, engaged, innovative, integrative, and transforming – that are anchored in strategy, leadership, structure, stakeholder relationships, and transparency.

- *Elementary* – Most organizations have a simple concept of citizenship. Their role in society is to provide jobs, pay taxes, and generate wealth. When it comes to sustainability, the primary strategy is simply to comply with laws and regulations. When issues concerning sustainability arise, the organization often reacts defensively and cites their compliance with the rules. Structurally, there are few if any resources dedicated to sustainability and little engagement with external stakeholders about it.
- *Engaged* – Companies in this stage espouse sustainability in an effort to legitimize themselves as a going concern. There may be philanthropic efforts to demonstrate sustainability's importance, but the public relations group handles most communication. The organization develops clear policies regarding social and environmental issues, there may be some dedicated staff groups, and there is an increasing dialogue with a variety of stakeholder groups.
- *Innovative* – The movement toward an innovative stage is signaled by the acknowledgment that sustainability issues are part of a business case. Leadership in the organization moves from supporter of sustainability to stewardship of the initiative. Leaders sponsor cross-functional projects to coordinate internal efforts and the organization works with external stakeholders to address areas of mutual interest. There are the beginnings of public reporting on sustainability progress.
- *Integrative* – In this stage, the organization has a sustainability value proposition. It works hard to proactively align the organization around a sustainability strategy, develop goals related to the "triple bottom line" (Elkington, 1994), and partner with stakeholders to accomplish change. Progress on sustainability is publicly available and confirmed by third-party sources.
- *Transformative* – In this final stage, the organization becomes an advocate for social change and moves to a leadership role within its industry if not more broadly. There is full disclosure regarding its sustainability activities and it works in multi-organizational alliances composed of governments, nongovernmental organizations, communities, and even competitors.

Modeled after Greiner's (1972) "evolution and revolution" framework, Mirvis and Googins proposed that particular challenges facilitated the movement from one stage to the next. They were quick to point out that the stages are by no means linear and determinant. Any particular organization may be quite advanced in some areas, demonstrating characteristics of an "integrative" stage but still having systems or perspectives that look very much "engaged." The *challenge of credibility* triggers the movement from an elementary to engaged stage. When an organization's meager support of sustainability becomes public, it must establish its credibility and legitimacy. For example, Loblaw is Canada's largest grocery and distribution chain. Interactions with WWF and Greenpeace over sustainable seafood challenged Loblaw's credibility, and the development of a sustainable seafood policy pegged the organization to specific improvements (Steele & Worley, 2011).

The *challenge of capacity* triggers the transition from engagement to innovation. During the engagement stage, the organization realizes that it will need additional resources, systems, and processes if it is to address successfully sustainability issues. Loblaw built and focused organizational capacity by appointing senior leaders to accountable positions and tasked with implementing the seafood policy. The challenge that moves the organization from innovation to integration is *coherence*. With the capacity added during the innovation stage, the organization must reconcile the capacity to address sustainability with its other capacities – to generate new products, to open new markets, to develop its leaders, and so on. All of these capacities must be rationalized into a coherent approach. As Loblaw's embedded new buying and merchandising procedures into the purchasing function and the stores, the organization had to learn to work with new stakeholders, deal with customer questions regarding availability of certain species, and build knowledge and skills related to sustainability. Finally, the transition to the transformative stage is triggered by the *challenge of commitment*. When sustainability has become a part of the organization's culture and identity, it moves to be an agent of social change. Loblaw's experience and success in sustainable seafood led them to become advocates for broader changes on the water and in the Canadian government.

Werbach (2009) suggests that organizations implementing sustainability strategies must pass through four phases of transparency. In the first phase, organizations are basically operating with a variety of "blind spots." They are unaware of their unsustainability. Many organizations, for example, are quite surprised at their carbon footprint once it is calculated, and it is often the sources of the footprint (e.g., travel, energy use) that are most surprising.

To move from "blind spots" to awareness, Werbach suggests that NGOs and activist protesting are often an important catalyst for change. Greenpeace and others have identified important (if sometimes dangerous) and visible violations of fishing practices, water pollution, and electronic waste. In awareness, organizations begin to take action. Efforts to address issues typically lead initially to compliance with regulation or other acceptable norms, and many organizations stop at this stage of strategy implementation and development. Werbach suggests that a higher level of implementation exists, which he calls "transparency." In transparency, the organization's actions and motivations are available and open. He suggests that the benefit of transparency is the speed with which change can occur. By being open and collaborating with others, any organization will become aware of more opportunities, more solutions, and more resources with which to approach sustainable goals.

A third evolutionary model of sustainability was proposed by Zadek (2004) who studied several organizations, and Nike in particular. Guided by an organizational learning approach, his observations suggested that organizations go through five phases – defensive, compliant, managerial, strategic, and civil. Similar to Mirvis and Googins' elementary stage and Werbach's "blind spot," the defensive phase is characterized by an organization that doesn't see sustainability as part of its mission or purpose. Suggestions that the organization should address these issues are met with resistance.

In the compliant phase, similar to Mirvis and Googins' engaged stage and Werbach's awareness phase, the organization complies with pressures to be more sustainable. Viewed as a risk management issue, the organization does what it needs to do to protect its brand, image, and reputation. The managerial phase is characterized by an understanding that addressing sustainability and corporate citizenship issues is part of the business. Managers are given the responsibility for integrating social and environmental practices into the operating model. The general belief is that to maintain the right to operate in the future, the organization must integrate sustainability into the organization and therefore resembles Mirvis and Googins' integrative stage. The strategic phase, also similar to Mirvis and Googins' integrative stage, views sustainability issues as a competitive opportunity. The organization uses sustainability as a criterion during new product/service development, in its marketing and sales materials, and in its recruiting messages. The final phase, civil, is similar to Mirvis and Googins' transformative stage. Here, the organization becomes an advocate for corporate responsibility.

Mirvis and Googins' model is the most comprehensive. It addresses both the stages an organization might go through as well as the triggers that spur movement from one stage to the next. Whereas Werbach slices the early stages more thinly by distinguishing between blindness, awareness, and compliance, Mirvis and Googins takes a finer grained approach to the latter stages by distinguishing between engagement, innovation, and integration. Similarly, Mirvis and Googins incorporate all aspects of organization design while Werbach's model is mostly concerned with strategy implementation, and Zadek's model is almost completely organization-centric. Zadek's model is more concerned with intra-organizational learning than interactions with the broader range of stakeholders. However, each model implicitly assumes or suggests that sustainability's maturity is reflected in its commitment – financially, strategically, culturally – to sustainable outcomes and embedding sustainability practices in operations. All models end up defining sustainable effectiveness as an enlightened, transformed, and proactive organization leading the charge for sustainability issues.

Unlike the models that suggest institutionalizing sustainability is the result of experience, the final model looks directly at the indicators and processes associated with embedding any change. Goodman and Dean (1982) proposed a model that describes how changes become institutionalized or persistent in organizations. While not aimed at sustainability per se, their models provide insights and measurements into how and why the implementation of large-scale changes like sustainability would "take hold" and persist in organizations. Goodman and Dean proposed that a change institutionalization could be assessed according to five increasingly stringent measures.

1. *Knowledge* refers to organization members understanding of the behaviors necessary to support a change.
2. *Performance* refers to whether people are actually performing those behaviors.
3. *Preferences* refer to a personal acceptance and belief in a change without organizational support.
4. *Normative consensus* is concerned with the extent to which people believe that the changes are the right thing to do and such support has become a part of the organization's belief system.
5. *Value consensus* goes a step further in looking at whether the organization supports culturally the values associated with the change, not the change itself.

These five measures constitute a "Guttman" scale, which suggests that achievement of any higher level of institutionalization automatically means that a lower level of institutionalization has happened. If an organization's approach to sustainability reaches the level of personal preference, then it is assumed that people understand (knowledge) and are behaving (performance) in ways that support sustainability.

Importantly, Goodman and Dean described the organization characteristics and mechanisms that must exist to support a change. First, sustainability is more likely to be institutionalized if it is "congruent" (Ledford, 1984) with the organization's environmental demands, its strategic intent and culture, and other changes taking place. For example, if there are strong pressures from customers, suppliers, buyers, communities, or other stakeholders, then sustainability should have a better chance of becoming a permanent feature of the organization. If sustainability is congruent with the organization's strategy, this too bodes well for institutionalization. Husted, Allen, and Rivera (2010) showed that when social and environmental projects were more central to an organization's mission and purpose, the organization was more likely to build collaboration capabilities with external stakeholders and more likely to develop internal sustainability capabilities. Lastly, sustainability should be easier to institutionalize if it aligns with and supports other changes going on. If an auto manufacturer is trying to implement a sustainability effort at the same time that it is fighting regulatory changes over exhaust or mileage requirements, organization members can be confused about the priority of such change efforts and less likely to support their implementation and institutionalization.

Second, Goodman and Dean suggest that when an organization supports a change with institutionalization processes, it improves the chances of persistence. The institutionalization processes include socialization, commitment, rewards, diffusion, and calibration. *Socialization* involves communicating the objectives of the change and its importance to the organization. *Commitment* involves a series of processes that invite people – personally and publicly – to accept and own a change. This type of personal commitment is different from the commitment of resources to a strategy. *Reward allocation* is concerned with linking knowledge and behaviors to execution of the change. People who are rewarded for supporting sustainability serve as role models for others. Institutionalization is supported when the organization *diffuses* solutions or best practices from one part of the organization to another. Finally, *sensing and calibration* involves using the organization's control systems – budgets, scorecards, performance management, information systems – to measure a change's impact on various outcomes and correct individual or unit behaviors that are not supporting sustainability. The institutionalization model is different from the evolutionary phase models and provides additional clarity about how a sustainability initiative might be managed to become embedded in the organization.

A NOTE ON METHODOLOGY

The Gap, Inc. case presented below draws from a number of published sources (e.g., Worley, Feyerherm, & Knudsen, 2010), publicly available information (e.g., www.gap.com), and original data collection efforts. For this chapter, I integrated the published and public materials into a chronological story that was compared with the sustainability evolution and change institutionalization models to assess Gap, Inc.'s journey. The opinions, conclusions, and recommendations expressed with respect to Gap, Inc.'s strengths and weaknesses are the author's and based on the data available.

SUSTAINABILITY AND THE APPAREL INDUSTRY

Sustainability in the apparel industry emerged as a concern in the late 1980s and early 1990s (Zadek, 2004; Frenkel & Scott, 2002). Individuals and NGOs concerned with the promotion of a more civil society created a wave of activism. The early targets of the activism – mostly Gap, Inc., Nike, Levi-Strauss, and Kathy Lee Gifford's line being sold at Wal-Mart – were charged with condoning sweatshop conditions, child labor, and forced labor in the factories producing garments. While the different apparel firms approached the media attention in their own way, the reality of the industry was that no one had a serious program in place to deal with the conduct of the factories. This lack of capability was mostly a function of the industry's structure.

The apparel industry's value chain consists of designing apparel, manufacturing and distributing garments, and marketing and merchandising them. As shown in Fig. 1, the manufacturing and distribution "supply chain" refers to the path from the farm where raw materials are grown to the stores where the clothes are sold. Virtually all apparel designers and retailers follow this stream of activities; however, the apparel brands do not own the farms, mills, or garment factories. To keep costs low, avoid duplication of invest-ment in specialized manufacturing capacity, and facilitate the ability to respond quickly to trends, a highly competitive and global system of factories exists. The large scale of the industry means that many governments and

Fig. 1. Apparel Industry Supply Chain.

cultures, thousands of people not directly employed by the brands, and a complex array of dyes, pesticides, and other environmentally sensitive activities are involved.

Social justice and ecological preservation have traditionally taken a back seat to profitability in this highly competitive and fragmented ownership pattern of factories, mills, ginners, and farms. Moreover, the lack of effective government regulation, poor management practices, or unethical owners resulted in unsafe working conditions, the nonpayment of legal wages, the denial of rights to freedom of association or movement, the support of child labor, and the pollution of land, air, and water. That the designers and retailers were surprised at being called to task for their role in this situation and the lack of capability to deal with it was understandable. The garment retailers were, for all intents and purposes, relatively blind to what was happening in the field.

GAP, INC.'S SUSTAINABILITY JOURNEY

Factory Compliance and Monitoring

The early 1990s thus represented an elementary, blind, and defensive period for nearly all of the apparel firms. Like others, Gap, Inc., currently a $14 billion (in 2009 revenues), 134,000 employee, global designer and retailer that is largely credited with the invention of the specialty retail segment, was relatively unaware of the conditions in the supply chain and their tacit role in supporting them. In response to credibility challenges raised by human rights groups, they moved into the engaged, aware, and compliance stage.

They began by employing a traditional "here's a business problem, let's solve it like we do other problems" strategy. Guidelines outlining general labor standards for vendors to follow were developed in 1992 and a vendor "code of conduct" was created in 1996. Gap, Inc. created a social responsibility function in the mid-1990s and appointed a vice president

(VP) for Global Compliance in 1996 to communicate the code to the factories. People were sent to monitor, visit, and work with factory management to address the violations reported.

This compliance and monitoring phase raised awareness of the industry's practices, established systems and processes of measurement, and did increase the number of factories adhering to basic labor and environmental standards. However, research conducted in 1996 by the Council on Economic Priorities (CEP) confirmed that early efforts focused on having suppliers sign a commitment to uphold a brand's code of conduct were generally ineffective. CEP's 1997 review of workplace codes showed that 80% of the codes failed to mention the right to freedom of association and 90% failed to mention the right to collective bargaining.

Moreover, the factories used by Gap, Inc. were also used by other apparel brands, some of which still did not have programs to address these issues. The different brands' codes of conduct were not standardized and each factory had to submit to multiple audits each year from each brand. Additional complexity could be added when factories were organized by multiple labor unions. Plants in Cambodia, for example, can have four or five different labor groups. Factory owners or plant managers found it difficult if not impossible to reconcile the often conflicting demands of the different brand buyers, the different labor groups' perspectives, the variety of monitoring organizations, and the diverse NGO community expectations. Without a comprehensive framework or systematic enforcement mechanism, the compliance strategy was often clumsy to enforce and its results inconsistent. Still, it represented an important building block.

Factory Capacity and Stakeholder Engagement

Gap, Inc.'s sustainability journey shifted from awareness and compliance and into a more innovative and managerial phase in 2001. The limitations of an imposed compliance approach and the inability to impact factory conditions resulted in Mirvis and Googins' challenge of capacity. When a new VP for corporate responsibility was hired, he spent a lot of time listening to both internal and external stakeholders and thinking about a new strategy.

Internally, the VP wanted to work with the sourcing organization to ensure that the factories heard a consistent message regarding the importance of human rights in the manufacturing of Gap, Inc. garments. Any brand's sourcing department is the key stakeholder from the factory's perspective because of its role in contracting for garment production. One of the early internal collaboration efforts involved the corporate responsibility group, the sourcing department, and laundries in China where fabric was washed prior to it being cut and sewn into garments. Many of the laundries were being dropped from contracts because of compliance violations. The sourcing manager noted that if the number of laundries available continued to decline, the organization would have to contract with new laundries with unknown compliance ratings in other countries at a higher cost and with some disruption in the supply chain. The regular meetings between corporate responsibility and the sourcing general managers to resolve issues of vendor compliance kept the laundries operating and helped to develop trust among the three groups. One of the biggest successes was an increased understanding of how denim fabrics could be washed without polluting local water supplies.

Externally, the VP engaged a local San Francisco NGO, Business for Social Responsibility, to conduct a stakeholder mapping process. The exercise produced two important conclusions: (1) stakeholders possessed information and experience that when combined with Gap, Inc.'s knowledge could be used to generate better solutions for the factory and (2) without an alignment of interests, even the best compliance system in the world would not be enough to build Gap, Inc.'s credibility as a voice for change. After much internal reflection, Gap, Inc. rejected the notion of going it alone or simply working with industry groups and competitors to solve the problem. They decided that a strategy of collaborating with others – even those critical of their efforts – would be a more productive path. Gap's 2005–2006 corporate social responsibility report outlined the perspective and philosophy that had been growing: " ... the preferred approach on the ground is increasingly moving from a strict monitoring model to one that can identify root causes and building the capacity of factories to address poor working conditions in a sustainable way. We hope to continue leveraging the independent monitoring groups' expertise, independence, local knowledge, and credibility with workers in ways that will help achieve this goal."

In 2002, the VP formed a separate stakeholder engagement function to develop an external stakeholder collaboration process. Combining the ability to mobilize multiple stakeholders to increase a factory's management capacity with the compliance and monitoring capability was an important step and signaled Gap, Inc.'s movement into the innovative stage. A good example of this new approach is provided by the CIMCAW (Continuous Improvement in the Central American Workplace) project.

THE CIMCAW PROJECT

China's admission to the World Trade Organization in 2001, the end of the Multi-fiber Arrangement in 2005, and the creation of the Central American-Dominican Republic Free Trade Agreement (DR-CAFTA) radically shifted the basis of competition for apparel workers in Central America. Through training and dialogue, the CIMCAW project sought to raise awareness that improved working conditions in Central America were important for the region to remain competitive in the global apparel industry.

The CIMCAW project was an inclusive, social dialogue among the key sector stakeholders. CIMCAW partners included the United States Agency for International Development (USAID), Social Accountability International (SAI), the International Textile, Garment & Leather Worker's Federation (ITGLWF), Development Alternatives Inc. (DAI), and several apparel brands including Gap. Together, workers and managers developed the management systems of local supplier factories, such as problem-solving teams, process improvement systems, and supervisory relations training. The joint training provided information on fundamental worker rights, and identified approaches for meeting national and international labor standards that enhance productivity and competitiveness. It also strengthened the capacity of local monitoring groups and government inspectors to carry out workplace evaluation now done by the multinational buyers.

As the CIMCAW project evolved and practices were reinforced at the local level, the critical role of government became apparent. An important innovation was the creation and development of multi-stakeholder Consultative Committees with representation from government, industry, and trade unions in three countries. Despite historical conflict among some of these actors, the committees successfully contributed to CIMCAW's direction, created a space to address broader industry issues, and brought government into the conversation. These committees, trainings, and projects have brought together factory owners and managers as well as local and international trade union representatives to create a dialogue where all actors have a shared interest and are free to work together without compromising the goals of their respective organizations.

The results from this expanded capability were very satisfying. Projects like CIMCAW increased Gap, Inc.'s organizational capability to engage in collaborative activities with multiple stakeholders, improved its visibility as a corporate social responsibility leader, and improved the performance of the factories in its supply chain. In particular, the factory ecosystem was becoming more capable, and workers in Latin America and Asia were benefitting from better working conditions and management relationships. Gap, Inc.'s multi-stakeholder collaboration capability was widely recognized as best in class, and their public reporting gained increased transparency. This reinforced Gap, Inc.'s approach of developing ongoing relationships instead of making each crisis an independent issue that required little follow-up. Their "social license" to operate was increased by working with and understanding other stakeholders in the community in which they practiced.

In addition, Gap, Inc.'s consistent work with the factories and involvement with SAI, Interfaith Center for Corporate Responsibility (ICCR), and other labor and environmental organizations built credibility and became an important network to address labor and social issues around the world. For example, when an inaccurate but potentially embarrassing news story about child embroiderers working on shirts was brought to Gap's attention by the NGO community, the stakeholder engagement group's ability to quickly investigate, respond, and take action allowed it to get in front of the story. When the BBC, Good Morning America, and the newspapers wanted comment, Gap, Inc. had the facts, took appropriate responsibility, and explained the actions it was already taking to address these industry-wide issues. The Gap, Inc.'s increased credibility as an authentic and progressive buyer served the company well during this incident. Not only were they trusted by the NGO community who informed them in advance of the story's release, a number of labor rights groups went on record with the media, highlighting Gap, Inc.'s handling of these issues. Gap, Inc.'s responses to the crisis were so prompt and clear that media coverage began and ended in a week.

Sustainability and the Supply Chain

The learnings from the combined monitoring, compliance, and collaboration capability revealed frustrating aspects as well. In particular, the focus on the factory left much of the supply chain – and many of the problems they were trying to address – out of scope. As Gap, Inc. and their partners worked to build capacity in the factories, they developed intimate knowledge of factory operations and contracting procedures. A recurring problem was getting the factories to avoid suppliers that were clearly in violation of human rights and labor laws. For example, even if the factories were certified, the fabric, materials, and accessories used to make Gap, Inc. garments could come from sources that were not in compliance with Gap, Inc.'s values and code of conduct. Many of these suppliers were simply "hidden" in the supply chain.

Despite the improved capacities and monitoring systems of the factories, controlling all the facets of the supply chain required tackling problems further up the supply chain, including the farms, the ginners, and the mills, and engaging an even broader range of stakeholders. For example, Gap, Inc.'s participation in a wide variety of networks and multi-stakeholder initiatives made it clear that a substantial amount of cotton from Uzbekistan, where child labor is routinely supported, was finding its way into the apparel manufacturing supply chain. Such practices are driven by diverse and deeply ingrained forces including a long history of forced labor for the cotton harvest, a "command economy" in the cotton sector that gave the government control over what farmers planted and where they sold their crops, and the ease and profitability of utilizing underage workers. The complexity of the supply chain – especially from the raw materials farmers to the ginners/spinners and the mills – meant that apparel designers and retailers, including Gap, Inc., had almost no way of knowing whether any of the cotton fabrics had been sourced with Uzbek cotton.

In deciding to use their knowledge and skills in sourcing practices, experience in collaborating with other stakeholders, and a deep understanding of the industry, Gap, Inc. was clearly moving into the transformation and civil phases – and in many ways skipping over the strategic and integrative stages. For example, involving the United States and European governments as key stakeholders greatly elevated a project's visibility and complexity. Moreover, expanding their lens to identify a raw material's point of origin and addressing the use of child labor at the farm level was challenging for Gap, Inc. since its primary problem solving and capacity building expertise was in the factories. As history had taught them, saying they were against a labor practice was important; however, ensuring that it wasn't happening would take time and collaboration.

In this case, Gap, Inc. initially made it clear to all of their factories that child labor was unacceptable and that they should not knowingly source yarn from

Uzbekistan farms. However, to encourage the Uzbek government to evolve its practices, Gap, Inc. joined a coalition of other like-minded organizations and groups, including the International Labor Rights Forum (ILRF), As You Sow, Center for Reflection, Education and Action (CREA), ICCR, Calvert Investments, the Environmental Justice Foundation, other apparel brands, investor organizations, and eventually the US government. Together, this diverse coalition of stakeholders built common ground, shared goals, action plans, and trust to develop solutions. Fortunately, many of these groups had worked together before and their successes over time brought trust and alignment.

The coalition not only wanted to insure that the factories and mills avoided sourcing cotton from Uzbekistan; they wanted to affect change at the farm level as well. The coalition agreed that a tracking system was needed to increase their visibility into the country point of origin for raw materials. To do that, the coalition is working with a supply chain traceability expert, and Gap, Inc. has started its own development effort to create a tool to trace and verify where materials come from.

Organizing and Institutionalizing Sustainability

The case makes clear that Gap, Inc. has been implementing design changes to support sustainability over the course of its journey. Beginning with the creation of a social responsibility function in the mid-1990s and the appointment of a VP in 1996 to the creation of a stakeholder engagement group, there have been changes in the structure, but mostly at the periphery. That all changed in 2008 and 2009 when the broader Gap, Inc. organization began to think about integrating sustainability into its strategy and operations.

Structurally, Gap, Inc. made important and integrative commitments to sustainability. First, the board of directors elevated sustainability's visibility in the organization. Rather than reporting into a subcommittee, the full board rearranged its agenda to receive regular updates on the company's social responsibility progress. Second, at the executive level, HR, sustainability, public policy, and communications were integrated and consolidated into the Global HR and Corporate Affairs function (see Fig. 2) under an executive vice president (EVP). Rather than creating a purely functional structure, Gap, Inc. created several integrated organizations. Reporting to the EVP were brand HR; global HR; HR strategy, rewards and operations;

Fig. 2. The Global HR and Corporate Affairs Function.

corporate communications; and the newly formed global responsibility group.

Leading up to the reorganization, the VP was promoted to senior vice president (SVP) of Global Responsibility in 2005, and in 2008 his duties expanded to include several human resource functions, including Global Employee Relations, Talent Management, and Diversity & Inclusion. Bringing these functions into the global responsibility organization integrates social responsibility practices with Gap, Inc.'s talent management strategy. For example, one of the first projects was to bring social responsibility training into Gap, Inc.'s Retail Academy, a program that provides product skills training to employees.

Expanding the scope of the VP's role also required that the social and environmental sustainability activities be given increased prominence and focus. In 2010, to support the ongoing factory-oriented compliance and capacity-building efforts as well as the broader industry and supply chain efforts, a reorganization was implemented that consolidated the ecological sustainability activities, the stakeholder engagement capability, and the factory monitoring groups under one leader (Fig. 3).

The newly created VP for Social and Environmental Responsibility (SER) was filled by a woman who had come to the sustainability organization from the North American production group in the brands. For three years prior to this appointment, she had been working to build out capabilities in strategic planning and environmental sustainability and leading one of the stakeholder engagement functions. Reaching into the brands helped SER gain further legitimacy and alignment with key functions in the organization. The social responsibility (field compliance), strategic planning, stakeholder engagement, and environmental affairs organizations all now rolled up into one singular focus. Prior to this restructuring, the social

Fig. 3.   Global Responsibility Function.

responsibility and environmental groups reported separately and coordination had been more ad hoc.

Concurrent with the reorganization, the SER leadership team and the SVP of global responsibility began a strategic planning process with a very different focus. They wanted to understand whether it was possible to leverage the group's 15 years of experience and learnings in the field to the broader Gap, Inc. organization. The result of the initial discussions was both very risky and very exciting. The aim of their strategy was to leverage Gap, Inc.'s credibility and trust among the ecosystem of external stakeholders and to use their multi-stakeholder collaboration capability as an asset for Gap, Inc. The focus of the strategic exercise was captured by the question, "How could our multi-stakeholder collaboration capability be applied to the larger Gap, Inc. organization?"

In the main – although certainly not exclusively – the compliance and stakeholder engagement teams were not working with the Gap, Inc. groups whose decisions often contributed to the problems they were solving. Despite the collaboration among stakeholder engagement, compliance, and the sourcing organization, they each worked primarily with the groups and organizations that campaigned against and challenged Gap, Inc.'s responsibility in the first place. There were few conversations about whether the garments were being designed for good labor practices or whether the specifications of fabrics and colors considered the environmental implications of their processing. In short, the social responsibility organization was managing the consequences of those choices, not the choices themselves. A variety of initiatives are being considered where the multi-stakeholder collaboration capability is being used to bring the relevant parties together earlier in the design process and apply a life cycle approach. The implementation of their strategy is ongoing and represents an important "next step" in Gap, Inc.'s sustainability journey.

DISCUSSION

It is relatively easy to tell the story of Gap, Inc.'s evolution in sustainability according to the phases described by Mirvis and Googins (2006), Zadek (2004), and Werbach (2009). The models provide an excellent frame for understanding how Gap improved its visibility as a CSR leader, increased their transparency regarding activities, and improved the performance of its supply chain. The case data support the conclusion that Gap, Inc. has many of the characteristics of a transformative, transparent, and civil organization. The organization's proactive actions to bring about change in the core processes and systems at the factory level and to work with other NGOs and like-minded retail brands to affect change along the entire supply chain would seem to be requisite behaviors for transformative status. While Gap does promote sustainability in its advertising, taking the sustainability message to consumers in a more proactive way may be the next challenge.

To operate in a sustainable manner, the ecosystem of firms, NGOs, and governments need to work together, and that requires learning in all parts of the system, including consumers. Gap, Inc.'s efforts, in collaboration with NGOs, other brands, and governments, set standards, structures, and processes that provided a basis for that coordination. The early work was necessary, if basic, because it set the foundation for different parts to work together. Doing so always carries the risk of losing a potential competitive advantage. Cooperation, collaboration, and standard setting levels the playing field for all. In the case of sustainability, however, Gap, Inc. cannot solve the problems of labor fairness or environmental harm alone even if it chose to fully integrate and own all of the assets in the supply chain – an untenable strategic choice in this industry.

But to answer the questions, "Is sustainability an important and institutionalized part of Gap, Inc.?" and "Is Gap a sustainable organization?" we need to look at the case through the lens of the other model.

Indicators of Institutionalization

The case provides *prima facie* evidence that the stakeholder engagement, compliance, and other groups related to social and environmental sustainability reflect all of the indicators of institutionalization. They possess the knowledge related to sustainability and they demonstrate behaviors that support sustainable activities. Most importantly, there is a strong normative and value consensus regarding sustainability.

Creating a sustainable organization is difficult in the best of circumstances, but it is much easier when the organization's values and identity are compatible with definitions of sustainable effectiveness. Since its founding, Gap, Inc. has lived according to a set of values that today are referred to as "wearing your passion." They include think customers first, inspire creativity, do what's right, and deliver results. The sustainability group's persistent pursuit of "doing what's right" – right for human rights, right for the business, right for the environment – can be traced to these core values. The group hires people who reflect these values and use them to influence hiring and promotion actions.

This normative and value consensus is the result of an open environment of information sharing. SER members spend a lot of time with each other discussing projects, industry and professional news, and their latest readings. It is also the result of an empowered group of people. Consciously or unconsciously, the organization has developed more quickly because there is a sense of "if you want to and you can, you may." While not written down or spoken that way, the members of the SER organization are accountable and responsible for sustainable actions. Their passion for and understanding of the Gap, Inc.'s values as well as the SER's mission and purpose have resulted in an empowered and engaged organization that takes initiative. The director of stakeholder engagement reflected, "I've seen some other companies have difficulty and lose patience when they approach collaboration as an add-on or a technique rather than an underlying philosophy of how to approach sustainability."

While there is a strong case for sustainability's institutionalization within the SER group, the indicators of institutionalization are less compelling at the enterprise level. There is good evidence that sustainability may be institutionalized at the knowledge and performance levels as well as some evidence of support at the preference level. For example, there were and are a variety of other "sustainability" initiatives taking place in different parts of the organization. Each brand within Gap, Inc., has their own (or shared) programs related to clean water, recycling, ethical sourcing, energy use, and other mostly environmentally related projects that can involve the engagement groups but do not necessarily include them. A number of these projects were generated in a "bottoms-up fashion." In other words, people are initiating activities because they want to, not because it is part of some program, which is a singular feature of the preference category of institutionalization (Goodman & Dean, 1982).

But there is little concrete evidence of strong normative and value consensus. The organization might be criticized from the perspective that despite all the visible work done by the stakeholder engagement and compliance groups, garments may still be designed according to cost and fashion criteria that are at odds with the use of sustainable materials or socially or environmentally sound manufacturing practices. It was this concern that led to the SER strategic planning objectives and process – to use their capabilities to bring a life cycle perspective to the rest of the organization. Practically, however, it probably reflects the simple notion that the organization responded to the places where they experienced pain. Their factory and other supply chain relationships were a source of risk that needed to be addressed. What the SER organization learned in those experiences has not yet permeated the economic logic of the rest of the organization. The more functional argument is that sustainability has a solid beachhead in an important part of the organization and in the organization's culture.

Levers for Driving Sustainability Deeper

There may be a stronger case for sustainability's institutionalization in the SER group than the broader Gap, Inc. organization. However, the firm is actively using many of the institutionalization mechanisms to drive sustainability into Gap, Inc.'s DNA. The use of a broad array of these mechanisms bodes well for Gap, Inc.'s future in sustainability.

First, they are actively managing sustainability's congruence with environmental pressures, strategic choices, and other changes. Sustainability, both as a specific capability developed by the SER group as well as its inclusion in the brands, sourcing, and facilities organizations, is being aligned with the pressures brought to bear by a variety of marketplace stakeholders. Similarly, Gap, Inc.'s strategies and values have increasingly reflected the tenets of sustainability. Whether it is the result of the engagement and compliance work or the result of some broader strategic awareness, the brand strategies at Gap, Old Navy, and Banana Republic are increasingly linking their product and advertising message to sustainability issues. For example, the Gap brand is advertising a denim-recycling program where old jeans are turned into housing insulation and a new pair of jeans is 20% off. Finally, sustainability is a complex change, including initiatives such as the denim and clean water projects, recycled price tags, and energy consumption; social initiatives, such as community involvement, diversity and inclusion projects, and employee engagement; as well as financial projects related to lowering costs. Almost any other change being implemented – facility/store redesigns, international expansion, or plans for revenue growth – can be designed to align with sustainability in mind.

Second, Gap, Inc. is using corporate communications, internal newsletters and communications, an extensive and maturing web site, and other traditional communication vehicles to ensure that people are exposed to Gap, Inc.'s social and environmental activities. However, the global responsibility and SER functions are aware that many of its efforts and results in the field are not widely known within the Gap, Inc. organization. In fact, some NGOs even commented that the dedication to social responsibility was more apparent in the group than in the enterprise. Gap, Inc. could improve the socialization of its members by exposing more of them to more of the work being driven in SER. This might be accomplished by rotating brand and sourcing managers through the SER organization as part of its leadership development process.

Third, Gap, Inc. is shifting its performance management systems to measure and reward sustainability-related behaviors. Sustainability objectives are now included in mangers annual performance goals and a portion of compensation changes is tied to their achievement. Most managers acknowledge, however, that this is a work in progress.

Fourth, Gap, Inc. is working hard to diffuse sustainability behaviors, values, and best practices throughout the organization. SER's recent strategic planning efforts are addressing this very issue and the concern that sustainability is more important in SER than in the rest of the organization. The global responsibility and SER organizations are building deliberate linkages into the Gap, Inc. organization. The reorganization of the HR function has made the transfer of skills and knowledge regarding sustainability to the rest of the organization a priority and a reality. People throughout the organization are being taught about the right way to do things and contributing to its institutionalization. In addition, the SER leadership team is expanding the internal collaboration process that had started with the source organization. SER recently invited an NGO expert on factory working conditions to engage the brands in a series of discussions on how design and purchasing decisions could create unintended consequences affecting the entire organization. The expert described the case of doubling an order of shirts due to higher than expected market demand. Without an understanding of supply chain dynamics, such an order could create pressures in the supply chain that would lead to a range of negative outcomes. Far from saying there should never be increases in orders, the SER group was suggesting that people stop and ask the questions. What are the impacts? Does the vendor have the capacity? Who all needs to be involved in this decision? Such broad involvement would pose less risk to the organization and create better outcomes for a broad range of stakeholders.

Another important diffusion attempt is the creation of an environmental council. The council's mission is to improve how Gap, Inc. uses resources to reduce the environmental impact with regard to ECO (Energy, Cotton/ sustainable design and Output and waste). It operates as a think tank for the senior executives and a cross section of mid-level managers to identify and prioritize opportunities to support the ECO focus, engage and influence senior leadership, share best practices, and participate on committees to tackle projects that cut across the brands.

Fifth, Gap, Inc. is working hard to reinforce its sustainability perspective through active reporting that calibrates progress. The sustainability section of Gap, Inc.'s website is full of cases, testimonials, measurements of factory and supply chain progress, and other activities that draw from SER's work as well as from contributions in the brand organizations. The organization actively manages and updates the website content, and sends a message to both internal organization members and external stakeholders that this is an important part of the Gap, Inc. organization.

CONCLUSION

The rhetoric around sustainability is clear. A recent global survey of CEOs by the United Nations found that 96% believe sustainability issues are critical to the future success of their firms. However, we need to go beyond the number of initiatives, advertisements about a company's commitment to the environment, and websites that list all the NGOs the corporation is partnering with to assess the extent to which sustainability is truly institutionalized.

Our theories and frameworks of sustainability's evolution within in an organization can provide very useful markers regarding progress. They identify behaviors, structures, and systems that need to change to move to higher levels of integration and effective indicators of implementation. Our models and frameworks of change institutionalization provide a slightly different but complimentary view on the extent to which sustainability practices are simple appendages to an organization's design or something that is truly integrated into the corporation's strategy and culture.

The Gap, Inc. case provides ample evidence of the utility of these frameworks and demonstrates their application. Gap, Inc. has clearly evolved in its sustainability maturity – in some parts more than others – but that differentiation, that the SER group is farther along than the rest of the enterprise, is an important benefit of the models. They help us to see that Gap, Inc. is still on the journey and is actively managing its way toward sustainable effectiveness.

REFERENCES

Amodeo, M. (2009). The Interface journey to sustainability: Identity dynamics within cultural incrementalism. In: P. Docherty, M. Kira & A. Shani (Eds), *Creating sustainable work systems: Developing social sustainability* (pp. 38–50). London: Routledge.

Elkington, J. (1994). Towards the sustainable corporation: Win-win-win business strategies for sustainable development. *California Management Review, 36*(2), 90–100.

Frenkel, S., & Scott, D. (2002). Compliance, collaboration, and codes of labor practice. *California Management Review, 45*(1), 29–49.

Goodman, P., & Dean, J. (1982). Creating long-term organizational change in organizations. In: P. Goodman (Ed.), *Change in organizations* (pp. 226–279). San Francisco: Jossey-Bass.

Greiner, L. (1972). Evolution and revolution as organizations grow. *Harvard Business Review, 50*(4), 37.

Husted, B., Allen, D., & Rivera, J. (2010). Governance choice for strategic corporate social responsibility. *Business and Society, 49*(2), 201–215.

Ledford, G. (1984). *The persistence of planned organizational change: A process theory perspective*. Doctoral dissertation, University of Michigan.

Mirvis, P., & Googins, B. (2006). Stages of corporate citizenship. *California Management Review, 48*(2), 104–126.

Steele, B., & Worley, C. (2011). Loblaw sustainable seafood initiative. (G 11-06). Los Angeles: University of Southern California, Center for Effective Organizations.

Werbach, A. (2009). *Strategy for sustainability: A business manifesto*. Boston: Harvard Business Press.

Worley, C., Feyerherm, A., & Knudsen, D. (2010). Building a collaboration capability for sustainability: How Gap, Inc. is creating and leveraging a strategic asset. *Organizational Dynamics, 39*(4), 325–334.

Worley, C., & Lawler, E. (2010). Built to change organizations and responsible progress: Twin pillars of sustainable success. In: W. Pasmore, A. Shani & R. Woodman (Eds), *Research in organizational change and development* (pp. 1–50). Bingley, UK: Emerald Press.

Zadek, S. (2004). The path to corporate responsibility. *Harvard Business Review, 82*(12), 125.

CHAPTER 4

TOWARDS A SUSTAINABLE HEALTHCARE SYSTEM: TRANSFORMATION THROUGH PARTICIPATION

Svante Lifvergren, Peter Docherty and Abraham B. (Rami) Shani

ABSTRACT

This chapter examines the developmental journey toward a sustainable healthcare system in the west of Skaraborg County in Sweden from 2000 to 2010. It tracks a stream of collaborative research projects within the context of the Swedish sustainability debate that were focused on achieving improved care quality, patient safety, efficiency, and efficacy. The case reports how a central government directive to integrate healthcare at the local level – the county – led to the establishment of a development coalition management group that designed and managed the transformation via broad participation and engagement mechanisms. The transformation process toward a more sustainable healthcare system raises theoretical and practical questions about sustainable effectiveness,

Organizing for Sustainability
Organizing for Sustainable Effectiveness, Volume 1, 99–125
ISSN: 2045-0605/doi:10.1108/S2045-0605(2011)0000001009

the role of partizcipation and learning mechanisms such as democratic
dialogue conferences in sustainable effectiveness, the tension between
planned and emergent change processes, and the challenge of integration
in the drive toward a sustainable healthcare system.

Keywords: Sustainability; sustainable effectiveness; participation;
learning mechanisms; transformation; development coalition;
democratic dialogue conference; sustainable healthcare system

The healthcare sector is facing extraordinary pressures and unsettling
challenges. Life expectancy is increasing, and thus proportionately more
people are developing multiple and complex diseases. Increases in the
capability of new treatment modalities and their costs, demographics and
economic forces in both developed and developing nations, and fragmentation in healthcare systems contribute to the pressures on healthcare systems.
New ways of organizing healthcare are required to provide and sustain high
quality care in line with patient expectations.

In Sweden, as in many countries in the European Union, healthcare needs
of all legally registered citizens are provided for by the state, at a moderate
cost and at a reasonable resource level, with good accessibility to care and
with good medical outcomes. This is mainly financed through individual
and corporate salary-based taxes. Healthcare answers for 9.2% of the gross
domestic product in Sweden, compared with 15.3% in the United States
(OECD Data, 2008). Swedish primary and hospital healthcare are organized
at the regional level, while after-care services are organized at the municipal
level.

This chapter describes the developmental journey of a local healthcare
authority in the west of Skaraborg County in Sweden toward a more
sustainable healthcare system. It tracks a stream of projects within the
county that were focused on achieving improved care quality, patient safety,
and efficiency. The case reports how a regional government directive to
integrate healthcare at the local level led to the establishment of a development coalition management group (DCMG) and the development of
participative learning mechanisms. Among the innovations described are
the use of democratic dialogue (DD) conferences – a structural learning
mechanism – as an engine for knowledge creation and knowledge transfer,
and the integration of a balanced scorecard (BSC) – a cognitive and
procedural learning mechanism – as a managerial tool to enhance sustainable
effectiveness.

THEORETICAL FRAMING: SUSTAINABILITY AND SUSTAINABLE HEALTHCARE

The emerging scientific body of knowledge about sustainability focuses on many different aspects of this transition (Mohrman & Shani, 2011, chap. 1, this volume). This chapter explores sustainability through the lenses of transformation and planned change, participation, learning mechanisms in general, and DD conferences in specific. Elkington (1997) defined the main *outcome* domains of sustainability as the "triple bottom line" – the ecological, the social, and the economic. The central theme of his thesis is the recognition that for a company to prosper over a long period of time it must find a way to meet society's needs without draining natural and social capital.

The point of departure in this chapter is that sustainability is not only an outcome but also entails the building of dynamic capacity within an organization to meet internal and external challenges of continual development. Although the *goal* of sustainability is to promote the continual regeneration of social, economic, and ecological resources, this chapter seeks to explore the "how" of sustainability. From this perspective, sustainability is viewed as the development of new capabilities and requires new ways of organizing and the design and implementation of a tapestry of learning mechanisms, leading to system-wide transformation (Docherty & Shani, 2009; Mohrman & Worley, 2010). We define sustainable capacity as an organizational ability to continuously learn from and cope with novel situations without losing options for the future. This entails the participation of coworkers and managers in recurrent and transparent dialogues at all levels to solve critical, emerging organizational challenges. Learning mechanisms provide the arena in which practitioners and researchers work side by side in the cocreation of actionable knowledge through dialogue. The complex nature of the situational context is an important aspect of transformational change where unforeseen events might disrupt the expected chain of events and complicate the linear logic of a planned change process.

Transformation and Change

There is a long history in the field of organization development and change concerning the conceptualization of planned change and transformational change. In the context of sustainability, we view transformation as a systematic effort by leadership to fundamentally change the system through the development of new capabilities. As such, transformation is a profound system attempt to either respond to environmental changes or to initiate such changes (Bartunek & Reis Louis, 1988); an effort directed at creating a new vision for the system (Porras & Silver, 1991); the creation of something new that is brought into being through a reformulation of old ways of thinking, structures, processes, and the emerging of new ones (Egri & Frost, 1991); a way to help the system become a learning entity (Sugarman, 2007); and a way to create new system capacities (Roth, Shani, & Leary, 2007).

Transformation presupposes a rational causality where someone is privileged to observe and reshape the system from the outside. From a complexity point of view, change emerges and is most often beyond the realms of detailed planning (Livne-Tarandach & Bartunek, 2009). A complexity view also implies that strategies seldom evolve the way they are intended. On the contrary, a strategy is created and recreated in multiple conversations, where coworkers bring their own meanings to what is formulated (Weick, 1995). New thoughts and proposals may emerge through dialogue, leading to unforeseen but often creative and fruitful activities in unpredictable directions. As such, transformation is a dynamic human endeavor that occurs within a complex context and involves a wide range of actors and activities.

From a change perspective, transformation processes are grouped into two broad categories: planned and emerging changes. Planned changes form the larger category and are usually characterized by the implementation of preconceived solutions. Yet, planned changes are almost always accompanied by unexpected consequences (Livne-Tarandach & Bartunek, 2009). There are varying definitions of emerging changes, including actions, adaptations, and alterations that produce fundamental change without an a priori intention to do so (Weick, 2000); the customizing of action to meet local conditions; local experimentation to develop organizational competences; and social innovation (Docherty, Kira, & Shani, 2009). The outcome of the (emerging) change process is not the preconceived solution, but the development of the most appropriate solution for the stakeholders concerned (Todnem By, 2005).

Sustainability transformation efforts include a hybrid of planned and unplanned change. Yet, some researchers argue that each seems to be appropriate in different situations. For example, according to Burnes, planned change is appropriate for structural changes, and emergent change is more appropriate for cultural change (Burnes, 1996). According to Beer and Nohria, planned change is appropriate for economic-based change, and less planned, emergent change is more appropriate for organizational capacity building (Beer & Nohria, 2005). In their studies at the British National Health Service, Bamford and Daniel (2005) found that directive planned change was more appropriate for new organizational structures, whereas a collaborative and participative approach was more appropriate for change processes targeting work processes. System-wide change that focuses on sustainability incorporates both planned and emergent dimensions and seems by its very nature to require the design and management of learning mechanisms (Docherty & Shani, 2009).

Learning Mechanisms, Participation, and Sustainability

Learning mechanisms are viewed as structures and processes that are designed to enhance sustainable dynamic capacities. They are planned proactive features that enable and encourage ongoing system learning (Shani & Docherty, 2003). An assumption is that the capability to learn can be designed rather than left to possibly evolve through the normal activities of the system. Although some may simply emerge informally, our argument in this chapter is that learning mechanisms can be purposefully designed to support sustainability, enhance sustainable effectiveness, and develop new capacities. Because system transformation occurs in the context of a complex activity system, the mechanisms must foster learning processes that are practice-based, multi-level, cross-community-based, and systemic and integrative.

Literature on learning mechanisms identifies three foci: (1) cognitive, (2) structural, and (3) procedural (Shani & Docherty, 2003). Cognitive mechanisms are concepts, values, and frameworks expressed in the value statements, strategy, and policies of the organization. Ideally they underpin practice-based learning processes at different organizational levels. Structural mechanisms are organizational infrastructures that encourage practice-based learning, such as lateral structures or DDs that enable learning of new practices within and across various organizational units. Procedural mechanisms concern the routines, methods, and tools that support and promote learning, such as problem-solving methods. Together these match the complexity of the new bundle of competencies and features that constitute a new capability. The literature suggests that most systems tend to develop some tapestry of learning mechanisms that fits its complex nature and dynamics (Roth et al., 2007).

A key ingredient of learning and learning mechanisms is participation. Participation is a foundation concept in the social sciences, such as social theory and philosophy (Habermas, 1987; Toulmin & Gustavsen, 1996), sociotechnical systems theory (Emery & Thorsrud, 1996), educational psychology (Shani & Docherty, 2003), and organizational theory (Pfeffer, 1995). The idea with inter- and intra-organizational learning mechanisms, such as the "development coalition" that is used in the Skaraborg case in this chapter, is to facilitate the breaking down of barriers between actors, units, organizations, and networks that prevent them from developing productive relations (Ennals & Gustavsen, 1998). Local commitment is based on the participants' joint efforts to develop new practice that by itself provides the opportunity to share experiences, to learn together, and engage in sense making with others. An example of an arena within which a high level of participation, relationship building, and learning occurs is a DD conference.

Democratic dialogue conferences, in general and in the healthcare context in specific, are structural learning mechanisms within and between organizations that are arenas for broad participation in addressing emerging societal issues (Ennals & Gustavsen, 1998). In Scandinavia, dialogue conferences are a means for participation among a broad spectrum of organizational stakeholders to forge a shared vision about change and devise concrete developmental action plans. The researcher's role is to establish the arenas for such dialogue and provide discursive tools to facilitate it (Gustavsen, 1992). Knowledge, seen as shared understanding generated by developmental action (Ford & Ogilvie, 1996), concerns both how the change process is organized and the content of the changes that are made to the social system.

Two further important aims in such conferences are to develop communicative competence within organizations and mobilize a broad level of participation by employees in developmental activities through creating a public arena for communication. Employees take part from agreed principles for good communication based on Habermas' (1987) idea of free communication (McCarthy, 1996). The notion of being "democratic" is tied to the right and obligation of all concerned to take part in the talk, to cooperate in the dialogue. The dialogue is based on a respect for experiences, equal to that for expert knowledge, as a basis for new and broader knowledge (Gustavsen, 1992; Shotter & Gustavsen, 1999; Pålshaugen, 2001).

Dialogue seeks to explore or alter underlying patterns of meaning. This entails people learning how to think together, not only to analyze a shared problem but also to surface fundamental assumptions and arrive at insights into why such problems might arise. Such an experience can thereby act as a springboard for new collective action (Isaacs, 1993). A key purpose of the conferences is mobilization (Docherty et al., 2009). For example, a concept such as "integrated care" only takes on meaning when all employees coordinate their everyday work and work processes in interaction with each other. The concept provides a frame of reference and a guideline for change. Dialogue conferences usually are concentrated into one to three days events, due to the difficulties in assembling people. Participants are expected to attend all the sessions and be actively involved in the process.

Action research methodologies are one of the tenants of the DD conference (Lifvergren, Huzzard, & Docherty, 2009). Collaborative research projects serve as both outcomes of the conference and as catalysts for the conference. They also function as learning mechanisms supporting the experiential learning cycle: planning, acting, collecting feedback, and reflecting on the outcomes achieved (Docherty & Shani, 2009; Stebbins, Valenzuela, & Coget, 2009). Action research facilitates individual and collective learning. For example, individuals who take part in the DD conference are responsible for sharing learning and new insights with their ordinary work groups and bring back lessons learned to the networks working along the care chain (Docherty, Huzzard, DeLeede, & Totterdill, 2004). In this respect, we define networks as inter- and intra-organizational nodes along the care chain, where cross-professional groups meet over organizational boundaries to share insights and ideas. Reflection meetings within the networks between the network members and their colleagues, in other networks or not attending any other network, serve as triggers for ongoing dialogue and exploration of additional collaborative research projects or experimentation of managerial actions.

In the remainder of this chapter, we describe Skaraborg County's healthcare transformation process through the theoretical lenses of dynamic sustainability, the planned and emergent change processes that were part of it, and the establishment of learning mechanisms, including its use of DDs. Next, the chapter provides a note about the research methodology and then provides a synopsis of a ten-year transformation journey of the Skaraborg Hospital Group (SHG).

A NOTE ABOUT THE METHODOLOGY

The Skaraborg County case study is a longitudinal field study that is based on an emerging cluster of collaborative research projects during the past ten years. The first author acted as one of three insider action researchers for the duration of the transformation, playing, and continuing to play a variety of roles in the ongoing inquiry process. The second and third authors were external action researchers for the past seven years and three years, respectively. The first years of the research, dealing with the integration of the work of the different care providers, including the functioning of the networks and the DD conferences, were conducted together with Marianne Ekman, Tony Huzzard, and Beth Ahlberg via the Skaraborg Institute. The later stages of the research, especially regarding quality improvement, learning and management systems, and system transformation were conducted together with colleagues from the Centre for Healthcare Improvement at Chalmers University of Technology – Bo Bergman, Peter Docherty, Andreas Hellström – and Rami Shani from California Polytechnic State University/ Politecnico di Milano.

Data collection began from the project get-go. During the past ten years, four systematic waves of assessment interviews have been conducted and performance indicators have been tracked, as the different collaborative research projects evolved and progressed. In the preparation for this case write up, an additional set of interviews were conducted in person and by phone with key stakeholders that had firsthand knowledge of the transformation process. Each round of interviews consisted of five to seven discussions with individuals or groups, and three stakeholders have been involved in every round. Transcripts of the interviews were compiled into a case description and shared with the members of the DCMG for shared interpretation, sense making, verification, and confirmation.

THE SKARABORG HOSPITAL GROUP'S TRANSFORMATION STORY

Background

In 2001, the Swedish national authority launched an effort to integrate local healthcare related activities of primary care centers, local hospitals, and municipal after-care facilities, in order to provide more effective and efficacious care and safety for patients. This led to collaborative activities to operationally integrate these three legally and organizationally separate entities. Five years into the project, the concept of sustainability was introduced and served as both an integrative mechanism and as a trigger for further collaborative effort. Skaraborg County had been chosen as one of the participants in the first phase of this integration program. Skaraborg County is situated in the eastern corner of Västra Götaland, one of the largest regions in Sweden. The 1.5 million people who live in the region's 49 municipalities make up 17% of the total Swedish population. The SHG is made up of four hospitals in the towns Falköping, Lidköping, Mariestad, and Skövde. The group serves 260,000 people with acute and planned care in most specialities, employs about 4,500 people, and has 800 beds.

Forming the Development Coalition

In response to the national directive to operationally integrate healthcare, Skaraborg County healthcare management decided to launch a transformation effort in one part of the county to lead the entire system change initiative. Due to its progressive orientation and reputation, the healthcare system in West Skaraborg, centered in Lidköping, was chosen to lead the effort. The healthcare providers in the West Skaraborg project are the Lidköping Hospital, two primary care centers (to be five later on in the project), and the after-care facilities in six municipalities, Essunga, Grästorp, Götene, Lidköping, Skara, and Vara. The Lidköping Hospital serves a population of about 85,000 people in West Skaraborg. It is an acute care hospital with complete departments and staff on call. It has about 160 beds and 700 employees.

The West Skaraborg coalition mechanism included the DCMG (described below), several project teams (later renamed as networks), representation from the four unions and patient associations, West Skaraborg healthcare politicians, all the municipalities concerned, and the researchers. Table 1 captures key milestones and their essence during the 2001–2010 period.

Management decided that the integration assignment would be carried out in a "development coalition." This choice reflected management values of "stakeholder participation" and "good work." Gustavsen, Colbjørnsen, and Pålhaugen (1998, p. 14) describe a development coalition in the following way:

> In a "development coalition" there are a number of actors who develop joint platforms and frameworks but otherwise function on the basis of complementarity: management manages, union representatives represent, workers take care of the operational processes, and researchers research. When they meet in joint arenas to create common platforms, they consider each other's points and arguments, but they are still there in the capacity of their ordinary role. When (they) agree on something, it is not because they have "taken over" each other's view, or, even, of necessity, developed a common view, it is because they have found it in their own best interest to support each other in a certain course of action.

Table 1. The West Skaraborg County's Transformation Journey:
Key Events.

2000–2001	The Västra Götaland regional office forwards a national directive concerning "integrated care" to the Skaraborg Hospital Group (SHG). SHG delegates the task to West Skaraborg. A development coalition is formed with politicians, healthcare providers, other stakeholders, and the researchers.
2002	A management group for the development coalition (DCMG) is created with the senior managers from the primary care centers, the hospital, and the aftercare departments in six local municipalities. The management group prioritizes the key issues to be focused in the project and selects cross-organizational, cross-professional, and cross-level networks/teams to work with the prioritized issues.
September 2002	The first democratic dialogue (DD) conference in the development coalition is held. Project groups (renamed networks), start their collaborative research work including exchanging experiences and reflection meetings within and between the networks, and with DCMG.
April 2003	The second DD conference is held: Reflections on the development work and process: An exchange of experiences and discussions of how one should proceed. Cross-organizational, cross-professional, and cross-level networks are established as the appropriate strategy for conducting development work.
September 2004	The SHG management system policy document is presented that includes both a clarification of management's value base and vision and also its process approach to development work. The policy document is converted to a balanced scorecard, which is introduced at all levels of SHG in order to improve dialogue but also its control over the costs of intangibles.
October 2004	The third DD conference is held, reflecting over several positive outcomes from the project. DCMG decides to make the development coalition a permanent part of the Skaraborg healthcare organization, with its own organization, personnel, budget, and balanced scorecard and recruits two people to build up a staff of internal consultants to aid the networks and to develop the development coalitions adaptive capacities.
October 2005	Some diffusion activities take place via a regional conference between West and East Götaland and the Southern Region of Sweden. Based on the experience to date, a comprehensive document is generated about both integrated healthcare and sustainability transformation roadmap.
2006–2010	The West Skaraborg coalition continues to lead the transformation process at the county. The West Skaraborg coalition provides guidance to other counties in Sweden on ways to design and manage efforts toward the enhancement of the development of a more sustainable healthcare systems and sustainable effectiveness.

The Development Coalition and its Management Group

The first step in the formal project was the creation of a *DCMG* that included the hospital director and the senior physician of the Lidköping Hospital, a senior civil servant from each of the six municipalities, and a senior management representative from each of the participating primary care centers. At the outset, the primary goals of the national assignment were improved care and safety for patients, and better utilization of the healthcare system's total resources. The members of the DCMG were very anxious that they themselves should perform as well and as soon as possible. Initially they met for several whole-day meetings, then settled on a full-day meeting every 14 days. Staff reported in interviews that management's behavior reflected that they actually meant what they had stated and were committed to integration. The first step in the West Skaraborg assignment was that the DCMG commissioned a document developed by an appointed project group describing the current situation of healthcare in the area. This listed the challenges that needed to be addressed and was an essential point of departure for the coming restructuring.

Identification of the Primary Networks/Projects in the Development Coalition

The next step was to select which improvement issues should be tackled in the cross-organizational, cross-professional, cross-level project groups, also referred to as networks. These networks were formally chosen and managed by the DCMG, but had a high degree of discretion in conducting their work. Several work processes or patient pathways were chosen, for example,

- *Örjan project*: To map out and improve the care chain for elderly patients (70+ years), concentrating on the transfers between different care providers. This project was already ongoing when the West Skaraborg project was formed.
- *Palliative care units*: To work for greater safety for patients with end stage disease by joint planning between the different care providers, including the patient and next of kin in the process. They were also responsible for designing a common education and conversational forum within this area.
- *Rehabilitation*: To produce suggestions for collaborative solutions between care providers and even involve the personnel from sick benefits authority to work out patients' benefits.

- *Personnel recruitment:* To examine the possibilities of trainee-appointments in which the employee can perform tasks at different care providers. They aim to increase the utilization of the employee's competence and encourage yearly trial positions in other care providers.

The First Democratic Dialogue Conference

The development coalition faced the difficult problem of involving many different actors with a diverse experience of healthcare work and potentially different conceptions of what the real problems are and how a well functioning healthcare system should be designed. Thus, implementing such a vision cannot be easily envisioned or controlled from the center. The need for more decentralized forms of working was widely acknowledged. The participants in *all* the coalition activities represented their own knowledge and experience; no one spoke for anybody else. All perspectives were important. The aim was to create arenas for reflection where the actors listened and dwelt on each other's perspective. The researchers' role was to facilitate the development dynamics, systematizing the participants' reflections and practical knowledge, facilitating the groups going from "words to actions." They also contributed their knowledge and experience in the discussions without adopting a consultancy role – sharing their knowledge in a genuine dialogue – as an experienced colleague, but registering and analyzing as well.

The conference generated dialogue as a precursor to developmental activities from within the organization itself rather than relying on the "expertise" of those from the outside. The format of the dialogue conference was successive group conversations, each followed by plenary report-backs. Between 75 and 100 people attended each conference. The group conversations encompassed four themes that followed naturally on from each other, working through four phases, each addressing a key issue: How do we wish the organization and the work organization to look in the near future (three to five years)? (The groups for this conversation were horizontal slices of homogenous groups); what are the obstacles to change? (The groups were diagonal slices of mixed groups); what can be done? (Dialogue groups were freely composed); and who is to do what and when? (The groups were vertical slices of heterogeneous groups). The teams from the development coalition's integration networks/projects were all participants in the DD conferences, and the fourth phase was their main opportunity to make their concrete plans for formulating and realizing their goals and to get critical, constructive feedback.

The broad methodology of working collaboratively on many levels – between healthcare providers, professions, hierarchical levels, networks, practitioners, and academics – has been applied in the majority of networks/ projects. A process improvement methodology was employed to build patient care pathways that cut across all of the organizations. In doing so they had to work through a number of intergroup dynamics that have been well discussed in the participation and process improvement literatures. In order to illustrate the magnitude of the transformation effort and its dynamics, we next focus on one of the collaborative research networks, the *Örjan network project*.

The Örjan Network: An Example

The Örjan project focused on the patient pathway for the treatment of the elderly (70 + years). The Örjan project group consisted of 18 staff members, including nurses and doctors from the hospital, the primary care centers, and nurses from all the six surrounding local authorities. The network members had meetings every second month in order to plan activities, to discuss, and to reflect. The complexity of elderly care became evident early on during the project. It was imperative to create a shared picture of how the pathway performed. Special action had to be taken to ensure that doctors could participate as their superiors had difficulty in prioritizing the project. Other difficulties encountered were staff's misgivings arising from earlier less fruitful change efforts, as well as suspicion toward other units and tiredness from the workloads when no resources were earmarked for development.

The project group applied research and improvement methodologies to a patient care pathway that cuts across all of their organizations: (1) mapping the patient pathway, (2) analyzing and measuring weaknesses in order to identify true problems in the pathways, (3) designing and introducing improvements, and (4) continuously evaluating implemented solutions. The identified problems and proposed solutions were presented and discussed iteratively at all workplaces along the actual patient care pathway to gain participation and commitment, thus inspiring joint action among coworkers. To get a better understanding of the patients' perspectives, focus groups were conducted with patients and their relatives. The investigation revealed that more than 80 steps were involved in the process of planning care outside the hospital for one single patient. The expenses of the process were estimated to be in the range of $285–565 per patient. Such findings prompted the group to explore a single procedure across the three levels of care for care planning, thereby reducing the number of steps dramatically.

The patient pathway project did meet obstacles and elements of resistance. Territorial thinking pervaded many of the workplaces across the three providers of healthcare and across different professional groups. Part of the problem here was that staff did not have the time or the capability to think from each other's perspectives, and coworkers were not always allowed by their managers to participate in project activities. But the Örjan project group made a point of keeping top management well informed with person-to-person "marking," i.e., specific project group members were given responsibility of updating specific individual members of the steering committee and of other critical management groups on progress in the project. This paved the way for allocated project time for front line staff.

The collaborative process involving coworkers across the three care providing organizations bore fruit. At the end of 2005, the network could present some key outcomes of its work: elimination of waiting times at the medical outpatient clinic (with the exception of heart ailments), reduction in number of visits to the medical clinic by 15–18%, initiation of process work in many other clinics and care units, and increase in staff awareness and learning regarding the patient pathways.

Implementing the Balanced Scorecard Management System

In 2004, a regional directive stated that all hospital groups in the region should use the BSC method. In response, the Skaraborg Hospital Management Group (SHMG) articulated its vision, strategy, and management system including long-term goals and critical success factors (short-term goals). The effort was also motivated by a need for the ongoing development dialogue to focus on results and to stimulate system-wide development at the SHG. The scorecard was initially drawn up for SHG at the corporate level. The corporate scorecard has since then been interpreted and modified in the main divisions in SHG-medicine, surgery, children/women, and the hospital in Lidköping – and in each of the underlying clinics in the different divisions.

The scorecard covers value statement, vision, strategy, and long- and short-term goals. The cornerstone of the *value base* is that all people are equal. Thus, all patients and their relatives, all staff and all other partners in providing healthcare have the right to respect and honesty, consideration and security, participation and fellowship/community, and development and understanding. The vision proclaims "excellent care in development" and underpins the different strategic perspectives of the scorecard model – patients, processes, personnel/learning, and a viable economy. The DCMG began to use the regional scorecard method to sustain the efforts of the development coalition. In 2004, the West Skaraborg coalition began to develop its own BSC covering the different care providers in the care value chain and focusing improvement, innovation, collaboration, and coordination. Participation at all levels and ongoing dialogue led to the integration of "promoting health" and "preventing sickness" into the scorecard – new directions that are fundamental to the notion of sustainable healthcare.

The Third Democratic Dialogue Conference

The third DD conference was held in October 2004 and marked the end of the first phase of the development coalition, at which time five of the collaborative research networks had produced concrete developmental outcomes. Inspired by the DD in 2004, there was a strong feeling in the coalition that the experience and knowledge generated, the formal and informal infrastructures that had been formed, the commitment, trust, and goodwill that had grown, were all too important to be allowed to be disbanded, to dissipate or just be postponed pending a decision to do one more project. Thus, following the third DD conference, the DCMG decided that the coalition and the development process should continue. Integrated healthcare development was no longer seen as a temporary initiative, but as a key ongoing process for the coalition. Resources were allotted to the coalition work in the budget process whereby each organization covered the costs of its own personnel. The "Excellent Care in Development" vision would now be supported with specific goals, management system and organization, and new positions were created and staffed.

The Emerging New Coalition

During 2005, the DCMG and the SHMG were in full agreement that the sustainability effort should continue under the umbrella of the Integrated Care Project (the new government directive) and accordingly decided to organize, staff, and finance the necessary organization within their own budgets. The DCMG was retained and still has the same full commitment from all the partners. The DCMG now has 12 representatives from the six municipalities' aftercare, five from primary care centers, and one from the hospital; all are senior managers. A new coordination group has been formed, staffed part time by one development individual from each of the medical sectors. Each organization is expected to cover the costs of its own staff's engagement.

The networks continue, and new networks are formed as others complete their tasks. They continue to be linked and activated by DCMG, who also oversees a regular joint one-day seminar where all networks present and share learning. During 2010, the ongoing collaborative networks included the "integrated care" team, palliative care, rehabilitation, dementia, Chronic Obstructive Pulmonary Disease (COPD), diabetes, and coordinated care planning. Each network has a representative from each of the partners in the coalition.

The DCMG meets for a one-day meeting four times a year. During the meetings, the coalition is represented by the CEO of the hospital and a public and a private primary care center, a departmental manager from each municipality, three coordinators, and representatives for a "guest" network that makes a special presentation. There are presentations from both the coalition and the politicians on recent experiences and plans ideas for future activities and processes. There is always a 100% turnout from the politicians, even from all the municipalities.

The BSC of the West Skaraborg Development Coalition is aligned with those at the hospital, the primary care centers, and some municipalities. Although the introduction of the BSC initially was a planned change governed by regional management to improve economic control, the development coalition uses it to support organizational development, sustainability, and sustainable effectiveness. This planned initiative has contributed to an emergent sustainability process. In the words of a coordinator:

> There is still much to develop, but the basic work done in grounding the BSC in our values and sustainability ambitions, and our frequent professional contacts have done much to create a positive climate and deep trust and helps us move forward in the healthcare sustainability drive.

Thus, critical resources in the form of budgets, emerging networks, and management structures have been incorporated as ongoing mechanisms – "the way of doing things" – in all three organizations. The whole system is transformed; resources for innovation and reconfiguration through learning and participation are allocated to address novel situations without disrupting established functions crucial for the stability of the system.

In other words, the system has adopted practices to foster its ability to continuously sustain and grow its capacity.

Skaraborg Hospital Group is progressing in its development activities and succeeds with 75% of its larger improvement projects, compared with 40% for the national average. Other results from SHG include the shortest length of stay at the emergency wards in the Western Region, cost efficiency above the national average in a number of care processes, above average in 24 out of 38 parameters in national quality registers concerning critical care results (e.g., 28-day-survival rate in myocardial infarction, proportion of stroke patients satisfied with the delivered care), and average or slightly under average in the remaining 12 parameters.

DISCUSSION

This section presents several reflections on the lessons gained in the collaborative process that evolved over a ten-year period, as the county was working on implementing an initiative that was directed by the state government. The emergent change process concerning the integration of activities of the three types of care providers in West Skaraborg aimed at developing their organizational capacities in order to provide improved healthcare through the use of planned networks. Stepwise learning development methods have resulted in a robust organization steadily working to attain sustainability.

Major features of these experiences were the level and extent of the wide participation of actors from all the relevant entities and units of the healthcare systems in the development projects, and the integration of learning mechanisms as a means toward sustainable effectiveness. Learning mechanisms and participation forums were designed and implemented to lead and transform the healthcare system.

Participation and Learning Mechanisms

Participation through working together in "home" units and "network" projects has been the norm in the coalition. All stakeholders have been engaged and their experiences, needs, and ambitions have been important contributions. Participation has involved defining issues, working to study the issues in collaboration with external researchers and experts, reflecting on and discussing analyses exploring solutions, and implementing them.

"Home" and "network" projects have been the arenas for individual and collective learning that have linked through subnetworks in the major projects, such as Örjan. These learning arenas have been complemented by others, with other stakeholders, the social partners, patients and their associations, and with management.

The BSC, a cognitive and procedural mechanism, has provided new language, new concepts, and models and values for thinking, reasoning, and understanding critical developmental issues in the different patient pathways. It is the basis for recurrent dialogues involving all caregivers along the pathway. Structural mechanisms provide organizational, technical, and physical infrastructures that enhance learning. These include different feedback and communication channels, arenas/forums, and networks for dialogue (Shani & Docherty, 2003).

The DDs, the DCMG meetings, and the project meetings are important structural learning mechanisms where new concepts, projects, goals, and vision are discussed regularly along the patient pathways (Docherty & Shani, 2009). The involvement of all stakeholders in dialogues has also been a key design feature. Procedural mechanisms pertain to the rules, routines, procedures, and methods that can be institutionalized in the organization to promote and support learning. In this case, the four-step process method that has been used during the projects has involved coworkers along the patient pathways, but has also provided a simple tool to coordinate the improvement efforts.

Achieving sustainable effectiveness requires managerial approaches that create synergistic effects by putting together different learning mechanisms:

- The use of DD conferences and other meeting arenas as an engine for knowledge creation and knowledge transfer
- The integration of a BSC
- An ongoing collaboration between internal and external action researchers.

Participation and Democratic Dialogue Conferences

Active participation by employees in the design of new forms of work organization becomes a central issue when management seeks to introduce and establish structural change in the health service such as integrated care. Securing commitment, will, and endorsement is sometimes beyond the capacities of many individual managers, yet these emerged from the conferences. The claim of "participation" in the design of the dialogue conferences entails allowing "all present to contribute to the dialogue" so that power differences can be set aside (Ekman Philips, Ahlberg, & Huzzard, 2003).

A strength of the dialogue conference as a working method is that it entails the connection between the developmental vision – including its difficulties – and concrete plans for action. The dialogue conference is thus an arena for rich sense making, where participants can generate change themselves from their own experiences (Weick, 1995). The change dynamic in the dialogues is mostly one of ongoing participative extension, discarding the notion of being in a "project," and becoming motivated to move onto genuinely developmental activities in a dialogical process underpinned by mutual trust and respect.

Leadership, Management, and the Balanced Scorecard

In the sustainability literature, the sustainability values usually cascade down through the organization from top management. In SHG, it was not sustainability that cascaded, but rather strong egalitarian values toward the organization's stakeholders, especially patients and staff. In West Skaraborg, the members of the DCMG saw the importance of firmly embedding these values in the development activities in their respective organizations, especially for all line managers. They had an important role in legitimizing the development work by underlining its tight coupling to operational activities in the different care organizations. The egalitarian power relations and values within the management structure of the project, not least within the DCMG, have mediated the dialogue conferences and the subsequent activities in West Skaraborg. However, this did not imply total delegation. The senior management team had a crucial role in interpreting the strategy of the politicians, and in deciding the priority areas for action and drafting the developmental assignments.

The meetings of the DCMG evolved from being simply administrative to allotting more time for sense making and a deeper level of reflection. The group regarded the reflection activity as invaluable. They appreciated the need for clear and precise communication with all the members in their networks. They decided to have special two-day reflection meetings with the heads of the different network/project managers.

The BSC is a model that has been introduced in a top-down fashion in most Swedish hospitals, as was the case with the National Health Service in the United Kingdom. The higher levels in the healthcare system usually see the model as a management control mechanism. At SHG, as well as in the development coalition, the model was viewed as an aid to organizational development, strongly coupled to learning, and development projects in the workplace that can enhance the effort toward sustainable healthcare delivery. In fact, the process of using the BSC framework has been a key integrative tool in engaging the personnel as a whole in the sustainability process. In particular, the goals formulated in the BSC have been important to identify remaining problems in the care pathways, thus inspiring new improvement projects.

Collaboration between Internal and External Action Researchers

A close collaboration between internal and external action researchers has been a key feature throughout the developmental journey. The notion of long-term action research as a potent tool in the development of complex healthcare systems has been brought forward earlier by, for example, Stebbins, Freed, Shani, and Doerr (2006), Stebbins, Valenzuela, and Coget (2009). The approach focuses on a close collaboration between researchers and practitioners in iterating action–reflection loops, where the researchers continuously contribute with special process and content inputs, for example, questioning taken for granted assumptions – the "way things are done" in the organization and introducing new methods and techniques for further development. The researchers have also provided design methods for increased participation and learning and inspired a more emergent, adaptive, and flexible but also critical approach to change processes. New insights have been acted upon leading to new experiences that were tested again in a continuous action–reflection spiral, the goal being to create actionable and useful knowledge from a pragmatic as well as a research perspective.

In the Skaraborg developmental journey, at least two researchers have been involved all the time. The researchers have facilitated DDs, DCMG meetings, and participated in a number of network meetings within the projects. In addition, the researchers, the development director of SHG, the quality consultant, and the hospital director of Lidköping have met every third month to reflect on the overall program and to learn from successes and failures. The reflections entailed a more pronounced focus on the importance of participation and learning mechanisms in the development efforts: permanent arenas for dialogue among coworkers were established along the patient pathways, but also arenas for involving all stakeholders from the different care providers. The importance of continuously discussing and agreeing on a shared vision and goals within the development coalition also became clear. In recurrent workplace meetings, vision and goals could be interpreted and translated to the daily operations. Other insights pertained to the importance of teaching coworkers different improvement techniques, for example, lean and six sigma, which were used to facilitate various improvement efforts within the projects. Finally, the joint reflections led to the employment of two full-time internal improvement facilitators coaching and supporting the activities of the DCMG but also of all the projects and their networks. In other words, the continuous collaboration with external researchers has enhanced the organizational ability to continuously learn from and cope with novel situations, increasing the dynamic capacity of the system.

Shortcomings of the Skaraborg Transformation Process

The learning mechanisms tapestry developed throughout the process no doubt was central for the emerging outcomes of the transformation – toward a more sustainable healthcare system. It became clear that there was more to the transformation than just learning mechanisms. Designing follow-ups on a regular basis created a pressure on management teams not only to listen and discuss but gradually to become much more expedient in implementing their own and others' ideas, thus supporting development of the care processes. Especially in the first five years, the investigations of issues and implementation of practices were somewhat slow and unevenly dispersed. Follow-ups and very consistent push from some managers made things move, but momentum took some time to develop. Effective tools for implementing could have resulted in a faster development pace. Learning mechanisms tapestries could be well complemented by more action implementation features not relying on action planning too much under the maybe false assumption that just because a plan exists, actions get implemented well enough.

IMPLICATIONS: ORGANIZING FOR SUSTAINABLE EFFECTIVENESS

The nature of the case and its ten-year duration raises a wide variety of issues on organizing for sustainability and sustainable effectiveness. Our basic point of departure has been to focus on management's ambition to maximize staff participation in their ordinary work and in development activities concerning their work – what some view is a key ingredient of a sustainable work system (Docherty, Forslin, & Shani, 2002; Docherty et al., 2009). Thus, our chosen areas of emphasis included the hows of a sustainable healthcare system, complex system transformation, participation, and learning mechanisms. In this concluding section we address few research and practical issues that are raised by this case.

The Need to Investigate the Relationship Between Tapestries of Learning Mechanisms and Their Impact on Sustainable Effectiveness

The nature and tapestry of the learning mechanisms that emerged overtime in the SHG constitute a new capability for the healthcare system, enabling it to continually generate enhanced outcomes and more sustainable effectiveness. The development of this new capacity, from a design perspective, requires the systematic exploration of different types and tapestries of learning mechanisms and decisions about the most appropriate tapestry that is likely to yield the desired sustainability outcomes. The case captured the learning mechanisms tapestry that emerged as the transformation effort progressed. Future research into possible different designs of a learning mechanism tapestries and the possible relationship between them and sustainable effectiveness is likely to be of significant added value.

Learning mechanisms tapestries to support the conduct of the current operational activities need to coexist with learning mechanisms that are designed to support and lead the system-wide transformation effort. The networks of relevant stakeholders are likely to vary. The demands made on different professions are likely to vary. Physicians, who are often the most necessary to include are often the most unwilling to participate, not least for cultural reasons. The Skaraborg journey suggests that DDs forums – as an example of one type of a structural learning mechanism – can be used to assemble "the whole system in the room," thus creating the understanding among managers of the importance of involving all coworkers in the transformation efforts while at the same time maintaining the balance between daily operation and sustainable development effort. Scientific-based knowledge is needed to learn more about alternative learning mechanisms and learning mechanisms tapestries that can facilitate the achievement of sustainable effectiveness.

The Need to Investigate the Relationship Between Learning Mechanisms Tapestry and Transformation Output Using Economic/Performance Indicators

The case presents data about the outcomes of the transformation as it was progressing, yet it is really hard to know how much of the success can be attributed to the development and deployment of the learning mechanisms and participation strategies. Most likely, the effectiveness of the learning mechanisms is difficult to measure, as they primarily worked through improving the implementation efficiency of other organizational processes such as process improvement practices.

Furthermore, the fact that a tapestry of learning mechanisms was used illustrates the difficulties of measuring the impact of a specific mechanism both on the transformation process and economic performance. Given the dynamic nature of healthcare systems as they respond to the many pressures they are experiencing, conducting traditional experimentations with control groups (some form of experimental design) is prohibitive. Furthermore, such controlled empirical studies do not fit the emergent change processes in which as the system learns the added value of the learning mechanisms, new mechanisms are created. These challenges require a research design that can capture dynamic transformation. The current study points toward the potential added value for a hybrid research approach that is based on collaborative research methodologies, longitudinal case study methodology, and grounded theory building.

How to Maintain Momentum Toward Sustainable Effectiveness?

This case represents a time span of ten years and as can be seen, the county is still using a number of learning mechanisms, while at the same time new learning mechanisms are developed. Persistence with the basic design (strategic learning dialogues, learning from experience, and learning across levels, units, and geographies) has been important. SHG has managed to sustain the situation by creating a balance between "cognitive mechanisms" on the one hand and "structural and procedural mechanisms" on the other. Strategies, policies, and management frameworks have provided explanations on where the system was and where management intend to go. On the other hand, practical projects have indicated that things are happening, and it is not simply a matter of a onetime transformation effort, but rather an ongoing process.

CONCLUSION

The recent *Second Annual Sustainability & Innovation Survey* of 3,000 managers that was conducted by MIT and the Boston Consulting Group claims that despite the effects of the financial crisis, a slow economy in much of the world, and continuing inaction by political bodies, the level of business investment in sustainability activities has been rising (Haanaes et al., 2011, p. 78). Development of sustainability capacity and achieving sustainable effectiveness, as we have seen in this chapter, requires a system-wide transformation. Many systems that embark on the sustainability track are likely to face decades long development to achieve sustainable effectiveness.

This case example captures how the West Skaraborg Healthcare Coalition in Sweden has in the last ten years made progress from tackling a challenging issue of integrating the work activities of three types of healthcare providers to provide a more sustainable and higher quality of healthcare delivery to its county's population. The adoption of an emergent strategy via high level of participation and a very open attitude to one's environment led to the development of a sustainability strategy, increasing the dynamic capacity of a complex healthcare system. The sustainability journey involves developing a clear sustainability strategy, finding approaches to participation and engagement, designing a tapestry of learning mechanisms, and establishing and being guided by measures of desired sustainable effectiveness. As we have seen at the Skaraborg case, the complexity of such effort suggests that very few shortcuts, if any, can be taken in the transformation process of the healthcare industry toward sustainability and sustainable effectiveness.

ACKNOWLEDGMENT

In particular, we want to dedicate this chapter to the late professor Peter Docherty. He has been the main inspirational force throughout the case, sharing his immense wisdom, kindness and vast experience. We will strive to continue our work in the spirit of Peter. We also wish to acknowledge our colleagues work, all of which forms a very important base to this chapter: Marianne Alärd, Owe Gustavsson, Marianne Ekman, Tony Huzzard, Beth M. Ahlberg, Bo Bergman, Elisabeth Ek, and Andreas

Hellström. We are also grateful for the excellent comments from our editor
Susan A. Mohrman.

REFERENCES

Bamford, D., & Daniel, S. (2005). A case study of change management effectiveness within the NHS. *Journal of Change Management, 5*(4), 391–406.
Bartunek, J. M., & Reis Louis, M. (1988). The interplay of organization development and organizational transformation. In: W. A. Pasmore & R. W. Woodman (Eds), *Research in organizational change and development* (Vol. 2, pp. 97–134). Greenwich, CT: JAI Press.
Beer, M., & Nohria, N. (2005). *Breaking the code of change*. Boston: Harvard Business School Press.
Burnes, B. (1996). No such thing as 'one best way' to manage organizational change. *Management Decision, 34*(10), 11–18.
Docherty, P., Forslin, J., & Shani, A. B. (Eds). (2002). *Creating sustainable work systems: Emerging perspectives and practices*. London: Routledge.
Docherty, P., Huzzard, T., DeLeede, J., & Totterdill, P. (2004). *Home and away – Learning in and learning from organisational networks in Europe*. Rapport för EU Commission (EU Innoflex Project).
Docherty, P., Kira, M., & Shani, A. B. (Rami) (2009). Organizational development for social sustainability in work systems. In: R. H. Woodman, W. A. Passmore & A. B. (Rami) Shani (Eds), *Research in organizational change and development* (Vol. 17, pp. 77–144). Bingley, UK: Emerald Group Publishing.
Docherty, P., & Shani, A. B. (Rami) (2009). Learning mechanisms as means and ends in collaborative management research. In: A. B. (Rami) Shani, S. A. Mohrman, W. Pasmore, B. A. Stymne & N. Adler (Eds), *Handbook of collaborative management research* (pp. 163–182). Thousand Oaks, CA: SAGE Publishing.
Egri, C. P., & Frost, P. J. (1991). Shamanism and change: Bringing back the magic in organizational transformation. In: W. A. Pasmore & R. W. Woodman (Eds), *Research in organizational change and development* (Vol. 5, pp. 175–221). Greenwhich, CT: JAI Press.
Ekman Philips, M., Ahlberg, B. M., & Huzzard, T. (2003). Planning from without or developing from within? Collaboration across the frontiers of healthcare. In: W. Fricke & P. Totterdill (Eds), *Regional development processes as the context for action research* (pp. 103–126). Amsterdam: John Benjamins.
Elkington, J. (1997). *Cannibals with Forks*. Oxford, UK: Capstone Publishing Limited.
Emery, F., & Thorsrud, E. (1996). *Democracy at work*. Leiden: Nijholt.
Ennals, R., & Gustavsen, B. (1998). *Work organization and Europe as a development coalition*. Philadelphia: John Benjamins.
Ford, C. M., & Ogilvie, D. T. (1996). The role of creative action in organizational learning and change. *Journal of Organizational Change Management, 9*(1), 54–62.
Gustavsen, B. (1992). *Dialogue and development*. Assen, NL: Van Gorcum.
Gustavsen, B., Colbjørnsen, T., & Pålhaugen, Ø. (1998). *Development conditions in working life: Enterprise 2000 development in Norway*. Amsterdam: John Benjamins.

Haanaes, K., Balagopal, B., Arthur, D., Kong, M. T., Velken, I., Kruschwitz, N., & Hopkins, M. S. (2011). First look: The second annual sustainability & innovation survey. *MIT Sloan Management Review*, *52*(2), 77–83.

Habermas, J. (1987). *The theory of communicative action* (Vol. 1–11). London: Polity Press.

Isaacs, W. (1993). Taking flight: Dialogue, collective thinking, and organizational learning. *Organizational Dynamics*, *22*(2), 24–39.

Lifvergren, S., Huzzard, T., & Docherty, P. (2009). A development coalition for sustainability in healthcare. In: P. Docherty, M. Kira & A. B. Shani (Eds), *Creating sustainable work systems* (2nd ed, pp. 167–185). London: Routledge.

Livne-Tarandach, R., & Bartunek, J. M. (2009). A new horizon for organizational change and development scholarship: Connecting planned and emergent change. In: R. W. Woodman, W. A. Pasmore & A. B. Shani (Eds), *Research in organizational change and development* (Vol. 17, pp. 1–35). Bingley, UK: Emerald Group Publishing.

McCarthy, T. (1996). Pragmatizing communicative reason. In: S. Toulmin & B. Gustavsen (Eds), *Beyond theory: Changing organizations through participation* (pp. 159–177). Amsterdam: John Benjamins.

Mohrman, S. A., & Shani, A. B. (Rami) (2011). Organizing for sustainable effectiveness: Taking stock and moving forward. In: S. A. Mohrman & A. B. (Rami) Shani (Eds), *Organizing for sustainable effectiveness*. Bingley, UK: Emerald.

Mohrman, S. A., & Worley, C. G. (2010). The organizational sustainability journey: Introduction to the special issue. *Organizational Dynamics*, *39*(4), 289–294.

Pålshaugen, Ø. (2001). *Som sagt, så gjort? Språket som virkemiddel i organisasjonsutvikling og aksjonsforskning [[As said, as done? Language as a means of organizational development and action research]]*. Oslo: Novus Forlag.

Pfeffer, J. (1995). *Competitive advantage through people: Unleashing the power of the workforce*. Boston: Harvard Business School Press.

Porras, J. I., & Silver, R. C. (1991). Organization development and transformation. *Annual Review of Psychology*, *42*, 51–78.

Roth, J., Shani, A. B. (Rami), & Leary, M. (2007). Insider action research: Facing the challenges of new capability development within a biopharma company. *Action Research Journal*, *5*(1), 41–60.

Shani, A. B. (Rami), & Docherty, P. (2003). *Learning by design: Building sustainable organizations*. Oxford, UK: Blackwell.

Shotter, J., & Gustavsen, B. (1999). *The role of 'Dialogue Conferences' in the development of the 'Learning Regions': Doing 'from within' our lives together what we cannot do apart*. The Centre for Advanced Studies in Leadership. Stockholm: Stockholm School of Economics.

Stebbins, M. W., Freed, T., Shani, A. B. (Rami), & Doerr, K. H. (2006). The limits of reflexive design in secrecy-based organizations. In: D. Boud, P. Cressey & P. Docherty (Eds), *Productive reflection at work: Learning for changing organizations* (pp. 80–92). London: Routledge.

Stebbins, M. W., Valenzuela, J. L., & Coget, J. F. (2009). Long-term insider action research: Three decades of work at Kaiser Permanente. In: R. W. Woodman, W. A. Pasmore & A. B. (Rami) Shani (Eds), *Research in organizational change and development* (Vol. 17, pp. 37–75). Bingley, UK: Emerald Group Publishing.

Sugarman, B. (2007). A hybrid theory of organizational transformation. In: W. A. Pasmore & R. W. Woodman (Eds), *Research in organizational change and development* (Vol. 16, pp. 43–80). Oxford, UK: Elsevier.

Todnem By, R. (2005). Organizational change management: A critical review. *Journal of Change Management, 5*(4), 369–380.

Toulmin, S., & Gustavsen, B. (Eds). (1996). *Beyond theory: Changing organizations through participation*. Amsterdam: John Benjamins.

Weick, K. E. (1995). *Sense making in organizations*. Thousand Oaks, CA: Sage.

Weick, K. E. (2000). Emergent change as a universal in organizations. In: M. Beer & N. Nohria (Eds), *Breaking the code of change*. Boston: Harvard Business School Press.

CHAPTER 5

EMERGENT COLLABORATION AND LEADERSHIP FOR SUSTAINABLE EFFECTIVENESS: THE METROPOLITAN HOUSING AUTHORITY

Ann E. Feyerherm and Sally Breyley Parker

ABSTRACT

Organizations are currently striving to become more sustainable, as resources dwindle and social desirability for sustainability increases. This is important in public sector organizations as well as private, and exemplars are needed. Therefore, this chapter provides a description of how a public housing authority in pursuit of a social mission parlayed an energy performance contract into a triple bottom line sustainability journey. The Cuyahoga Metropolitan Housing Authority's (CMHA) sustainability journey has been shaped most significantly by the commitment of CMHA leadership to collaboration (internal and external) as a core strategy. The chapter provides a rich description of CMHA's emergent partnerships with various organizations in their environment; focusing first on energy and later encompassing social, ecological, and economic sustainability. It describes and analyzes the leadership that emerged which played an essential role in supporting the

Organizing for Sustainability
Organizing for Sustainable Effectiveness, Volume 1, 127–153
Copyright © 2011 by Emerald Group Publishing Limited
All rights of reproduction in any form reserved
ISSN: 2045-0605/doi:10.1108/S2045-0605(2011)0000001010

complexity of increasing collaborative involvement. New theories of leadership, most specifically Complexity Leadership Theory (Uhl-Bien & Marion, 2008), emergent leadership (Goldstein et al., 2010), and adaptive leadership (Heifetz, 1994) are used to make sense of the leadership philosophy and actions that worked in the sustainability journey.

Keywords: Leadership; sustainability; collaboration; public housing; complexity

EMERGENT COLLABORATION AND LEADERSHIP

This chapter examines the role of leadership in the transition underway in the Cuyahoga Metropolitan Housing Authority (CMHA) as it has used many forms of collaboration and partnership to deal with the complex challenge of becoming a more sustainable system. Public agencies like CMHA manage systems in which resources are constrained and projected to decline (Hemphill, McGreal, Berry, & Watson, 2006). For such systems, the "triple bottom line" presents and represents an apparent paradox of having to take on even more with less. This forces new perspectives and different ways of working, thus exacerbating the complexity and uncertainty in which the organization is already operating (Wood & Gray, 1991). Partnerships and collaboration are a common and necessary strategy for managing the impact of complexity and optimizing opportunities that come with advancing sustainability (Trist, 1983; Pfeffer & Salancik, 1978). CMHA provides a rich empirical case from which we can extract learning about the nature of leadership required to carry out such a sustainability strategy.

Sustainability is by nature an interdependent and multifaceted phenomenon that integrates the traditional and predominant economic bottom line with social and/or environmental imperatives. The Brundtland Commission's report (United Nations General Assembly, 1987) is the starting point for most definitions of sustainability: "In essence, sustainable development is a process of change in which the exploitation of resources, the direction of investments, the orientation of technological development, and institutional change are all in harmony and enhance both current and future potential to meet human needs and aspirations."

Just as organizations need to consider different modes of organizing to work in a complex environment, they need to understand the leadership modes and attributes most suited for times of turbulence, uncertainty, and rapid change. While there is the temptation to "hunker down" and become more controlling, what is needed is leadership that will enable collective intelligence and informal dynamics in human systems (Uhl-Bien & Marion, 2008, p. xiii). Dess and Picken (2000) suggest that:

> The demands of the changing environment present a complex set of challenges – and require a shift in focus and emphasis – for organizational leaders ... To meet the challenge, organizational leaders must "loosen up" the organization – stimulating innovation, creativity, and responsiveness, and learn to manage continuous adaptation to change – without losing strategic focus or spinning out of control. (p. 19)

Recently, literature about organizational sustainability points out the importance of leadership (Crews, 2010; Epstein, Buhovac, & Yuthas, 2010) to the success of this complex transition. In this chapter we examine CMHA's transition through the lens of leadership theories aimed at dealing with complexity, including Complexity Leadership Theory (CLT) (Uhl-Bien & Marion, 2008), adaptive leadership (Heifetz, 1994), and generative leadership (Goldstein, Hazy, & Lichtenstein, 2010). Leaders fostered and enabled the collaborative partnerships that contributed to the growing vibrancy of CMHA in their quest to provide sustainable, low-cost public housing. We start with a brief review of complexity-oriented leadership theories that we believe help articulate new forms of leading that are necessary in organizations pursuing a sustainability course of action.

Leadership Theories Relevant to Collaboration for Sustainability

Recent theories of leadership that specifically rely on principles of complexity, emergence, and adaptability are presented as the lens to examine leadership in the CMHA case. Managing for sustainable effectiveness encompasses energy efficiency, social welfare, wise use of public resources, and leveraging resources in an increasingly turbulent field; it calls for a new perspective on leadership. CLT (Uhl-Bien, Marion, & McKelvey, 2007) distinguishes leadership from leaders and frames "leadership as a complex interactive dynamic from which adaptive outcomes (e.g., learning, innovation, and adaptability) emerge" (p. 299). Leaders are individuals who act in ways that influence this interactive dynamic and may hold formal roles in the organization. Implicit in this definition is that leadership is a property and dynamic of those involved in producing outcomes. It includes three "entangled" roles of "adaptive leadership, administrative leadership and enabling leadership that reflect a dynamic relationship between the bureaucratic, administrative functions and the emergent, informal dynamics of complex adaptive systems (CAS)" (p. 186).

The premise of this leadership theory is that within current bureaucratic structures, complex adaptive systems are also active. Thus, to foster sustainability, leaders not only have to manage hierarchical coordination but also must foster emergent creativity, learning, and processes to deal with the inherent complexity. The role and function of leadership must address both stability and emergence.

Adaptive Leadership
CLT includes the concept of adaptive leadership. Heifetz (1994) was the first to propose this construct, which involves fostering adaptations through influencing dialogue, embracing disequilibrium to create the urgency for change, and generating leadership throughout the organization. In this light, adaptive leadership as a process requires empathy, depersonalizing conflict, creating courageous conversations, "standing in the balcony" to see the whole picture, empowering others, and bringing an authentic self to the work. This contrasts with more traditional leadership for "technical" problems, in which the necessary knowledge is already discovered and available, and where organizational procedures and roles guide what should be done and by whom. In a more traditional case, leadership would shield the organization from external threats, clarify roles, stabilize and restore order, and reinforce norms.

By comparison, adaptive leadership is required when there are inadequate responses to certain situations, no clear expertise can be found, no single person has the credibility required or there are no established procedures. In this scenario, leadership is more likely to frame key questions, let the organization feel the external pressures, challenge existing roles, surface conflict, and challenge unproductive norms.

Enabling Leadership
"The role of enabling leadership in the CLT framework is to directly foster and maneuver the conditions (e.g., the context) that catalyze adaptive leadership and allow for emergence" (Uhl-Bien, Marion, & McKelvey, 2007, p. 205). Enabling leadership must also manage the interface between adaptive and administrative leadership, oftentimes disseminating innovative outcomes "upward" and throughout the organization. Setting conditions that enable adaptive leadership can include establishing interactions through networks both internal and external to the organization, monitoring the

environment, creating interdependencies so there is pressure to act on information, and fostering appropriate tension.

Administrative Leadership
The third component of CLT is administrative leadership, which refers to the actions of people who occupy formal managerial roles that plan and coordinate activities. This can range from top-level managers who establish strategy, acquire and distribute resources, and set policy, to other managers who engage in planning, coordination, setting work systems and standards. To deal with complexity, administrative leaders exercise their authority with consideration of the organization's need for creativity, adaptability, and learning. They may help institutionalize innovations that have been created through adaptive and enabling leadership and that create value for the system.

These three aspects of leadership are intertwined in CLT and offer a way to look at leadership for sustainability through the lens of complexity.

Generative Leadership
Also instructive is the concept of generative leadership, which according to Goldstein et al. (2010), focuses on the mutual interplay and influence of people in the processes of innovation. It is the influential interactions between people that will create the novelty necessary for innovation. In this sense, generative leadership is about interaction and mutuality, not about one leader. Generative leadership is not a "laissez-faire orientation which just allows emergence; rather, it is about intentional hands-on building up of ecologies of innovation, the construction of more effective social networks, and the search and amplification of experiments in novelty, which result in the emergence of innovation" (p. 4). Table 1 summarizes CLT, adaptive leadership, and generative leadership.

In the next section, we describe the evolution of CMHA and its cascading partnerships in their sustainability journey. Even though CMHA is a bureaucracy and has a defined hierarchy that must manage the assets of the organization and be mindful of spending public funds, it also represents the challenge of needing to be adaptable and innovative in its journey toward sustainability. Collaboration is inherent in the sustainability literature and emerged as an overarching strategy in CMHA's journey to become sustainable. The nature of successful collaboration requires many elements, but the most frequently found in literature are: common or complementary aims, establishing and maintaining trust, credible and open process, broad-based stakeholder involvement, interim successes, and leadership

Table 1. Complexity Leadership Theory (CLT), Adaptive Leadership, and Generative Leadership Functions.

Functions	Definition	Examples of Actions
CLT – adaptive (includes adaptive leadership concepts)	Refers to adaptive, creative, and learning actions that emerge from the interactions of complex adaptive systems as they strive to adjust to tension[a]	• Originates change as conflicts resolved in new ways • Fosters adaptation • Confronts loyalty to legacy practices • Embraces disequilibrium • Runs numerous experiments • "Stands in the balcony" • Generating leadership throughout the organization regardless of hierarchical job position • Mobilizes everyone to generate innovation • Creates culture of courageous conversations
CLT – enabling	Works to catalyze the conditions in which adaptive leadership can thrive and to manage the entanglement between bureaucratic and emergent functions of the organization[a]	• Fosters interactions • Fosters interdependencies • Injects appropriate tension – internal and external – and helps manage it • Manages the "entanglement" between administrative and adaptive leadership • Helps disseminate innovative processes and products
CLT – administrative	Refers to the actions of individuals and groups in formal managerial roles who plan and coordinate activities to accomplish organizationally prescribed outcomes in an efficient and effective manner[a]	• Structures tasks • Engages in planning • Build vision • Acquires resources • Manages crises • Manages conflict • Forms organizational strategy
Generative	Focuses on mutual influence and capturing the benefits of the mutual interplay[b]	• Hands-on building up of ecologies of innovation • Focuses on nexus of relationships linking individuals • Engages in novel experiments • Recognizes, amplifies, and disseminates seeds of innovation

[a]From *Complexity Leadership Theory* (Uhl-Bien, Marion, & McKelvey, 2007).
[b]From *Complexity and the Nexus of Leadership* (Goldstein, Hazy, & Lichtenstein, 2010).

(Crislip & Larson, 1994; Huxham & Vangen, 2005). These were all evident in the CMHA case, to a great extent.

PROVIDING AFFORDABLE AND SUSTAINABLE HOUSING

The CMHA is a political subdivision of the State of Ohio, serving Cuyahoga County through two federally assisted housing programs: Low-Income Public Housing and the Housing Choice Voucher Program. While it is first and foremost a property manager, it is a property manager with a social mission. As CMHA endeavors to improve property management practices and reduce costs, it does so in an attempt to help fund its social mission of providing safe, quality, affordable housing and its goal of creating strong communities that residents are proud to call home, that are not isolated from surrounding neighborhoods but are linked to the social, education, economic, and religious institutions of the community at large, and which support individuals and families (residents and employees) to be strong contributing members to the community (CMHA website, 2010).

As federal funding for public housing has continued to shrink and the U.S. Department of Housing and Urban Development (HUD) has pressed for increasingly effective property management practices, CMHA (along with other public housing authorities) faces a world of declining resources and increasing need. When CMHA embarked on its sustainability journey in the mid-2000s as a way to decrease costs through reduced energy consumption and increased energy conservation, it did so as a strategy for sustaining what it was already providing residents – not as a strategy for increasing monies for new products and services. The early sustainability efforts drove a need for collaboration both internal and external, which in turn spurred new, more entrepreneurial ventures within CMHA.

History and Context

The CMHA was established in 1933 as the first housing authority in the State of Ohio. Responsible for the management and operation of the local public housing program, CMHA is now the seventh largest housing authority in the United States, consisting of 47 public housing developments and serving nearly 14,000 households. The mix of housing includes high-, mid-, and low-rise buildings, townhouses, duplexes, and single-family homes.

CMHA also maintains an accredited police department and a social services department that develops programs to enhance the quality of life of its residents.

The CMHA case study is a longitudinal qualitative field study. Two sets of interviews have been conducted by both authors; the first in preparation for a case presentation in October 2008 and the second in preparation for this chapter in September 2010.

The Journey Begins: An Energy Performance Contract and the Transformative Partnership with Siemens Building Technologies

As the cost of energy began to consume more of CMHA's operating budget, CMHA's Chief Executive Officer George Phillips-Olivier and Chief of Staff and Operations Jeffery K. Patterson wanted to establish a comprehensive program that would reduce energy use throughout their buildings and incorporate energy savings practices into the daily routines of their residents. With limited capital funds available, CMHA turned to HUD's energy reduction incentive funding program, Energy Performance Contracting (EPC), to provide third party financing for the initial energy-related improvements. In 2005, CMHA selected Siemens Building Technologies – through the HUD-approved procurement process – to be a partner in this twelve-year, $33.6-million dollar project. Siemens Building Technologies, Inc. is an operating group of Siemens AG, one of the world's largest engineering conglomerates. Founded in 1998, Siemens Building Technologies is a leading provider of energy and environmental solutions, building controls, fire safety, and security system solutions making buildings comfortable, safe, productive, and less costly to operate.

The Siemens contract was not CMHA's first energy performance contract with a major energy solutions provider. From its previous experience, CMHA had learned the importance of partnership and of engaging residents to implement sustainable solutions. Therefore, with the Siemens contract, CMHA leadership fostered an intentional and more deeply collaborative partnership that was grounded in a shared commitment to education and to partnering with CMHA residents, NGOs, local businesses, and other public agencies.

In this initial project, the sustainability focus for both organizations was cost reduction for CMHA through reduced energy consumption. For both Siemens and CMHA, however, the goals were bigger than just satisfying a contract, completing construction, and reducing energy costs. In addition to reducing energy costs, Phillips-Olivier and Patterson of CMHA saw an opportunity to explore and implement energy efficiency/green building concepts that were not typical part of a HUD Energy Performance Contract. Similarly, Siemens wanted more than a single project out of the energy efficiency contract. They saw this as an opportunity to build an ongoing relationship with CMHA. As the collaboration progressed, Siemens' primary project lead, Bill Davis, realized this was also an opportunity to learn from CMHA and improve Siemens' own internal processes for working with customers to establish truly sustainable approaches to energy reduction. The combination of each organization's individual objectives with a shared, yet more implicit commitment to something bigger than the project helped build a strong foundation for collaboration.

To provide a home for this project, CMHA established an Office of Energy Conservation, which was to be led by Mark Novak, formerly an internal auditor for the organization, in a new role as Director of Energy Conservation. Siemens acted as general contractor, pulling in a team of national Siemens housing experts to work in tandem with local Siemens professionals who provided the day-to-day project management and supervision of CMHA's upgrades. CMHA provided the procurement function and oversaw the implementation of the energy efficiency improvements. The project was structured to support communications within and between the different components of the project team inside the two organizations, from executive leadership to construction implementation, and to facilitate decentralized decision-making within the established parameters of the project. A structure of formal and informal meetings kept people apprised of project status and focused attention to key issues. As part of this structure, senior leadership from both CMHA and Siemens maintained their own regular meetings as a forum to resolve issues that required higher-level intervention. Everyone knew this communication structure was in place which, according to Patterson, helped "facilitate flow and minimize games that get played at lower levels" in construction projects.

Leadership capacity and personality also contributed to the project's success. As part of a core leadership team from Siemens and CMHA, Patterson and Davis were instrumental in helping to create a culture of collaboration and communication. Both told the authors that many of the team members possessed both the ability and the willingness to collaborate and that a spirit of cooperation between Siemens, CMHA staff, and CMHA residents was contagious. People within both organizations realized they had to put egos aside, cut through bureaucracy, and figure out how to get things done. Jeff found it was helpful to "sit people down and explain why" CMHA was doing what it was doing and to be "clear on end results."

Patterson also emphasized the importance of process to the project, a significant shift from his normal mode of operation as a self-proclaimed "get it done kind of guy." He knew success would require that staff and residents be willing to do things differently; consequently, the process demanded that residents be engaged in planning and construction and be trained on energy efficiency. At CMHA's request, Siemens hosted information meetings at each housing site to let residents know what was going to be happening in their homes, why the energy efficiency improvements were important, how long the process would take, and the benefits to them. Although Siemens had some prior experience working with other public housing authorities, they had never hosted these types of meetings for residents. At first, Davis didn't understand why CMHA wanted to do this; he was a bit apprehensive that they would be opening the door to all kinds of complaints and challenges. However, after the first few meetings, he found that the process was in fact helpful to Siemens as well as to the residents.

Resident engagement, training, and education were critical parts of the process. Phillips-Olivier and Patterson have long recognized the importance of engaging residents and encouraging their leadership, working closely with CMHA's resident leadership body, the Progressive Action Council (PAC), established in 1989. The residents of CMHA elect delegates to PAC, which in turn, serves as their resource for information, as well as an advocate when residents want to voice opinions. PAC also oversees elections for resident leaders of the Local Advisory Councils (LAC) at each CMHA property. All residents are considered part of their development's LAC, and vote to elect their own officers (CMHA website). The PAC Executive Board, consisting of eight volunteers elected by the PAC delegates and appointed by the PAC president, works closely with the CMHA administration to address resident issues and comment on related policy. PAC collaborates with the CMHA administration, providing the residents' perspective on new opportunities and modifications to existing procedures, including the Agency's Annual Plan and Capital Fund programs. According to Lillian Davis, President and Budget and Training Committee Chairperson for PAC, Phillips-Olivier "keeps us abreast of everything" and knows "he can't make anything happen unless each and every one of us buys into it. He listens, he learns from us and us from him."

When it came to accomplishing CMHA's energy efficiency goals, Phillips-Olivier knew that resident buy-in through engagement and education would be essential. "We recognized that it's easy to install new toilets, but if we don't change habits, then nothing really changes." Siemens led the training, working with a contractor who made the training process fun by creating contests and fact cards with questions like "What is the first thing you should do when coming into your house?" "What saves energy?" Residents could win prizes and have fun at the training sessions, which encouraged people to pay attention. For example, energy-efficient toilets operated differently from traditional toilets. Many residents were in the habit of lifting the top of the tank and putting in automatic blue toilet cleaner products. The trainer looked for a creative and fun way to tell people not to do this and came up with a simple and memorable saying – "No blue in the loo."

Training always occurred before any actual construction took place on a site. Throughout the project, there was a continual cycle of training, construction, and debriefing. After construction had started on a site, CMHA and Siemens hosted resident feedback meetings, receiving both positive and critical feedback from residents that helped them improve their process. Although Davis acknowledged that this kind of process required more up-front time and costs, he came to realize that the investment is "well worth it!" It ultimately helped to streamline resident relations during the construction process, a process improvement that Siemens transferred to their work with other housing authorities.

The outcomes from the CMHA/Siemens collaboration were many and varied. The facility improvements resulted in minimum guaranteed energy savings for CMHA equivalent to $47 million. Energy conservation and optimization upgrades were made to 45 of CMHA's 47 housing developments, with improvements made to approximately 7,000 of the CMHA's 10,000 building units. Siemens worked with contractors to employ CMHA residents for 28 percent of the total hours worked on the project exceeding original goals for the project and providing on-the-job training and employment opportunities for the residents. In addition, Siemens started modeling the process adopted during the CMHA project as an offering for other clients across the country, and the CMHA/Siemens team has hosted sessions with HUD and other authorities to focus on best practices for sustainability implementation and partnership.

The Journey Continues: CMHA's Emerging Sustainability Initiatives

Having had the positive experience of the energy audit and Siemens partnership, CMHA began to initiate and/or respond to an expanding variety of sustainability opportunities and new partnerships. These have included an after-school program for CMHA youth, a teen leadership development program for high school students living in CMHA housing, recycling in administrative and resident facilities, Leadership in Energy and Environmental Design (LEED) based design construction standards, and urban gardening.

As the key players in the CMHA have taken on each new initiative, the meaning of sustainability has expanded and gained clarity. Four particular elements shape the agenda. First, the formal sustainability movement started with an explicit focus on energy conservation and cost saving, a focus that has remained central. Second, while the explicit focus was cost savings through energy conservation, the sustainability agenda has always been implicitly grounded in the social mission of CMHA. These two elements are illustrated in Phillips-Olivier's description of his approach to sustainability. "For me, sustainability has to make sense in the business environment. Take recycling. It is not yet mandated in the City of Cleveland; in fact, when we started it was costing us more." This statement was quickly followed by, "We need to do it because it is good for the region. We did it [recycling] primarily to provide jobs for the residents – it was enough of a synergy."

Third, a spirit of innovation and entrepreneurship, particularly on behalf of Phillips-Olivier and Patterson, has shaped the basic nature of the initiative from the beginning. Starting with the energy performance contract, Phillips-Olivier emphasized to Siemens that, "Everything is on the board – we want to go outside the box – solar, wind, etc. Then we can pare back from that. We like to push the envelope." As a result, CMHA ended up with improvements that were not traditionally part of a HUD energy efficiency project, like new roofs. According to Patterson, the next step beyond energy efficiency was a green roof (also known as a "living roof," as it is a roof with "vegetation and a growing medium") at one of the properties. Admitting the payback was not that great, he added, "We did it because we wanted to break that threshold. If we had not done the green roofs, we knew we might not have had the chance to do it again. We took the green roof and built on recycling and gardening. We are trying to get residents to be more conscious about these things."

Phillips-Olivier has also expanded the leadership group beyond a body defined solely by position. Both he and Patterson have increasingly engaged individuals not in formal positions of leadership but who are willing and able to get in and figure out how to get things done. Together, they all have been working across departmental lines and across organizational lines – finding and engaging others both within and outside of CMHA who may or may not be in formal positions of leadership. Whereas in the past, positional leadership may have been a primary determinant for who they chose to work with – these people appear to look first for will and skill. This expansion of the leadership group has and continues to cause tension within members of the formal leadership group.

The fourth element has been a commitment to education and engagement. It started with the Siemens participation at resident training and has remained constant as a core strategy for advancing and embedding sustainability aligned behavior. Beginning with residents, education and engagement efforts have expanded to include youth and staff, thus strengthening the "people" part of CMHA's triple bottom line. A discussion of some ongoing specific initiatives follows.

CMHA After-School Program
While the energy performance contract was underway, CMHA and Siemens initiated another collaboration, this one with a social focus on providing greater access to educational intervention programs for young residents in CMHA units. While public housing was originally intended as a social safety net for individuals and families who, for various reasons could not afford market rate housing, CMHA's leadership realizes that this safety net has, in many instances, become a way of life, a repeating cycle where generations continue to live in public housing. CMHA also knows that education, particularly for youth, can play a critical role in breaking this cycle. Just as the energy performance contract with Siemens was a means for reducing property maintenance costs (the economic and environmental legs of sustainability), collaboration with Siemens to win a 21st Century Community Learning Center grant, represented the social leg. The 21st Century Grant is a program of the U.S. Department of Education that supports the creation of community learning centers to provide academic enrichment opportunities during nonschool hours for children, particularly students who attend high-poverty and low-performing schools. The program helps students meet state and local student standards in core academic subjects, such as reading and math; offers students a broad array of enrichment activities that can complement their regular academic programs; and offers literacy and other educational services to the families of participating children (U.S. Department of Education website). For CMHA, this program provided more youth with an educational intervention at a critical age and reinforced the efforts of the public school system, Cleveland Metropolitan School District, by supporting their day-to-day efforts with after-school learning and enrichment programming. For CMHA, the result has been an increase in test scores, grades, and attendance for

students who have consistently participated in this 21st Century program. Based on their success, Patterson indicated that they will continue to seek grants and other funding opportunities to support this program. Siemens, as part of their corporate social responsibility commitment, donated the grant-writing expertise and participated on the CMHA 21st Century steering committee.

CMHA Teen Leadership Development Program
As a part of the CMHA 21st Century Grant, CMHA was able to initiate a young leaders' academy called Generation Success-Teens Achieving Greatness (GS-TAG). A vision of Patterson's, GS-TAG is a program that helps CMHA high school youth achieve their potential as productive members of the community by developing leadership capacity and promoting educational attainment. The program encourages student empowerment and engagement through a curriculum that promotes self-awareness, creativity, healthy relationships, abundance thinking, civic engagement, effective communication, and neighborhood stewardship.

To initiate the program, CMHA partnered with Currere, Inc., a local organizational development firm, to lead the design and early stage implementation process. Under the guidance of one of Currere's principles, the GS-TAG program was designed and is delivered through a collaboration that includes CMHA, the GS-TAG students, Currere, an independent youth facilitator, the Cleveland Scholarship Program, and other partners who bring in special program components. Currently, GS-TAG program collaborators are compensated for their participation in delivering the program, but in the design phase, the initial group of collaborators came together as volunteers to cocreate the program with CMHA. A number of the early collaborators fell out of the process, due most often to two factors: (1) the potential collaborator ultimately was not interested in customizing their program to work in a larger CMHA context; and/or (2) the potential collaborator was not interested in sharing credit with other contributors. With an initial collaboration team in place, the program kicked off in June 2008.

It has taken a while to solidify the GS-TAG collaboration team. Individual team members have continued to change over the course of three years, with Patterson and Currere being the only original team members remaining. Others have either left the partner organization (as is the case with the original CMHA program staff), have not been asked to continue in the collaboration due to a perceived lack of alignment with program intention and design, or have decided to opt out voluntarily due to divergent goals, lack of alignment, etc.

From the start, there has been a certain ambiguity about which member of the collaboration is actually charged with leading which aspects of the GS-TAG program. This has created challenges and tension among certain members of the internal CMHA team and between those CMHA team members, Currere, and other members of the collaboration. Key individuals have brought different expectations and benchmarks to the program, including graduating from high school and supporting the GS-TAG students in getting out of public housing by going to college. As the program has progressed, expectations, originally set by Patterson as graduation from high school, have been raised. His new bar is graduation from college. Regardless of differences in expectations, the current collaborators do share a strong commitment to the development of the GS-TAG youth.

The development consultant from Currere was surprised to find that one of the major roles she occupied and continues to play in the program is serving as "the glue" for all of the partners and component parts. "My first thought was, who would weave all these parts together? Who was going to be the glue? I asked myself, is this what I signed up for? Do I have this mission and passion? I would bring snacks – that was my biggest strategy." Snacks and all, she did become the glue for the collaboration, a role that would create tension between her and the two CMHA direct program staff. "There were too many cooks in the kitchen. There weren't explicit roles," and there was a "lot of internal bumping up against each other. I contributed by not being as good of a communicator as I needed to be. I got overwhelmed by it sometimes and didn't think about all of the people I needed to be communicating with and didn't live up to my own rules of what supports partnerships." Now, the GS-TAG program is early into its third year and a new internal CMHA team is in place. As Patterson steps in to help orient the CMHA internal team, his focus has shifted to the development of a plan for sustaining the program once the 21st Century Grant is up.

CMHA Recycling Program

The energy efficiency audit also catalyzed a significant focus on recycling within CMHA for administrative as well as resident housing facilities. The office of Energy Conservation morphed into the Office of Energy Conservation and Sustainability and doubled in size from one to two staff: Mark Novak, the director of energy efficiency and sustainability and Larry Davis, the manager of sustainability.

The CMHA executive office, along with Novak and Davis, have continued to use education and partnerships with other community organizations to drive home the importance of recycling. Phillips-Olivier organized field trips to an area landfill for different CMHA teams. "Talk about an educational experience, when you look at the Styrofoam plates out there and see that these will be here in one hundred thousand years, you get the impact of the decisions we make." Davis and Novak continue to take the recycling message to their residents, emphasizing the what's, how's, and why's of the program with a touch of humor. Although their efforts meet with different levels of success at different sites, the overall process has been effective. Novak shares the story of one site where a woman, who for years has been vocal in professional action councils, approached them after the presentation saying, "You changed me, I'm doing it." Now Novak realizes, "She will be an ambassador."

To support its educational objectives, CMHA has formed partnerships with other organizations including Cleveland Metro Parks Zoo and the County Solid Waste District. For instance, Novak and Davis have organized a variety of outings to the zoo so that different groups, including the executive staff and a troop of CMHA Girl Scouts, could learn about the value of composting through the zoo's program, *What Do They Do With the Poo at the Zoo*. Davis also communicates regularly with a Business Recycling Specialist at the Cuyahoga County Solid Waste District to share information and provide updates. Neither can remember who approached whom, but both agree it has been a good partnership and "a two-way street." By helping CMHA expand and institutionalize their recycling efforts, Solid Waste is able to advance its mission of landfill diversion. For the County specialist, he is just doing his job. "All I do is challenge and push gently to let them know of options to increase recycling cheaply and easily." The relationship has deepened over time. With every interaction building trust, both people better understand what the other is up against and they become more invested. While the County specialist may just be doing his job, it is obvious that CMHA views him as a significant resource and as a partner. As the specialist noted, "It touches me that he does – really touches me to know that he views us as a partner."

Internal partnerships have been a tougher nut to crack. In 2005, CMHA began a major reorganization from a centralized to a decentralized structure. It is now organized around property units called asset management properties (AMPs). AMPs are headed by AMP leaders who are measured against a set of performance metrics for their respective property units. When it comes to sustainability and recycling, there are no institutional incentives for AMP leaders to take on these new initiatives.

"Some AMP leaders have bought in, some have not, and some are in the middle." Both Davis and Novak recognize that the AMP leaders have "pressures they have to deal with, and developing the necessary internal partnerships has been challenging, including getting green teams throughout the organization with members whose hearts are in it." At the end of the day, AMP leaders' evaluations are "going to be based on occupancy, not on how much they have recycled."

Another barrier to embedding recycling and sustainability internally has been CMHA's traditional silo mentality, although it has significantly lessened over the past five years under Phillips-Olivier's leadership. Personnel have long been dispersed in offices and properties throughout the county, making it easy for each department to choose and set their own rules. According to Novak, this will change with the move of the majority of departments to a new CMHA campus, emphasizing that co-location of most departments will make it easier to institutionalize sustainability practices and harder to hide actions that don't align.

When it comes to recycling and sustainability education, Novak and Davis have found work with youth particularly meaningful. When they took the CMHA Girl Scout troop to the zoo program, they asked them about the main tenets of recycling. "One little girl said, 'Reduce, reuse, recycle, respect' – just like that. We can sit here and talk about the adults, but when we talk to the youth we know it is their world that we are doing the sustainability bit for – it is a wonderful moment." Davis also took a group of young people on a stream cleaning initiative with the Metroparks as part of a program called Bug City for which he volunteers. "They started out grumpily and then learned about nature and jobs. We are talking about the winning of hearts and minds and getting this message out there that this is for the kids. Let's leave something behind for them. People seem to get that youth focus. The focus of our residents isn't sustainability, but they get the kid piece."

From Novak's and Davis's perspective, CMHA needs to take a stronger top-down approach to further institutionalize recycling and sustainability and to drive a culture of sustainability (and recycling) throughout the organization. "The key to achieving our 2011 goals right now is to get everyone at CMHA into the program. We are going to ask Phillips-Olivier and Patterson to say 'CMHA is sustainability.'" Novak and Davis would "love to see this in the resident's lease; either you recycle or you get a 30 day notice – to see it is part of the organizational culture that you are expected to recycle." "Top down support will allow us to leverage CMHA's historically top down culture and police it. Top down is the engine; beyond that you need groups of people talking about it, enforcing in, taking ownership – top down will force or push grass roots." This presents an interesting contrast to Phillips-Olivier's and Patterson's more entrepreneurial approach.

Green Construction
The energy efficiency audit also drove changes in construction practices and policies, as energy conservation standards were incorporated into more and more construction specifications. "We started by looking at the energy efficiency of equipment and fixtures, like stoves and toilets in the apartments, and have gone beyond equipment and fixtures to what things are made of, to the next level ... " Today, LEED methods and practices are fairly standard for all new construction. The new CMHA campus will be LEED Silver certified. The head of the construction project illustrates this commitment. "We will have recycling stations everywhere we can, plus making people aware of shower rooms in the building on the first floor," which will "encourage people to run or bike to work."

Members of the Construction department help link together the Office of Energy Conservation and Sustainability, the Purchasing Department, and the Executive Office. Within this group, there appears to be a culture of learning by doing, learning with each other, and partnering. "Partnering is part of the culture," and CMHA is partnering more and more with other organizations in the community on different construction projects like the splash park and the CMHA garden at Outhwaite Estates. As Phillips-Olivier expressed, "If you put creative people in a room and let them go, that is what you get – and see that continuing."

Community Gardens and CMHA Green Teams
Patterson had a dream to build parks within CMHA's housing units. As a start, he initiated a partnership with the executive director of the Cleveland Botanical Garden to turn a blighted and dangerous vacant lot where two children had been killed into a learning garden. He brought together folks from construction, resident leadership, the Housing Choice Voucher program, area nonprofits, and a daycare center. Co-led by Jeff and the Botanical Gardens, they found a private donor, garnered additional funding from two major area foundations, and built a splash park with the help and collaboration of CMHA residents, local businesses, community non-profits, and KaBOOM! (a national nonprofit dedicated to creating

playgrounds). According to Lillian Davis, a resident leader and long-time CMHA resident:

> Everyone was pitching in to make this a success. We met with residents, let them know this is what we planned to do, what we want to see by 5 PM. They helped build it, so they take care of it; total ownership is there because they built it. At Outhwaite, they now grow vegetables; residents keep the kids involved in it. The children who were killed led to a splash park – it is like throwing new seeds. We were successful in getting the grants because Mr. Patterson had the resident input and trust. If you don't have the partnership, nothing will be successful. You have to put everything on the table: the good, the bad, and the ugly. And be truthful – you have to let everyone know what is going on. If you are truthful, they will buy into what you are talking about. Anything that is going on at CMHA, the residents are involved, the partnerships are involved. We will sit around the table and discuss it. When we go out to build KaBOOMs it is for the children.

In the process of building the first park and garden, CMHA hired away the project liaison from the Botanical Gardens to work at CMHA. As CMHA's first "real green person," Brittany Barski quickly became the go-to person for questions about landscaping, the CMHA Green Team, and community partnerships around land use, food, and community gardening. Reporting into the construction department, Barski is the leader and manager for CMHA's Green Team, and she teaches a group of residents at three sites about sustainability and gardening. She recounted that, from her perspective, the first round of planting at one of the community gardens was not received with much interest on behalf of residents. As she sought to understand why, she learned through conversations with residents that a local food bank was dropping off the very same food products (e.g., corn) that had been planted in the garden. Now she understood that rather than lacking interest in the garden, the residents just wanted alternative vegetables from the garden. For Barski, there was great learning and now she manages a growing group of residents, currently totaling 11 people ranging in age from 30 to 70, that works in the gardens two days a week. "The gardens are growing. Gardening brings a lot of truth – you get to supplement your income – learn about what you eat, learn who you are, learn patience. It can change lives. I have one guy I taught about dill and how you use it. He grew it, and now he is harvesting it. He is excited about this!"

The first garden continues to catalyze a growing number of new community gardens in which CMHA takes part. One of these, the Ohio City Farm, is situated on six acres of land directly behind the largest public housing high-rise in the state. This farm is the result of a collaboration that was initiated with CMHA in January 2010 by Ohio City Near West (a nonprofit community development corporation). The collaboration also included the Great Lakes Brewing Company (a rapidly growing brewery with a local restaurant that wanted to source agricultural products locally) and The Refugee Response (an NGO founded to help refugees adapt to life in northeast Ohio and which now operates at the farm, providing resettled refugee trainees with employment, education, and training). The executive director of Ohio City Near West first approached Phillips-Olivier in January 2010 to propose a community farm on the site, and just five months after this initial conversation, the land was being tilled. Now there are 3½ acres of growing space being farmed by Refugee Response, CMHA residents, and the Great Lakes Brewing Company. As Phillips-Olivier declared, "Trust is critical. If don't have trust you have nothing."

According to the Eric Wobser, executive director of Ohio City Near West, everyone he worked with at CMHA actively assisted him in moving through the necessary process and getting the essential buy-in and agreements. When Ohio City Near West and the CMHA staff team first presented the proposal to the CMHA board, it was rejected. He recognized that, "We didn't have the right information. There was no compelling story." With the help of CMHA leadership and staff and further informed by meetings with the CMHA Board, the proposal was presented again at the next board meeting and approved without a hitch. Historically known as hard and slow to work with, "CMHA was the fastest moving partner on the whole project. They made it a priority." From his perspective, the Ohio City Farm has been a great example of collaborative leadership. "This would not have happened without CMHA (the land), Great Lakes (seed money), Refugee Response (the know-how), and Ohio City Near West (the instigators). Had any one of those not stepped up, this would not be here today."

Summary

In 2005, CMHA embarked on a sustainability journey, starting with an energy performance contract (with Siemens Building Technologies, a global technology company) and a strong desire on behalf of CMHA leadership for a collaborative partnership. For CMHA, the energy performance partnership with Siemens was a success – economically, environmentally, and socially. Through the collaboration with Siemens, CMHA team members effectively advanced their organization's energy performance objectives. They also expanded their own collaborative capacity – providing the foundation for developing numerous partnerships that CMHA has taken on over the past six years with a growing number of NGOs, for profit entities, and governmental agencies. These collaborations have resulted in various additional capacities/programs – such as CMHA's recycling initiative, LEED-based construction standards, and green teams; the 21st Century Grant sites and GS-TAG; the Ohio City Farm; and the Splash Parks and community gardens – all of which enhance CMHA's ability to deliver its social mission in an environment of constrained resources.

DISCUSSION

Theories of leadership based on complexity, adaptability, and emergence are useful in understanding and learning from CMHA as it becomes more and more sustainable, using a strategy of collaboration and partnerships. Elements of CLT (enabling, adaptive, and administrative), and generative leadership were evident in this case, and provide a basis to demonstrate what is useful to an organization developing its capabilities to increase sustainability through partnerships. These leadership theories are built on the premise that the environment is increasingly complex, the work of organizations includes problems that have no easy solution and opportunities not yet realized, and that there are complex adaptive systems at play. The theories all presume that there is a tension between bureaucracy and innovation – or between control and chaos. To make the most from these conditions, leadership must be energized throughout the organization as well as from people in appointed authority positions. Specific categories of actions include building and enabling networks of people (internal and external to the organization), challenging the status quo and not immediately "fixing" the disequilibrium that ensues, fostering innovation and experimentation, and disseminating and instituting the new capabilities, processes, and structures that emerge.

In the CMHA case, there was an intentional building of networks of different people to allow for "ecologies of innovation." From regularly scheduled meetings between Siemens and CMHA to mutual training of construction engineers to resident boards to people being co-located, there were plenty of opportunities – formal and informal – to create dialogues that led to innovation. This supports the idea that collaboration is a way to handle the complexity which has to be addressed as the organization works to achieve greater sustainability.

Leadership was able to live with disequilibrium and wait for emergence. Pushing the envelope on the green roof provided a challenge to the norm, and was done to stretch the residents, the city, and CMHA to think outside their comfort zone. This caused questioning but later provided an example of what could be done for sustainability. Fostering a recycling program was another initiative that challenged the status quo, and is creating some tension between those "believers" and those who do not participate in recycling. Some are hoping for a mandated solution, but thus far, leadership is holding the tension while a better solution is found.

One of the major skills in adaptive leaders is the ability to see "from the balcony"; this perspective allows leaders to not get caught in the disequilibrium. This ability was evident with CMHA; Patterson and others remarked on his own talent to see things that others could not. Others also noted his ability to have vision, yet at the same time be pragmatic. Phillips-Olivier remarked that one of his roles was to help people make sense of what is emerging. Both of these leaders were able to manage the inherent tension of order and emergence.

Fostering innovation and experiments were evident with various people and projects in the system. For example, in the early community garden the first planting could be classified as a failure, the experiment was valued for the learning that resulted. The GS-TAG educational program went through a series of iterations on the definition of success and who to get involved. The recycling program started with residents and is now part of the planning for the new headquarters building, with learning gained from what worked and what doesn't. From talking to involved residents, staff members, and external partners, one gets the sense that CMHA is willing to try anything that will lead to sustainability.

Trust was a component that was the precursor of innovation and collaboration. If administrative leaders have trust from the people within the organization, then enabling the innovation is made more possible. As Phillips stated, "people have to believe in whoever is at the top in whatever levels or it falls back into a bureaucratic trap." This was also true with collaboration external to the organization, from LEED consultants to the Botanical Gardens to Ohio City Near West.

Disseminating new processes and instituting innovation was evident in restructuring roles that occurred with the advent of the sustainability position and subsequent department. The new LEED building planning was a tangible institutionalization of CMHA's focus on environmental sustainability, not only as following requirements of LEED building itself, but in the clear intention to build in recycling, elements that would contribute to a healthy lifestyle (e.g., showers for those who bike to work), and physical structures that would add to processes of internal collaboration. The green teams and the active involvement of presidents in the resident organizations were mechanism for residents' voices to be heard.

This case demonstrates two dynamics critical to the ability of this resource constrained organization to become more sustainable: the use of collaborative partnerships to expand the knowledge and resources of the organization, and building leadership throughout the organization that catalyzes and supports innovation and networks of action that are part of the adaptation of the organization to better accomplish its mission in a sustainable manner. The leadership approaches that allowed progress in achieving more sustainable ways of functioning are those that are described in CLT.

Leadership had to catalyze a lot of variation in approaches to sustainability. Some were more structural, as in appointing a director of sustainability, and some were emergent such as the children's programs. Formal training was necessary for those who were in charge of the LEED certification and other learning was done while in the process of "doing" something like gardening. The formal leaders had to tolerate the tension of how to handle recycling (emergent or command and control), the continual shifting in the GS-TAG teen leadership program (in house or external leadership), the messiness of working with new partners while under time pressures (Ohio City Near West). Collaborative partners varied in the degree of commitment and the extent to which they were almost part of the organization. This all made for a complex, emergent, and adaptive system that required new vision and skills for leadership – those elaborated in Table 1.

Contributions to Theory

This case offers an opportunity to understand the application of CLTs to entities making the transition to a more highly sustainable organization. By looking at an example of a public organization successfully moving to be more sustainable, we have learned that a move toward sustainability adds complexity, which leadership can and should leverage by collaboration and partnering.

This case highlights the evolution of ever-widening circles of collaboration, with the original partnership of Siemens starting the trajectory of collaboration. CMHA demonstrated an evolving capacity to collaborate in many arenas – from environmental to social, and with many partners – from businesses to residents. CMHA employees relied on cyclical trust building and transferred that knowledge and the trust in collaboration to new partners (not just a trust of the initial collaboration). They developed an ethos of collaboration that applied to growing the capacity of CMHA and the residents of the projects to partner. They also developed a learning orientation that made collaboration possible as a system dynamic, and not just a "one-shot deal."

Therefore, we propose that success in partnering makes it more of a known dynamic and also makes it possible and desirable to look for additional collaborations. Theorists and practitioners should not just look at any one particular collaboration, but rather the constellation of collaborations and its evolution over time. This also challenges the entrenched organizational belief of "only collaborate when you have to." CMHA started embracing opportunities to partner as a strategy to pursue their goals of sustainability. Part of this was a strategy to obtain resources – both time and talent – since sustainability is multifaceted and organizations don't always have the knowledge or personnel required for success. Collaboration also became essential inside the organization, as it became evident that sustainability would touch resident lives, would impact environmental stewardship through recycling, gardens, and advanced construction methods, as well as affect long-term financial planning.

The second area of contribution to theory is leadership. Much of what we saw in this case substantiated the premises of the literature on leadership in complex situations. Innovation was enabled through creation of networks of people having the right conversations. Leaders who saw things differently – "from the balcony" – were able to mobilize energy. People learned to manage the tensions and paradoxes that otherwise could have had led to a state of confusion and inappropriate short-term solutions. Through making inclusion a regular aspect of sustainability initiatives, formal leaders extended their leadership to others and leadership became a product of the interactions among people and not just of position. Leaders took on a series of experiments, and when something didn't go well, there was learning and not blame. Appropriate new structures and processes were instituted, thereby reinforcing a new emphasis on sustainability. This would suggest that as organizations move toward sustainability, different models of leadership are appropriate.

The key role of values and leadership has not yet been called out to any great degree with CLT. Throughout the process, the value system played a major role in the actions taken with partners. For example, there was a shared concept of being stewards for the residents and a belief that the role of leadership was to win "the hearts and minds" of residents. This stance made a difference that informed their actions in moving toward sustainability. The director acknowledged that the mission focus influenced their work with partners – and created some tensions, because some of the people that have came to work with them did not share the same values. What role do values play in addressing the complexity we face in creating a sustainable organization, community, or society? We believe that this is a fruitful area for further exploration and understanding.

Contribution to Practice

Since the optimization of planet, profit, and people by definition involves a complex set of issues and players, changes must happen in a wider domain than one organization, and this wider domain may be full of tension between competing goals. Examining leadership through the lens of complexity and using the strategy of collaboration in CMHA has yielded lessons for others who are engaging in the sustainability transition.

Unleashing the potential energy in the system requires a willingness to go beyond the traditional business case. Although this was the original reason why CMHA engaged in an energy audit, the players involved soon realized that achieving true change required expanding the domain to social, environmental, educational, and economic domains, and to use education, partnership, and involvement in a manner that released transformative power in individuals and for the organization. CMHA employees and their partners were guided by a set of values regarding social good, importance of trust, and inclusive leadership. This set of values may have served as a surrogate for a shared definition of sustainability. In this case, different groups of people were enacting the different components of sustainability – each remaining true to their own definition. However, they did share the values, which happened to be supportive of sustainability. Projects and initiatives that employed the values of education, partnerships, and inclusion resulted in interesting and innovative solutions and opportunities to emerge that did lead to a more sustainability-focused organization.

Formal leaders in systems aspiring to become sustainable must develop the ability to share leadership, thus tapping into the potential that exists in its own system, as well as other outside entities that can become partners and collaborators. Power sharing enables and emboldens other leaders in the organization, creating ideas, experiments, and initiatives that will lead to sustainability. In this case, the willingness to trust others and inspire others' trust was important in sharing leadership.

Sustainability relies on champions and enablers, and structures and processes need to be created to support adaptive actions and committed people. CMHA needed to make structural changes, create project teams, and establish new roles and departments, and those in authority were willing to make these happen. Internally, a department was added, and job positions within other parts of the organization were created. In addition, they had others who were not formally in CMHA act as leaders of initiatives. They gave agency and legitimacy to others in the community – residents, consultants, and people from other organizations – to create and act.

CONCLUSION

To truly energize the potential for becoming sustainable, leaders must have adaptability and create organization systems and initiatives that go beyond their traditional boundaries. Leaders need to go beyond just "rational" acts and operate in the realm of connecting with passion and purpose of all of the individuals involved. There are always pressures in the environmental context of a public housing agency or any other organization, whether it be scarce resources, social problems that need solving, or the expectations of residents and the public. The question is will there be leaders who see opportunities to use collaboration to creatively respond? Will they be able to create partnerships inside and outside of their heretofore-defined organizational boundaries? CMHA provides a rich example of leadership approaches to deal with complexity by fostering partnerships that create necessary innovation and extend the capabilities of the organization to carry out its mission sustainably.

REFERENCES

CMHA website. (2010). Available at http://www.cmha.net/.
Crews, D. E. (2010). Strategies for implementing sustainability: Five leadership challenges. *SAM Advanced Management Journal*, 75(2), 15–21.
Crislip, D. D., & Larson, C. E. (1994). *Collaborative leadership*. San Francisco: Jossey-Bass.
Dess, G. G., & Picken, J. C. (2000). Changing roles: Leadership in the 21st century. *Organizational Dynamics* (Winter), 18–34.
Epstein, M. J., Buhovac, A. R., & Yuthas, K. (2010). Implementing sustainability: The role of leadership and organizational culture. *Strategic Finance*, 91(10), 41–47.
Goldstein, J., Hazy, J. K., & Lichtenstein, B. B. (2010). *Complexity and the nexus of leadership: Leveraging nonlinear science to create ecologies of innovation*. New York: Palgrave Macmillan.
Heifetz, R. (1994). *Leadership without easy answers*. Cambridge, MA: Harvard Publishing.
Hemphill, L., McGreal, S., Berry, J., & Watson, S. (2006). Leadership, power and multisector urban regeneration partnerships. *Urban Studies*, 43(1), 59–80.

Huxham, C., & Vangen, S. (2005). *Managing to collaborate.* New York: Routledge.
Pfeffer, J., & Salancik, G. (1978). *The external control of organizations.* San Francisco: Harper & Row.
Trist, E. (1983). Referent organizations and the development of inter-organizational domains. *Human Relations, 36*(3), 269–284.
Uhl-Bien, M., & Marion, R. (2008). *Complexity leadership.* Charlotte, NC: Information Age Publishing.
Uhl-Bien, M., Marion, R., & McKelvey, B. (2007). Complexity leadership theory: Shifting leadership from the industrial age to the knowledge era. *The Leadership Quarterly, 18,* 298–318.
United Nations General Assembly. (1987). *Report of the World Commission on Environment and Development: Our common future.* Transmitted to the General Assembly as an Annex to document A/42/427-Development and international co-operation: Environment. Available at http://www.un-documents.net/wced-ocf.htm. Retrieved on December 1, 2010.
Wood, D. J., & Gray, B. (1991). Toward a comprehensive theory of collaboration. *Journal of Applied Behavioral Science, 27*(2), 139–162.

CHAPTER 6

MANAGING SUSTAINABILITY: THE PORT OF LOS ANGELES AMONG AN ECOLOGY OF ORGANIZATIONS

Jan Green Rebstock and Hilary Bradbury-Huang

ABSTRACT

Purpose – *The purpose of this chapter is to discuss managing sustainability across an industry and examine the catalyst, enablers, and challenges for systems-level change through a case study of one organization, the Port of Los Angeles (POLA), and its participation in the Sustainable Enterprise Executive Roundtable (SEER) action learning network.*

Methodology/approach – *The chapter uses a case study approach, written by reflective practitioners in action.*

Findings – *The challenges and enablers of achieving organizational change for sustainability within the POLA ecology are addressed as part of a forcefield of enablers and obstacles. Action learning in the context of collaborative projects across the ecology becomes a key process for managing change toward a sustainable goods movement ecosystem.*

Research/practical implications – *The chapter is addressed to those scholar-practitioners who struggle with issues of organizational change for sustainability outcomes. The core work is to align organizations, within and around the node organization, for sustainability. By analyzing*

Organizing for Sustainability
Organizing for Sustainable Effectiveness, Volume 1, 155–185
ISSN: 2045-0605/doi:10.1108/S2045-0605(2011)0000001011

the systems forcefield, we can better perceive the implications for action and identify leverage for change.

Social implications – *Organizations are the key unit for culture change for sustainability within society. Engaging with other organizations involved in the work of sustainability is required to create systems-level change.*

Originality/value – *The scholarly contribution is based on revisiting the usefulness of Lewin's Change Forcefield, which the authors have adapted by integrating the concepts of the learning organization and systems thinking to help understand change and redesign efforts for sustainability within and among organizations.*

Keywords: Sustainability; organizational change; learning; systems thinking; green technologies; sustainable business; port; goods movement

INTRODUCTION

This chapter discusses managing sustainability in the context of an ecology or system of interdependent organizations with global and local stakeholders intersecting in Southern California. The case study focuses on the Port of Los Angeles (POLA), a global trade gateway, and its internal and external sustainability initiatives, including its participation in the Sustainable Enterprise Executive Roundtable (SEER), a regional collaborative action learning network. The challenges and enablers of achieving organizational change for sustainability within the POLA organizational culture and ecology are addressed as part of a forcefield of enablers and obstacles. Action learning in the context of collaborative projects across the ecology becomes a key process for managing change toward a sustainable goods movement ecosystem.

The chapter is addressed to those scholar-practitioners who struggle with issues of organizational change for sustainability outcomes. The core work is to align organizations, within and around the node organization, for sustainability. By analyzing the systems forcefield, we can better perceive the implications for action and identify leverage for change.

The case study offers the reader: (1) an understanding of the core enablers and features of a sustainable organizational culture and ecology, (2) a discussion of key obstacles and future challenges, and (3) an assessment of the value of engaging with other organizations involved in the work of sustainability. The scholarly contribution is based on revisiting the usefulness of Lewin's Change Forcefield, which the authors have adapted by integrating the concepts of the learning organization and systems thinking to help understand change and redesign efforts for sustainability within and among organizations.

SUSTAINABLE ORGANIZATIONS

Futurist Robert Olson writes that "the image of a sustainable future provides an integrative sense of perspective and suggests there are 'simultaneous solutions' that make sense from multiple points of view – actions that will increase economic opportunity, protect and restore the environment, stimulate the emergence of environmentally advanced technologies, revitalize community, and improve the actual conditions of daily life for people everywhere" (Olson, 1995, p. 32). Organizations play a crucial role in creating this vision of a sustainable future, as they are microcosms within the greater society (Greenwald, 2008). It has been argued that much of the heavy lifting toward achieving sustainability in society will be done in this arena (Starkey & Welford, 2001; Meynell, 2005).

Managing for sustainability in an organization challenges us to look at balancing environmental, economic, and social or equity issues in relation to each other. Therefore, we must learn to identify systemic interconnections and seek solutions where elements ideally support or reinforce one another in a beneficial reciprocal relationship (Capra, 1996; Metzner, 1999). The parsimonious framework of the "triple bottom line" (Elkington, 1997), which refers to focus on profit, people and planet, has led to popular adoption of a Triple Bottom Line (TBL) assessment approach that helps organizations balance economic, environmental, and social responsibilities when considering overall corporate performance (Sauvante, 2002; McDonough & Braungart, 2002). However, even with the TBL approach, discerning competing interests and negotiating among the tradeoffs to balance economic, social, and environmental objectives is a challenging and complex process (Jamali, 2006).

We assert that organizations with learning cultures, where systems thinking, high-performance teams, and collaborative projects are employed, are best suited to address evolving challenges and achieve the adaptive change needed to manage for sustainability. As illustrated in the POLA case study, we find that organizational culture is an essential component of creating organizational change for sustainability and maintaining cohesion and coordination of sustainable practices both within and across an organization's boundaries. In turn, these cultural forces can reciprocally influence broader cultural change in society (Harris & Crane, 2002).

Kurt Lewin, father of social psychology and committed to positive social change, suggested that all people and organizations exist within a forcefield that holds them in place, or in homeostasis, because one set of enablers meets a set of obstacles to the desired change. We build on Lewin's perspective and view the focal organization POLA as a major node embedded within an interdependent system that itself exists within an ecology of organizations, all linked to a greater or lesser extent, and influenced in varying degrees by changes in the organizational culture of the focal entity.

ORGANIZATIONAL CULTURE

The orientation of an organization is dictated and reinforced by its culture, with culture understood as "a system of ideas and perceptions about the meaning of life in an organization" that characterizes how individuals should act and the nature of their relationships with others (Greenwald, 2008). Relationships within the organization can impact how the organization relates to others. Specifically, Greenwald (2008) has found that organizational cultures can both reflect and influence the main culture within a society, while Post and Altma (1994), Welford (1995), and Harris and Crane (2002) find that "green culture change" in society as a whole is what drives the movement toward sustainability. We highlight the link between sustainability and culture because it is one of the most challenging yet critical enablers of embedding sustainable practices within an organization and helps reinforce systems-level change more broadly (Harris & Crane, 2002).

Through organizational culture, employees absorb the social knowledge of an organization's objectives, methods, and values, which helps them navigate through the uncertainty and complexity in their work (Khademian, 2002). "Commitments" deeply embedded within an organization can be used to align actors so that there is a general level of agreement governing what work gets done and how it is performed (Khademian, 2002). Adopting sustainable practices requires behavioral changes among employees; a sustainability ethic must be communicated as an organizational commitment for this to occur. These explicit and implicit commitments guide the decision-making of employees and help employees understand their role within the organization. We are reminded that culture ultimately exists only in the thinking of individuals (Greenwald, 2008) even as it may appear reified, which reinforces the link with and importance of organizational learning.

LEARNING ORGANIZATIONS

Senge (1990) popularized the notion of the learning organization for multinational corporations. Core to the set of concepts and practices associated with the learning organization is the high-performance team that functions as the fundamental learning unit for modern organizations. An organizational learning culture that embraces learning and change can foster sustainability (Senge, 1990; Jamali, 2006, p. 813). Jamali (2006) asserts that as organizations integrate sustainable practices, they must create and apply the knowledge and insights needed to institutionalize the use of a sustainability decision-making framework. This work requires that organizations must learn how to consistently develop and apply this knowledge to address the evolving challenges that come with rethinking and innovating business practices and responding to feedback as new approaches are developed and implemented (Jamali, 2006). Therefore, skill development for adaptive management seems essential for managing for sustainability.

Learning how to think systemically within the organization is required for managing the complex issues related to sustainability. For example, a global understanding of the environmental, social, and economic impacts of a proposed action and the stakeholders involved is required to create strategies that avoid or mitigate those impacts and effectively implement them. Systems thinking contributes to higher organizational performance and allows for the development of the tools, skills, and processes needed to understand and manage the structures of complex systems (Skarzauskiene, 2010). The competencies a systems thinker develops, such as managing alliances, reinvention, strategic planning, and building effective teams (Skarzauskiene, 2010), are important for managing sustainability issues and relationships within an organization and across networks.

An organization adopting a systems thinking approach would study the system it was in (natural, political, economic) and recognize the interdependent relationships over time that are key to managing sustainability issues. A thorough understanding of any system requires "knowledge of the nature of interactions among its parts as well as the nature of its interdependencies with other parts of the larger system(s) in which it is embedded" (Robertson, 2006, p. 7). Through systems thinking, employees learn to observe how they and their actions relate to the system they are in and can note what sustainable practices are occurring, what problems are ignored, how business units are interacting, and where leverage points for change or improvements exist (Zulauf, 2007).

As the structure of a system influences the behavior of its members (Zulauf, 2007), it is important to understand these dynamics when designing sustainability initiatives. Zulauf (2007) suggests that self-awareness might be the starting point for thinking systemically. Additionally, developing the powers of observation of employees is required to foster their ability to read systems, where they can identify signals and understand when subtle changes occur (Zulauf, 2007). As skill development for systems thinking increases, organizations are better able to identify how their actions impact the systems they operate within and how to anticipate the changes needed to achieve sustainability goals.

Learning organizations can help develop employees as systems thinkers. Over time, employees can build their capacity to identify complex relationships and linkages among issues and begin to reason and make judgments within holistic contexts (Davis & Somerville, 2006, p. 128). These skills are needed to make the best strategic investments in sustainability planning and program management within an organization. This work includes identifying the issues most material to the organization, designing approaches to address causal issues, and managing resources, processes, and stakeholder relationships to produce effective outcomes.

At a time when organizations are trying to grasp the causal issues related to sustainability, a particularly salient criticism of learning organizations and systems thinking is the difficulty of the delayed nature of feedback loops, which are supposed to show interrelationships, but one can never be sure of causality (Grieves, 2008). It can take a while to recognize the effects of relationships, and the longer time passes, the more likely it is that intervening variables will obscure causal relationships. Another criticism related to systems theory is its lack of accounting for power relations, so we must be mindful of this when trying to understand system dynamics and designing policy options.

Senge, Lichtenstein, Kaeufer, Bradbury, and Carroll (2007) stress that meeting the sustainability challenge will require extensive collaboration *across* organizational boundaries, rather than "merely" within organizations to drive system-wide change. They find that there is still no widespread precedent for this kind of cross-sector collaboration and argue that it must be cocreated by various stakeholders by interweaving work in three realms: the conceptual, the relational, and the action-oriented. Through action learning, when there is space for thinking together, creating trust and undertaking meaningful projects collaboratively, organizational leaders can collectively manage the strategic complexity that comes with managing sustainability. In subsequent work, Senge et al. have stressed the particular importance of establishing a strong network of trusting relationships – a relational space – as a prerequisite for meaningful outcomes of dialogue and collaborative projects (Bradbury-Huang, Lichtenstein, Carroll, & Senge, 2010).

ACTION LEARNING

Action learning is both a process and a program of outcomes that involves a group of people collaboratively engaged in problem solving and learning through experience with a consciousness about improving their learning process. It is an iterative process that adds value to the organization(s) in which it happens (Marquardt, 1999) and supports the innovative and adaptive approaches needed to manage sustainability. Reg Revans, the original articulator of the action learning concept (Pedler & Burgoyne, 2008), suggested six main features of action learning: a learning group, a reflection process, followed by a questioning process, a resolution to take action, a commitment to learning, and a facilitator.

This case study of POLA illustrates the practical implications of taking an action learning approach to organizational sustainability. As noted above and demonstrated in the following discussion of POLA's evolving journey to become a sustainable organization, organizations must balance pressures from many complex issues and stakeholders as they continuously work through sustainability challenges. By focusing on POLA, a major node within a complex interdependent web of organizations, we are able to explore the forcefield of enablers and obstacles to creating change for sustainability.

THE SUSTAINABILITY STORY FOR AMERICA'S PORT: HOW BREAKTHROUGHS HAPPEN

The POLA, America's busiest port, is part of a port complex located in the San Pedro Bay, 20 miles south of downtown Los Angeles. Over 40% of the nation's containerized imported goods move through the global gateway created by the POLA and Ports of Long Beach (POLB). A major economic engine, POLA contributes to over 900,000 jobs in the region and over 3 million nationwide (POLA, 2010). POLA is a public enterprise, a proprietary department of the City of Los Angeles that operates on the revenue generated from lease agreements related to its 7,500 acres of land and water along 43 miles of waterfront.

Increases in US consumer spending starting in the 1990s led to a sharp increase in imports from China. These cargo volumes grew exponentially through 2007, when throughput reached 8.4 million twenty-foot equivalent units (TEUs) compared to 2.9 million TEUs in 1997. POLA was concerned about constructing enough infrastructure capacity to accommodate the growth, as cargo volumes in the region were expected to triple or at least double by 2025. This level of forecasted growth has since been revised and is now expected to occur in 2035. Regardless, past unmitigated growth has created cumulative negative environmental impacts and increased health risks to the region and local community.

POLA is a major node within the global goods movement system with mobile emissions sources from ships, trucks, trains, and cargo handling equipment that have historically been unregulated and run on diesel fuel. It is located in an area with the poorest air quality in the nation and a high regional background residential cancer risk. In 1998, diesel particulate matter (DPM) was designated by state regulatory agencies as a toxic air contaminant (cancer-causing agent). The San Pedro and Wilmington communities adjacent to the Port became concerned about the public health impacts of the increasing diesel emissions created by goods movement. Over time, the regional air quality agency conducted two studies (Multiple Air Toxics Exposure Study (MATES) II (2000) and MATES III (2008) regarding the increased cancer risk to residents associated with DPM from diesel exhaust and identified the POLA and POLB as major contributors. Regulatory and political pressure, combined with community and environmental group opposition through an environmental lawsuit, prevented any major port expansion projects from moving forward between 2000 and 2007.

Green Growth Challenge

POLA's evolving journey to become a sustainable organization began in response to the increase in cargo imports, the inability to expand, and the need to improve existing infrastructure. Therefore, POLA was forced to focus on addressing the cumulative impacts of existing port operations and planned expansion efforts. A settlement agreement in 2003 that resulted from the China Shipping Lawsuit (filed under the California Environmental Quality Act (CEQA)) established a port community advisory committee, which forced more transparency and community input into Port decision-making, along with a $50 million dollar mitigation fund for community aesthetic and air quality projects. Specifically, as a result of the settlement agreement, POLA committed to researching and developing technologies that could be used within the port to reduce air emissions from port operations. POLA also began to conduct port-wide studies on a range of environmental issues related to light and glare, noise, transportation, biological resources, and historical resources.

As the major public health impacts from goods movement were related to air quality, POLA started to address these concerns by conducting inventories for all mobile sources of air emissions within the port. Partnering with adjacent POLB for the first time on environmental policy, in 2006 both Ports released a joint Clean Air Action Plan (CAAP), which provided a comprehensive approach to aggressively reduce air emissions by 45% within the world's seventh busiest container port complex as capital development projects moved forward. POLA's move toward sustainability began with the philosophy of green growth: implement aggressive environmental mitigation policies and programs and allow for continued port expansion and investment in infrastructure. The CAAP is considered a living document that is updated approximately every five years to guide policies and investments towards reinvention as a zero emissions port.

Emissions reductions were achieved by a combination of voluntary market-based incentives, new POLA tariffs and policies, and contractual requirements integrated into the lease agreements for new capital development projects. A 2010 POLA air quality report card shows that significant voluntary reductions of overall air emissions have been achieved since 2005, with a 52% reduction in DPM port wide. Between 2007 and 2009, POLA approved six major capital improvement projects. In 2008, $383 million in construction contracts were awarded for these projects. Port wide, in 2010 over 18 multiyear construction projects were underway, including a cargo terminal expansion project, a road-widening project, a new marina, channel deepening project, and a large 30-acre community park.

POLA Sustainability Initiatives for Green Growth

In addition to the landmark CAAP, the following initiatives and best practices demonstrate POLA's management approach for sustainability:

- *Green Leases* – Starting in 2007, POLA created a new standard template for lease agreements that allows for the implementation of an unprecedented number of mitigation measures and project requirements to reduce the environmental impacts of terminal operations to the greatest extent feasible.
- *Project Incremental Residential Health Risk Threshold* – In 2006, POLA and the POLB established a policy that no project shall be approved unless it complies with the CAAP. Further, the incremental increase in residential health risk created by the project must not exceed a threshold of 10 in a million. While challenging, since its adoption, all of the new POLA projects evaluated and approved under the Port's CEQA environmental review process have met this requirement.
- *San Pedro Baywide Health Risk Reduction Standard* – In 2010, as part of the CAAP Update, the POLA and POLB adopted a health risk reduction standard that aims to lower the residential cancer risk due to DPM by 85% in the port region and communities adjacent to the ports by 2020.
- *Increased Community Involvement and Transparency in Port Decision-Making* – Better communication with the community is achieved through the creation and support of the Port Community Advisory Committee (PCAC), greater outreach and coordination with the local neighborhood councils, and widespread noticing and information sharing through the environmental review process for new development projects.
- *Community Mitigation Agreements* – The China Shipping Settlement and TraPac Community Benefits Agreement, which combined total almost $100 million, have required POLA to make significant investments in green growth policies and mitigation programs.
- *Restructuring the Southern California Trucking Industry* – A cornerstone of the landmark CAAP is the award-winning Clean Trucks Program (CTP), in which the POLA and POLB and the trucking industry cooperated to achieve 80% reductions in DPM emissions from port-related trucks in only two years. This was facilitated through incentive grant funding, fees, and by introducing a concession licensing contract mechanism to regulate the engine and model years of trucks allowed within the Ports. The CTP was praised in 2009 by the U.S. Environmental Protection Agency as "the largest, most aggressive air quality program at

any port complex in the world" (EPA, 2009). Several ports around the country, including New York/New Jersey, Seattle, and Oakland, are now implementing their own versions of this program.

- *Advancement of Clean Technologies* – One component of the CAAP is the Technology Advancement Program (TAP), a $15 million fund created by the POLA and POLB to provide grants to emerging port-related clean technologies and help facilitate demonstration pilots. Over $9 million in grant funds have been distributed as of January 2011. Regulatory measures from the CAAP and technologies from the TAP are integrated into the Port's environmental review process and lease requirements for cargo terminal expansion projects. Some of these projects include the development of the world's first hybrid diesel-electric tugboat, a seawater scrubber filtering technology for vessels, and an electric short-haul drayage truck. A key part of the CAAP strategy is the adoption of technology-forcing performance standards, such as the new long-term CAAP goals for 2023: reducing port-related emissions of DPM by 77%, 59% for nitrogen oxide (NOx), and 93% for sulfur dioxide (SOx). Achievement of these goals will depend on technologies that have not yet been developed or are not currently commercialized. The TAP addresses this need for port-related technologies that continue to improve in efficiency and emissions reductions. In addition, the Port's lease agreements have a standard condition requiring that no less than every seven years new technologies under the TAP shall be reviewed and evaluated for adoption by cargo terminal operators and the Port based on feasibility.

- *Promoting International Adoption of Clean Technologies* – As POLA is sensitive to ensuring that its progressive policies are feasible for a world shipping community to implement, POLA is engaged in international collaboration to reduce environmental impacts. The Port is working with other ports, terminal operators, fuel providers, and truck and vessel engine manufacturers to drive innovation and accommodate the implementation of mitigation strategies. One example of this work includes the Port's advocacy of Alternative Maritime Power (AMP), an emissions-reduction technology that enables ships at berth to shut down their on-board engines and plug into the land-based electric grid for power. Previously used by the Navy and Alaskan cruise ships, POLA was the first port in the world to apply AMP technology to a container terminal. To facilitate the use of AMP by other ports worldwide, POLA patented a design for the connection from the ship to the shoreside infrastructure that has been finalized by the International Standards

Organization (ISO) and is now under review by the International Electrotechnical Commission (IEC), pending adoption. The use of AMP is shown to reduce DPM, NOx and SOx emissions by 95% while a vessel is at berth. In late 2007, the California Air Resources Board (CARB) passed a state regulation that 50% of a vessel fleet's visits to a California port must use shoreside power while at berth by 2014, and this requirement ramps up to 80% in 2020. POLA plans to construct the shoreside infrastructure for AMP at 24 berths within the next five years (POLA, 2010).

- *Development of Human Capital and Local Economic Development* – In partnership with the local chambers of commerce, POLA has recently created PortTech LA, a nonprofit green tech business incubator designed to help entrepreneurs and small companies commercialize their technologies and act as a bridge to and beyond the TAP. Services provided to scientists and inventors include assistance with business administration and development, marketing, and guidance through the technology commer-cialization process, with opportunities for pilot projects and contracts in the port and throughout the City of Los Angeles. By investing in human capital, focusing on innovation, and building on the dense networks already in place, PortTech LA was born from and is contributing to an ecosystem where the Port and the City of Los Angeles have learned through crisis and are on the road to reinvention for a more sustainable future. Exporting these technologies to other ports helps create a cohesive regulatory landscape for international shipping companies and will reduce the cost of compliance over time. PortTech LA is part of the larger CleanTech LA initiative, a collaborative effort among the City of Los Angeles, the business community, and the area's research universities USC, UCLA, and CSU to position Los Angeles as the "clean tech capital of the world," where maritime goods movement, renewable energy, research, and clean tech clusters create green jobs. Balqon Corporation, the nation's first heavy-duty electric truck manufacturer, was one of the first companies to receive TAP funding from the Port. The truck's prototype was first tested within the port and POLA became its first customer. As a result of the Port's investment of approximately $5 million, the company opened a manufacturing center in Harbor City near the ports, and POLA collects a royalty payment of $1,000 for each vehicle it sells worldwide. In January 2011, Balqon announced it had received a $15 million order for 300 electric drive systems from a company in China to integrate them into private and government bus fleets. The new business is expected to create 150 local jobs related to fabrication and assembly, along with engineering and research.

- *International Port Management Leadership* – POLA has also taken a strong leadership role among ports worldwide thorough industry organizations like the International Ports and Harbors Association (IPHA) and the American Association of Ports Authorities (AAPA), which have provided a platform for sharing sustainability initiatives. For example, in 2008 the Environment Committee of the IPHA and POLA sponsored an international symposium on managing climate change in the port context. Building on previous efforts of the Clinton Climate Initiative, the symposium officially launched the World Port's Climate Initiative (WPCI). Through this effort, port authorities from around the world share best practices toward implementing sustainability and climate change policies. POLA currently leads the carbon footprinting workgroup of the WPCI and has created a footprinting guidance document for ports, along with a dynamic carbon calculator that helps capture the complex relationships of multimodal transport. Collaborative projects taken on by the 59 member ports of WPCI include the development of a toolbox for port clean air programs, a shoreside power informational website, and an Environmental Ship Index.
- **Sustainability Assessment** – In 2008, POLA conducted a sustainability assessment that identified 32 specific POLA programs and policies that reflect the importance given to stewardship and environmental, social, and economic sustainability. Some of these initiatives include a joint baywide Water Resources Action Plan (WRAP) with the POLB, POLA's LEED Green Building program, recycled water infrastructure program, ISO 14001-certified Environmental Management System (EMS) for the POLA Construction and Maintenance Division, protection of a 15-acre nesting site for the endangered California Least Tern, and a 10 MW solar energy program, with the first megawatt completed in 2010 on the roof of the Port's cruise terminal.

Leading an Ecology of Organizations

Many of the Port's initiatives demonstrate how public agencies can transform from being regulators to collaborators with industry and contribute to the advancement of sustainable societies by using a mix of regulatory and market-based approaches (Mazmanian, 2008). POLA's role as a facilitator and collaborator within an ecology of organizations is illustrated by Fig. 1, which shows the relationships among regulatory

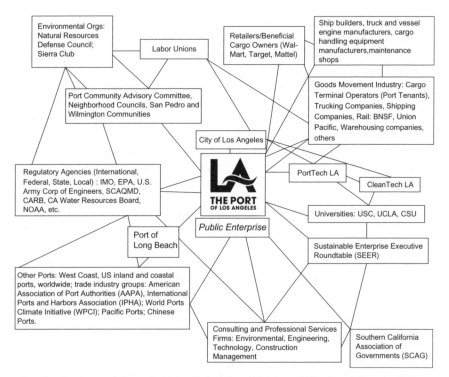

Fig. 1.   Ecology of Organizations Related to POLA and Regional Sustainability.

agencies, companies within the global goods movement industry and related support services, local stakeholders, and other ports. Most easy to note is the sheer complexity of the ecology, with the Port embedded in a local, regional, and global network of ecological, social, and economic relationships and stakeholders exercising overlapping and differing interests and jurisdictions. Visually this systems map provides a compelling reminder that no organization exists alone, nor can an issue as complex as sustainability be treated as it so often is, internally. It also hints at how difficult implementing systems-level change can be without engaging the right stakeholders.

Many of the initiatives described in the POLA case study involved complex multistakeholder processes with a myriad of interests and constraints to be negotiated. In the case of the CTP, much of the work focused on how to establish a direct relationship between the Port and the trucking community so that changes in operations could occur. Creating the contractual link was important because the Port was taking responsibility through its emissions inventory for the air pollution caused by port drayage trucks but initially did not have any power or authority to require cleaner trucks for port operations.

While a court case started the sea change at POLA, lawsuits from laggards have been obstacles to the Port's attempt to create mechanisms for addressing emissions sources outside of the Port's direct jurisdiction. For the CTP, the use of a new contract mechanism, the concession agreement, sustained challenges in district court brought by the American Trucking Association (ATA). The judge had found that because POLA was a "market participant," the CTP requirements were exempt from the claim of federal preemption under the Federal Aviation Administration Authorization Act (FAAA) that protects interstate commerce and guards against local regulations that could impede the free flow of trade. Further, the judge found that the new CTP requirements were a business necessity to protect the government's financial interests and that reducing pollution was key to maintaining viability for port operations (*Supply Chain Digest*, 2010).

Challenges Remain

Despite these great achievements, many challenges remain as POLA works to institutionalize sustainable practices and expand operations. Some worth highlighting include

- *Ad Hoc Approach* – There remains an ad hoc approach to sustainability within the organization. The need to reduce health risk and air emissions initially sparked the Port's move toward more sustainable practices, so extensive data, metrics, and targets related to air quality and health risk have been collected and developed. In 2009, the POLA and POLB jointly approved the WRAP, which addresses water and sediment quality with various control measures within the ports. However, currently there is no comprehensive sustainability program with port-wide metrics or targets to measure performance outcomes or interdependencies across air, water, land, biological resources, or social and economic development programs. Further commitment is needed to develop and manage a comprehensive systemic assessment of POLA's sustainability performance using the TBL approach with strategies that demand continuous improvement. Much of this work consists of defining short- and long-term sustainability goals and meaningful metrics, and then strategically integrating, coordinating, and further developing some of the aforementioned 32 existing POLA sustainability initiatives, policies, and programs.

• *Distributing Costs* – The financial costs of being a first mover to implement new technologies and best practices for achieving air emissions reductions have presented challenges for POLA, the private cargo terminal operators, and the Southern California goods movement industry in general. Balancing who should bear the costs to implement mitigation measures that comply with the CAAP (i.e., the CTP, AMP, and new terminal equipment), while considering how they impact the competitive advantage of the region and among POLA customers is an ongoing challenge, as POLA cannot afford to subsidize all of the CAAP programs. When the CAAP was first approved in 2006, initial estimates put full implementation costs from $1.2 to $2 billion. Acknowledging the CAAP was underfunded, the POLA and POLB committed in 2006 to a total of $400 million over the following five years, with the intention of seeking grant funding and using fees to reassign costs of reducing emissions back to the Beneficial Cargo Owners (market retailers) who own the cargo moving through the ports. According to the 2010 CAAP Update, funds spent and budgeted by POLA on the CAAP from 2006 to 2014 are $235 million. Similarly, the POLB budget for the same period is $330 million. In addition, from 2006 to 2009, state and federal sources contributed over $63 million for CAAP measures. Planned contributions from the same agencies from 2010 through 2014 total almost $58 million. Through the Port's use of cargo fees, significantly less Port funds were needed for the CTP, as private industry invested an estimated $600 million to help retrofit or replace the Southern California port trucking fleet (POLA and POLB, 2010).

• *Lack of Diffusion of Sustainability Ethic Throughout the Whole Organization* – While "adopting a sustainability ethic throughout the organization" is a strategic objective of the Port, POLA has honed the policy infrastructure and focus of staff development on the implementation of specific sustainability policies and not a learning orientation to sustainability in general. Most of this focus has been on the implementation of policies and programs that reduce air emissions and health risk and mitigation measures related to impacts from new expansion projects undergoing the CEQA environmental review process. All employees are not aware of the Port's suite of sustainability best practices or policies, which impacts how effectively the sustainability ethic is integrated and reflected throughout Port operations. Further, many of the approximately 900 Port employees still need to understand

and internalize the concept of sustainability and its framework for decision-making to reflect it in their daily practice. In short, further investment in building the human capacity within the organization to learn for sustainability will help the Port achieve its goal of truly being grounded in a sustainability ethic.

- *Social Aspect of Triple Bottom Line* – POLA is still struggling with right balance of the social/community aspect of sustainability. Regarding the community's influence over port decision-making, one could liken this to a pendulum swing. After what some had termed "a hundred year war" between the Port and the community, the China Shipping Lawsuit filed under CEQA ushered in an unprecedented amount of communication, coordination, and community involvement in Port policy-making, reaching a point where one could argue port decision-making was almost paralyzed. However, with the successful completion of some "green growth" projects, out of this conflict a new appreciation and way of relating between local community groups and POLA has developed, albeit tenuous. Still, the Port acknowledges that its projects do result in disproportionately high and adverse human health and environmental impacts on minority and low-income populations. The Community Benefits Agreement signed by POLA and a coalition of 17 environmental, community, and labor groups was approved in late 2010 to establish a nonprofit with a mitigation fund of up to $50 million from port revenues. Projects from the fund would include air filtration systems for schools and a study of off-port impacts related to health, land use, and other issues in the adjacent communities of Wilmington and San Pedro. Deciding on the right level of substantive public engagement in port policy-making, along with developing agreement on the social impacts of port operations and the extent to which the port should mitigate for those remains a challenge. Recent discussions among the Port, regulatory agencies, and community groups have focused on whether and how to conduct health impact assessments (HIAs) within the context of the CEQA environmental review process to perform a broader analysis of the human health impacts from port operations and consequently how to mitigate for those impacts. Currently, the Port conducts health risk assessments (HRAs) for proposed projects that examine cancer risks and acute and chronic noncancer health risks on local communities. This information is displayed in the form of a cancer risk isopleth map to show how risk patterns are distributed throughout the community. Included in the current analysis is the incidence of premature death and morbidity rates. The HIAs under debate would look at a broader range of health impacts.

POLA Culture Change

While challenges remain, an unmistakable sea change toward managing for sustainability has occurred at POLA. Specifically, the lessons learned from meeting the challenges of reducing air emissions and health risk impacts while still moving forward with future capital development projects have been memorialized and preserved within department policies, environmental documents and plans, and the mental maps of the Port staff members involved in the project teams who helped achieve these outcomes. Some of the elements that helped create and preserve the culture change at the POLA include:

- *New Port Leasing Practices* – These practices have changed the business climate at the Port and throughout the maritime industry, sending a firm message about what future sustainable port operations must look like. This paradigm shift from legacy property management practices was accomplished through the *top-down leadership* and political momentum provided by Los Angeles Mayors Jim Hahn and Antonio Villaraigosa and POLA Executive Director Dr. Geraldine Knatz, along with past and present POLA Board members.
- *Transparency* – Significant public disclosure of in-depth environmental studies and increased monitoring and reporting continue to occur. Community oversight through the PCAC, the local neighborhood councils, and environmental groups created the *bottom-up political conditions* for change and maintain pressure for performance and continuing innovation. Major plans and programs for the Port, such as the CAAP, WRAP, and CTP are designed with input from stakeholder committees.
- *Collaborative Partnerships for Innovation* – During this pivotal time, collaborative partnerships between POLA and the state regulatory agencies, industry, local community, and POLB have formed to design and implement studies, test regulatory policies through voluntary incentive programs, and pilot new technologies.
- *High-Performance Project Teams* – Representatives from environmental, engineering, planning, real estate, city attorney, and public affairs departments created high-performance project teams to improve internal communications and interdisciplinary perspectives. The project teams focused on designing and constructing new facilities, conducting environmental reviews, and drafting green lease agreements with new requirements.

- *Robust Policy Toolbox and Staff Resources* – Port-wide plans to achieve air and water quality goals are memorialized in the CAAP and WRAP, along with a suite of mitigation measures, best practices, reporting mechanisms, and monitoring programs reflected in the environmental assessments conducted by the Port. These policies are then applied port wide through tariffs, lease agreements, contracts, incentive programs, voluntary measures, and grant funding. The Port has invested significant resources in building the expertise and scope of its environmental management staff. In 1973, POLA was the first port in the country to establish an environmental management division. While the Port employs over 250 engineers, the environmental division had grown from 5 people in 1999 to almost 30 people in 2010 to respond to the demands of conducting environmental studies, preparing environmental impact reports, managing the CAAP and the WRAP, and coordinating this work within the Port and with regulatory agencies, the public, and the business community.

Action Learning Capabilities and Orientation

Through action learning, the Port has built the capacity to identify leverage points for change and pioneer new concepts and technologies to systemically improve the operations of its tenants. Here action learning is seen in a context of desired social or organizational change that evolves in cycles of reflection on action (Reason & Bradbury, 2001). The six main features of action learning as conceptualized by Reg Revans (learning group, reflection process, questioning process, resolve for action, learning commitment, and facilitator) were present throughout the various processes the Port undertook to establish many of its sustainability initiatives, including creating the CAAP, conducting more rigorous environmental reviews while drafting new analysis protocols, and drafting new lease agreements. The following mechanisms reflect and enable the action learning approach employed by the Port:

- Lease requirements and mitigation measures serve as leverage points with tenants to stipulate best management practices and the use of green technologies for pollution reduction; requirements are constantly evolving and responding to new information.
- The Port's comprehensive emissions reduction plan with progressive targets and a road map for implementing new technologies allows for

continuous improvement toward a zero emissions port; long-term health risk reduction goals for 2023 are technology forcing.

- Funding for emergent technologies that can lead to future emissions reductions and local economic development is provided.
- PortTech LA provides a forum for attracting and nurturing green tech businesses to allow for the further commercialization of technologies by providing business support services and pilot project opportunities. These activities contribute to a cluster of business and technology innovation at the ports.

POLA has set new international standards of best practices for sustainability within the maritime industry. This required strong leadership, interactive cross-functional project teams, a robust policy toolbox, and reporting mechanisms, which in turn have contributed to an organizational culture based on innovation, policy feedback loops, and the use of green technologies. This increasing adaptiveness for managing sustainability is reflected in how the Port now interacts with its customers, the community, regulators, and industry competitors. Specifically, the Port takes more of an active role in education, advocacy, and outreach, monitoring its own performance and that of its tenants, funding, and initiating research and pilot projects, reporting data and outcomes, and creating recognition programs for tenants and technology innovators. Let us now turn to the role of the SEER in advancing collaborative learning for sustainability within Southern California.

AN EXPERIMENT IN REGIONAL SUSTAINABILITY PRACTICE: SUSTAINABLE ENTERPRISE EXECUTIVE ROUNDTABLE

In December 2006, the POLA began participating in a regional collaborative learning network, the SEER, to gain some insight into how it might help redesign a sustainable goods movement system. Participants in the group understood that their actions were reinforcing a harmful set of dynamics within the global logistics supply chain. Within this environment for mutual dynamic learning, members felt comfortable sharing information and engaging in a systems approach to problem solving. As the practitioners explored the interdependencies of their related businesses and the cumulative impacts of the global goods movement system, they realized their potential to become leading change agents within the system and within their own organizations. Transforming the interactions between government, business, general society, and the biosphere in support of sustainability is a key challenge (Healy, 2006, p. 49). SEER created the framework to do this by enabling participants to focus on organizational learning, collaboration, and opportunities to create systems-level change.

SEER was an interdisciplinary group of researchers, consulting firms, business leaders, and public agencies led by the second author and hosted by the USC Center for Sustainable Cities. After inception (for details, see Bradbury-Huang, 2010), the first author partnered in convening a group focused on the global goods movement system. This executive education endeavor began to look reflexively and collaboratively at how impacts within the system could be reduced, potentially changing the entire system dynamics. The mission of SEER was not directly tied to the study of sustainable goods movement, but to enable collaborative learning among regional business leaders so that more sustainable practices may result, benefiting the TBL through the implementation of projects that promote sustainability.

Bradbury-Huang (2010) characterizes learning inside SEER as "the transformation of experience through reflection and conceptualization, so that it enables new projects to be undertaken collaboratively." Business participants were invited to participate in systems thinking exercises, dialogue, and field trips to help them better observe and understand the perspectives of each other within the goods movement industry. Participants from each organization were additionally invited to bring a decision maker, technical staffer, and guest so that executive decision-making power could be informed by technical expertise. While attendance among workshops varied, eight core companies invested in the design phase and engaged throughout the process. Some of the collaborative projects included redesigning product packaging to reduce waste, cataloging leadership efforts in Southern California related to regional sustainability, and the development of a goods movement carbon calculator.

POLA Participation

POLA joined SEER to share and learn best practices related to sustainability and engage other stakeholders within the goods movement network. Port staff was especially interested in the action learning focus of the group, with emphasis on creating a project that could be a demonstrative learning tool. These interests were met by participation in the soft systems mapping exercises, creating a carbon calculator systems dynamic model that traced a container from a factory in inland China to a distribution center in Kansas based on actual transportation and emissions data provided by participants, and the ability to hear from others within the supply chain how Port policies affected their operations. Because the group members were from the business community, as opposed to mixed with community activists, some of these conversations were especially candid. In the past, forums where these groups interacted were often highly politically charged environments, which can preclude authentic dialogue among actors. Introductions among members in SEER have influenced current POLA projects, as described further below, and laid the groundwork for future projects.

Both POLA management and technical staff participated in the ten SEER workshops. Representatives from POLA environmental management, planning, economic development, and engineering divisions attended. All of the feedback was positive, especially the focus on the systems approaches to problem solving, which was identified as an area of skill development needed among POLA staff. Political deadlines often drive staff toward completing projects without the time to reflect on perhaps more insightful ways of doing things, so this forum provided an opportunity to gain a wider perspective. A defining feature of the SEER experience for the Port was the role of the university as a neutral convener and facilitator of dialogue and projects. This was significant because of the effort made to engage practitioners with theory and ground the collaborative projects with concepts from systems theory, life cycle analysis, and sustainability frameworks like The Natural Step and TBL. The focus on a learning network was also key, as opposed to a forum hosted by a regulatory agency, community group, or business that may have a different agenda for garnering participation.

Carbon Calculator Project

POLA's greenhouse gas (GHG) modeling efforts include creating a carbon footprinting guidance document and leading efforts in the WPCI on how ports can create and manage their GHG emission inventories. Early discussions and data from a SEER group member, a major toy manufacturer, contributed to POLA's understanding of the inland distribution network and helped refine assumptions used by POLA for that portion of the goods movement chain in the footprinting analysis. SEER provided the first opportunity to POLA to obtain this type and specificity of data from a Beneficial Cargo Owner (major retailer) whom with Port staff normally has no direct contact. Early efforts by USC academic researchers to create a carbon calculator model were helpful to POLA, who went on to develop its own dynamic carbon calculator and benefited from observing the SEER team approach. While one could argue that these efforts might have evolved anyway, independent of the collaborations through SEER members, efforts were definitely enhanced and accelerated by the interactions.

Bradbury reiterates that to enable innovative collaborations, organizations must support a learning culture. POLA has definitely become an innovation lab for addressing air emissions from mobile sources within the goods movement supply chain, and one could argue that it has adopted a learning organization culture around this focus. Work related to the CAAP, TAP, PortTech LA, and WPCI are good examples of its commitment to action learning. Throughout this process, POLA has developed one of the most comprehensive air emissions inventory at three scales – local, port footprint, and extended to China. Some of this work was done in collaboration with SEER researchers and participants. The Port has shared these inventory methods with other ports around the world and is encouraging them to adopt similar mitigation measures to standardize technologies.

Navigating POLA's Forcefield: Lessons Learned

Building on Lewin's Change Forcefield, we offer Fig. 2 as an illustration of general enablers and obstacles to change. Features of a learning organization that negotiate between opposing and enabling forces, as experienced in the POLA case study, include a corporate culture with strong but ad hoc sustainability approaches, high-performance teams with exceptional leadership, a systems thinking approach, and collaborative projects. These features build on and respond to the enabling forces of transparency, meaningful metrics to show progress, and the establishment of technology-forcing performance standards and backstop regulations that require at least some incremental improvement in performance across the industry.

Despite confronting contentious issues, through an alignment of interests, recognition of mutual dependency and interconnectedness, collaboration and trust, individuals among organizations can find shared meaning and achieve system-wide changes. As people can be caught in this forcefield too, it is helpful to reflect on the view that individuals are neither fully autonomous within society nor mindless cogs without influence (Healy, 2006). Rather, "we live through culturally bound structures of rules and resource flows, yet human agency, in our continually inventive ways, remakes them in each instance, and in remaking the systems, the structuring forces, we also change ourselves and our cultures. Structures are shaped by agency just as they in turn 'shape' agency" (Healy, 2006, p. 47). Sufficient

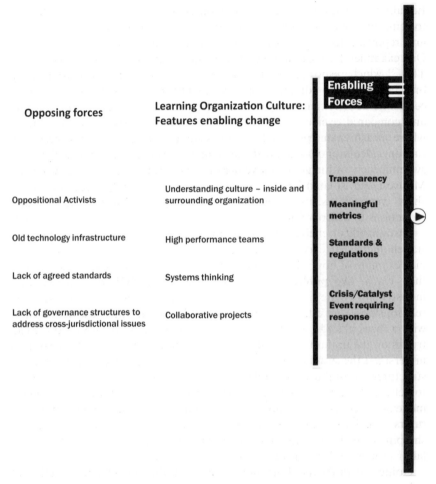

Fig. 2.   General Forcefield of Enablers and Obstacles to Change.

awareness of these structural constraints and power relations can lead
people to change rules and resources flows and transform our perceptions
and actions (Healy, 2006).

Measurement has been crucial to defining and implementing sustainability initiatives at the Port. For example, once the Ports started conducting
air emissions inventories to identify pollution sources, they began to
understand what contributed to the problem and how to target solutions.

Equally important is showing the outcomes of behavioral or policy changes to reinforce changes in the organizational culture. Performance monitoring and reporting to provide transparency and measure effectiveness are key. One example of a meaningful metric created at the Port was "emissions per TEU," which responded to the concern that pollution levels would drop only because cargo volumes (measured in TEUs) decreased due to a drop in economic activity. In this way, emissions reductions could be understood and compared over time, regardless of economic cycles. Another example where measurement provided insight is the carbon calculator project. The carbon calculator was a great learning tool because it provided both a systemic view of the goods movement journey from China to the American Midwest and isolated key factors (such as time, route, and fuel source) to show comparisons and tradeoffs when trying to manage efficiency and reductions in carbon emissions.

Sustainability challenges often involve environmental impacts and stakeholders that exist beyond clearly defined jurisdictions. The CTP is a nice example of how when faced with a wicked problem that initially defied their reach, two public agencies (the POLA and POLB) partnered with industry to create a new model with great success. New contractual relationships were established between the Ports and the trucking industry, with a focus placed on outcomes that resulted in approximately 9,000 clean trucks on the ground. While structure matters, organizational leadership to understand the systems issues, work collaboratively, and create governance structures to establish new relationships mattered more to overcome the forcefield of inertia to change. Understanding the complexity of the goods movement ecosystem, involving the trucking companies, engine manufacturers, regulatory agencies, market retailers, cargo terminal operators, shipping companies, community activists, environmental organizations, and labor groups, adds to the appreciation of this feat.

Going forward, the Port must focus on the power and practice of reflection to achieve deeper institutionalization of sustainable practices among the employees within the organization. Learning for sustainability relies heavily upon the development of skills for conscious reflection and the ability to understand interdisciplinary connections. One successful example of this occurring is among the POLA Construction and Maintenance Staff (painters, roofers, carpenters, mechanics, gardeners, etc.), who were independently recertified under ISO 14001 in 2010 for the division's EMS. Creation of the EMS required the written formalization of procedures that employees perform every day. The C&M staff had to reflect upon the steps in their daily tasks as they formalized the procedures and recorded best management practices to reduce environmental impacts and comply with health and safety regulations. Many have since created new more efficient procedures after better understanding EMS objectives and the impacts of their previous approaches. Improvements have been measured in recycling rates, significantly reduced hazardous waste streams, and increased pollution prevention activities and environmental awareness.

As discussed earlier regarding internal organizational change, changing behaviors of POLA staff to apply a TBL approach to decision-making for tasks ranging from purchasing cleaning products to designing marine cargo terminals requires the creation of feedback loops. However, the response to feedback is only as effective as the power of observation, reflection, and practice exhibited by the people performing the work and identifying opportunities for innovation within this framework. The culture at POLA has resulted in finely tuning these skills for staff focused on certain priority issues, such as reducing air quality and health risk impacts. Developing these adaptive management skills throughout the organization is key to managing sustainability effectively. As our understanding of the challenges and tradeoffs that result from implementing TBL strategies grows, we must learn how to reframe obsolete approaches, rewire through better learning (Kettl, 2006), and develop the judgment that allows us to collectively practice adaptive management.

When leaders enable cross-organizational interconnections and partnerships, the approach must emphasize responsiveness, understanding of the organization's potential impact on other organizations, and active outreach to build relationships (Fenwick, 2007, p. 641). The demands on executive leaders and requirements for cognitive and emotional self-development are particularly intense, given the diversity of stakeholders and general high degree of complexity associated with sustainability issues (Akrivou & Bradbury-Huang, 2011). Further, *Complexity leadership theory* (Marion & Uhl-Bien, 2001; Uhl-Bien, Marion, & McKelvey, 2007) posits that performance success depends on the degree to which networks of interdependent (individual) agents can bond in cooperative dynamics. For executives leading such efforts, the future remains open to emergent redirection, which allows for emergent and complex group dynamics (Uhl-Bien et al., 2007). Complexity leadership scholars also argue that system performance outcomes are produced (Uhl-Bien et al., 2007) by the nexus between individual leaders and collective expression of leadership. The distinction between leaders and *leadership* in the organization (Uhl-Bien et al., 2007) is a key feature of complexity leadership. The distinction is based on the assumption that *leadership* is socially constructed. Leadership has been defined as "an emergent interactive dynamic that is itself productive of adaptive outcomes" (Uhl-Bien et al., 2007).

POLA's leadership in port environmentalism through creating voluntary initiatives and incentive programs has produced effective test beds for policy and technological innovation, future regulations, and lease requirements. It is acknowledged that complementing regulations are essential to achieve gains in some areas, such as health-based air quality standards. Effective partnerships with regulatory agencies to help craft technology-forcing performance-based regulatory standards that are feasible for industry to meet is key. For purposes of designing the CAAP, the Ports created a technical advisory committee composed of state and local air regulatory agencies. Going forward, continued coordination with shipbuilders, engine manufacturers for vessels, trucks, rail, and cargo handling equipment, terminal operators, and shipping, trucking, and rail companies, along with scientists, inventors, and investors will be required to meet future goals. To keep up in a world of continuous improvement, collaborative learning through partnerships within and among organizations is required. This effort will especially be significant when designing and constructing future green infrastructure systems to help meet regional air quality, health risk reduction, and GHG reduction targets. Implementing the Port's vision of a zero emissions container movement system (ZECMS) with new technologies and infrastructure systems will require a coordinated market response throughout the region, whether based on a fixed guideway system using technologies like maglev or electric rail, or building electric or hydrogen truck networks, or some combination of these options. On the waterside, global collaboration will continue to be required to address vessel emissions both in transit (through fuel use, engine standards, and alternative technologies) and at berth (for those vessels and ports that are not good candidates for the AMP technology) to reduce the shipping industry's significant contribution to harmful criteria pollutants, GHGs, and human health impacts.

IMPLICATIONS FOR FUTURE RESEARCH AND PRACTICE

It will be interesting to note in the future the actual costs and benefits for system changes in the POLA case, both within the Southern California region and across the goods movement industry. How the costs for implementing system-wide changes get distributed and whether the cost structures evolve to sustain future changes will be fodder for future research. For example, in the case of the CTP, will shipping prices be restructured to reflect the increased costs associated with upgrading and maintaining clean truck fleets? The majority of trucks in service in 2006 were worth under $20,000 and affordable for independent owner-operators to lease and purchase – the industry was largely built upon this model; new clean diesel trucks with 2007 engines average about $100,000 each. When the regional port trucking fleet must upgrade again by 2021 to meet new engine regulations, who will bear those costs?

Thinking back to the tragedy of the commons, it has long been understood that one actor must not create such externalities and systems-level costs from its operations that it would cause a collapse to occur. For example, costs estimates associated with health impacts from port-related goods movement in California at approximately $19 billion (CARB, 2006) speak to the dangerous lack of balance in the system. However, the price of implementing change at a systems level should not be assigned to any one actor or group. Ultimately, consumers in the Midwest receiving furniture, clothing, or electronics from China have just as much responsibility as the shipping companies, terminal operators, engine manufactures, and other players within the goods movement system for creating the air quality and health impacts experienced by Southern Californians. The CAAP tries to address this issue by shifting the burden from residents to cargo owners and consumers. The Port accomplished this by implementing cargo fees targeted at cargo owners, where the revenues collected are reinvested to achieve emissions reductions. Cases such as this provide good examples for exploring policy responses, solutions for cost sharing, and the benefits of transformation through innovation. There is much anticipation regarding the amount of business investment in green technologies and local economic development that will center on the greening of goods movement in the future.

In addition, the Port's status as a public enterprise seems to make it well suited for tackling the challenges of becoming a sustainable organization. The plurality of needs it serves (i.e., directives of an elected official – the Mayor – as a public agency, duty to manage port resources as State Tidelands assets in a fiscally responsible manner, and need to maintain industry competitiveness while contributing to the regional and national economy) certainly puts the balancing act of attaining TBL objectives into sharp focus. The collaborative multistakeholder approaches needed for green growth seem to be the only way to effectively deal with these issues. Greater investigation into the accountability of public enterprises to stakeholders and the use of these institutions to promote sustainability may be helpful. More so, examining the learning processes that must occur in complex ecologies to create systems-level change is needed, as much of the progress must be made by private organizations that adopt sustainable practices and change legacy operations.

Absent a federal freight policy, it has been suggested by Pisano, Mazmanian, Little, Linder, and Perry (2008) that new governance structures are needed for megaregions that can help guide planning for regional strategic investment that supports TBL objectives. As a regional economic engine that needs to upgrade to green infrastructure systems this decade, the Port would benefit from the Southern California region organizing around sustainable transportation infrastructure. Further work that explores how this might be accomplished, either through "Centers of Excellence" that reflect a larger vision of SEER or some other version of a regional sustainability collaborative that fosters learning, planning and coordinated investment across organizations would be helpful.

Finally, it is not likely that many organizations are training employees on how to learn for sustainability. Likewise, they probably don't grasp that this process must be continuous. Rather, most organizations are struggling with implementing specific initiatives ranging from energy efficiency and water conservation to waste reduction and climate action plans, without acknowledging the action learning opportunities these experiences can provide. As planning for sustainability and climate change depend as much on behavioral changes as they do on technological innovations, focusing investment on building the human capacity for sustainability learning within organizations and collaboratively across organizations is a prerequisite for greater cultural change and the successful visioning and implementation of sustainable public infrastructure systems in the future. How to create sustainability learning networks within and across organizations will be a key challenge for practitioners and researchers over the next decade. Some nonprofits are just beginning to address this need. Practitioners and researchers will need to work together to capture and utilize insights gained from action learning and academic research to advance systems-level change for sustainability.

REFERENCES

Akrivou, K., & Bradbury-Huang, H. (2011). Predicting executive success: Catalyzing organizational sustainability. *The Leadership Quarterly*. (Forthcoming).

Bradbury-Huang, H. (2010). Sustainability as collaboration: The SEER case. *Organization Dynamics*, 39(4).

Bradbury-Huang, H., Lichtenstein, B., Carroll, J., & Senge, P. (2010). Relational space and learning experiments: The heart of collaborations for sustainability. *Research on Organizational Change and Development. 18*, 109–148.

California Air Resources Board. (2006). Final emissions reduction plan for ports and goods movement in California. Available at http://www.arb.ca.gov/planning/gmerp/plan/final_plan.pdf

Capra, F. (1996). *The web of life: A new scientific understanding of living systems*. Chapter 1 – Deep ecology – A new paradigm, and Chapter 2 – From the parts to the whole. New York: Anchor Books/Doubleday.

Davis, H., & Somerville, M. (2006). Learning our way to change: Improved institutional alignment. *New Library World, 107*(1222/1223), 127–140.

Elkington, J. (1997). *Cannibals with forks: The triple bottom line of 21st century business*. Oxford: Capstone Publishing.

Environmental Protection Agency, Office of Environmental Justice. (2009). Environmental justice achievement awards fact sheet. Available at http://www.epa.gov/environmental justice/resources/publications/awards/2009/cleantrucks.pdf

Fenwick, T. (2007). Developing organizational practices of ecological sustainability: A learning perspective. *Leadership and Organization Development Journal, 28*(7), 632–645.

Greenwald, H. (2008). *Organizations: Management without control*. Los Angeles: Sage.

Grieves, J. (2008). Why we should abandon the learning organization. *The Learning Organization, 15*(6), 463–473.

Harris, L. C., & Crane, A. (2002). The greening of organizational culture: Management views on the depth, degree and diffusion of change. *Journal of Organizational Change Management, 15*(3), 214–234.

Healey, P. (2006). *Collaborative planning: Shaping places in fragmented societies* (2nd ed.). USA: Palgrave Macmillan.

Jamali, D. (2006). Insights into triple bottom line integration from a learning organization perspective. *Business Process Management Journal, 12*(6), 809–821.

Kettl, D. (2006). Is the worst yet to come? *The Annals of the American Academy of Political and Social Science, 604*, 273–287.

Khademian, A. (2002). *Working with culture*. Washington, DC: CQ Press.

Marquardt, M. (1999). *Action learning in action: Transforming problems and people for world-class organizational learning*. Palo Alto: Davies-Black Publishing.

Marion, R., & Uhl-Bien, M. (2001). Leadership in complex organizations. *The Leadership Quarterly, 12*, 389–418.

Mazmanian, D. (2008). *Los Angeles' clean air saga – Spanning the three epochs*. University of Southern California School of Policy Planning and Development, Environment & Sustainability, WP-March 2008-1. Available at SSRN: http://ssrn.com/abstract=1523966

McDonough, W., & Braungart, M. (2002). Design for the triple bottom line: New tools for sustainable commerce. *Corporate Environmental Strategy, 9*(3), 251–258.

Metzner, R. (1999). *Green psychology: Transforming our relationship to the earth*. Chapter 11 – Transition to an ecological worldview. Rochester, VT: Park Street Press.

Meynell, F. (2005). A second-order approach to evaluating and facilitating organizational change. *Action Research, 3*(2), 211–231.

Olson, R. L. (1995). Sustainability as a social vision. *Journal of Social Issues, 51*, 15–35.

Pedler, M., & Burgoyne, J. (2008). Action learning. In: P. Reason & H. Bradbury (Eds), *The handbook of action research* (2nd ed., pp. 1–4).

Pisano, M., Mazmanian, D., Little, R., Linder, A., & Perry, B. (2008). *Toward a national strategic investment framework*. Working Paper: Megaregions Governance and Finance. Project of America 2050, The Judith and John Bedrosian Center on Governance and the Public Enterprise, and The Keston Institute for Public Finance and Infrastructure Policy.

Post, J., & Altma, B. (1994). Managing the environmental change process: Barriers and opportunities. *Journal of Organizational Change Management, 7*(4), 64–81.

Port of Los Angeles. (2010). Facts and figures. Available at http://portoflosangeles.org/pdf/POLA_Facts_and_Figures_Card.pdf

Port of Los Angeles and Port of Long Beach. (2010). San Pedro Bay Ports Clean Air Action Plan 2010 Update. Found at http://www.cleanairactionplan.org/reports/documents.asp

Reason, P., & Bradbury, H. (Eds). (2001). *The handbook of action research*.

Robertson, P. (2006). *Ecological governance: Organizing principles for an emerging era*. Unpublished manuscript.

Sauvante, M. (2002). The triple bottom line: A boardroom guide. *Director's Monthly, 25*(11), 1–6.

Senge, P. (1990). The fifth discipline: The art of practice and the learning organization. *Classic Readings in Organizational Behavior*, 438–444.

Senge, P., Lichtenstein, B., Kaeufer, K., Bradbury, H., & Carroll, J. (2007). Collaborating for systemic change: Conceptual, relational and action domains for meeting the sustainability challenge. *Sloan Management Review, 48*(2), 44–53.

Skarzauskiene, A. (2010). Managing complexity: Systems thinking as a catalyst of the organization performance. *Measuring Business Excellence, 14*(4), 49–63.

Starkey, R., & Welford, R. (2001). *The Earthscan reader in business & sustainable development*. London: Earthscan Publishing.

Supply Chain Digest. (2010). Logistics news: Federal judge rules for port of LA in drayage truck emissions case, perhaps ushering in era of more local control over trucking. *Supply Chain Digest*, September 7.

Uhl-Bien, M., Marion, R., & McKelvey, B. (2007). Complexity leadership theory shifting landscape from the industrial age to the knowledge era. *The Leadership Quarterly, 18*, 298–318.

Welford, R. (1995). *Environmental strategy and sustainable development*. London: Routledge.

Zulauf, C. (2007). Learning to think systemically: What does it take? *The Learning Organization, 14*(6), 489–498.

CHAPTER 7

BUILDING MULTI-STAKEHOLDER SUSTAINABILITY NETWORKS: THE CUYAHOGA VALLEY INITIATIVE

Christopher G. Worley and Sally Breyley Parker

ABSTRACT

This chapter provides a rich and thick description of a collaborative, place-based, interorganizational process in the domain of social, ecological, and economic sustainability. Governmental agencies, businesses, philanthropic organizations, NGOs, consulting firms, and private citizens tried to move from an underorganized and tacit set of ineffective relationships toward a structural collaboration in service of a "place" known as the Cuyahoga River Valley. While the process built momentum and expectations among its participants and other stakeholders, an important outcome of the collaboration did not materialize as planned. The leading actors struggled with scaling a "negotiated order" and leveraging the high levels of commitment among the participants. Despite the setback, many of the aims of the collaboration continue to be achieved, albeit at a slower pace and without a high regional priority. The chapter explores whether the trans-organization development (Cummings, 1984) perspective is a useful model for intentionally intervening in a

Organizing for Sustainability
Organizing for Sustainable Effectiveness, Volume 1, 187–214
Copyright © 2011 by Emerald Group Publishing Limited
ISSN: 2045-0605/doi:10.1108/S2045-0605(2011)0000001012

multi-stakeholder collaboration and the roles that negotiated order (Nathan & Mitroff, 1991) and referent organizations (Trist, 1983) play.

Keywords: Sustainability; collaboration; trans-organization development; stakeholders; networks

SUSTAINABILITY AND TRANS-ORGANIZATION DEVELOPMENT: THE ROLE OF NEGOTIATED ORDER AND REFERENT ORGANIZATIONS IN THE CUYAHOGA VALLEY INITIATIVE

The "tragedy of the commons" is a popular metaphor and economic phenomenon where the quality of a shared resource – air, water, open space, grazing land – and the ability of that resource to sustain economic activity over a long time horizon degrade because no single stakeholder must account for it. Each rational stakeholder accelerates degradation and mortgages future benefits in the name of current opportunities. As each stakeholder reaps the benefits of their decision, the future costs of those decisions are borne by the interdependent set of actors. Daniels (2007) suggested that the rate of resource degradation would depend on the number of stakeholders using the resource, how much damage each use caused, and the ability of the resource to rejuvenate itself.

When applied to issues of social and environmental sustainability, the number of stakeholders using natural resources, such as land and water, is large and the consequence of each use can be small, thus leading to a decline that is barely perceived until it is too late. Also known as messes (Ackoff, 1981) or meta-problems (Chevalier, Bailey, & Burns, 1974), a variety of issues, problems, and opportunities facing the world, including global warming, social unrest, child labor, water quality, and poverty, can be conveniently viewed through the tragedy of the commons metaphor. The tragedy results from tacit and unplanned coordination among loosely coupled (Weick, 2001) organizations, governments, groups, and individuals. Through no single stakeholder's fault, there is no common understanding of the problem, no agreed upon method for addressing it, and no formal mechanism to act on behalf of the commons. Yet the quality of the commons degrades, bit by bit, because each stakeholder acts in its own self-interest and has no accountability for the externalities of its operations.

Rather than focusing on Daniel's rate of decline in the resource, organizational scholars and practitioners concerned with social and environmental sustainability address how to reverse degradation through conscious intervention. Theories of trans-organization development (Boje, 1982; Cummings, 1984), collaboration (Gray, 1989; Huxham, 1993), and social entrepreneurship (Bornstein, 2007) focus on the conditions and processes that can help to restore resources to earlier levels of quality.

In this chapter, we use the process of trans-organization development (TD) (Cummings, 1984) to frame our understanding of intentional intervention and the concepts of negotiated order (Nathan & Mitroff, 1991) and referent organizations (Trist, 1983) to understand the dynamics and outcomes of a collaborative, place-based attempt to restore the vitality of the Cuyahoga River Valley near Cleveland, OH, USA.

Understanding Collaboration and Trans-Organization Development

Open systems models presume that organizations are dependent on their environments for inputs that are essential to their functioning (Thompson, 1967; Katz & Kahn, 1978). When such resources are scarce, organizations tend to compete with one another, attempting to gain power and control over essential inputs while also trying to remain autonomous (Pfeffer & Salancik, 1978). A second possible response focuses on coping with environmental complexity and change by forming multiorganization collectives. Working together, competitors reduce the uncertainly associated with acquiring the input resources or reducing the negative consequences of producing undesirable outputs. However, doing so means the organization must forgo some autonomy and the opportunity to establish competitive advantage on this dimension. When the input is free, as in the case of the commons, there is no competitive pressure and organizations are incented to use the resource at a rate that exceeds the resource's ability to rejuvenate. The organization mortgages its own future and destroys the resource that is literally and figuratively giving life to the system, resulting in the tragedy.

Building on open systems frameworks and the work of Emery and Trist (1973) and Trist (1983), Cummings (1984) integrated social problem solving and interorganizational research to propose a planned change process he called trans-organization development (TD). To provide a context for TD, Cummings first defined a trans-organization system (TS) – a group of organizations that are joined together for a common purpose (p. 368). Understanding this definition is critical to solving the tragedy of the commons and the role TD can play. The terms "joined together" and "common purpose" cannot be defined too literally. All that is required for a TS to exist is that a set of organizations have some awareness that they share an issue or problem.

Collaboration researchers have labeled this common purpose a "negotiated order." Trist (1983) suggested that a negotiated order included the process of "domain formation," a socially constructed view or shared appreciation of a phenomenon/issue. He emphasized the importance of recognizing that "domains are cognitive as well as organizational structures, else one can only too easily fall into the trap of thinking of them as objectively given, quasi-permanent fixtures in the social fabric, rather than as ways we have chosen to construe various facets of it" (p. 273). Nathan and Mitroff (1991) suggested that a negotiated order exists when organizations have jointly determined the terms of their future interactions with one another. It is an agreement about the rules of the game. When there is a negotiated order, the members of a TS know what is expected of them as part of the network.

A negotiated order, because it is socially constructed, has both planned and emergent elements and is subject to change. That is, members of the TS have to become aware of their role and contribution to the tragedy and see some benefit in further participation. If a member of the TS believes there has been a change in the ratio of costs to benefits or that there has been a shift in their assessment of the common resource, their motivation to participate and contribute to the TS can change.

However, there have been few studies of negotiated order (Pasquero, 1991; Nathan & Mitroff, 1991). In the most comprehensive study on negotiated order, Nathan and Mitroff (1991) carefully interviewed members of a "product tampering" TS (e.g., manufacturers, the FDA, grocery stores, etc.) to determine how each stakeholder viewed the problem, their role in a crisis, and most importantly their expectations of other's behaviors in a crisis. They found, for example, that manufacturers wanted to see tampering as "their" problem alone and expected to handle the crisis without assistance. They missed the interdependent nature of the problem. Without a negotiated order, the TS was relatively unprepared to effectively handle product tampering crises.

In contrast to most organizational systems, TSs tend to be under-organized (Brown, 1980). Potential member organizations may not perceive the need to join with other organizations. They may be concerned with maintaining their autonomy or have trouble identifying potential partners. U.S. firms, for example, are traditionally "rugged individualists" preferring to work alone rather than to join with other organizations. Even if organizations decide to join together, they may have problems managing their relationships, and because members typically are accustomed to hierarchical forms of control, they may have difficulty managing lateral relations among independent organizations. They also may have difficulty managing different levels of commitment and motivation among members and sustaining membership over time. These characteristics make creating and managing TSs difficult (Gray, 1985; Harrigan & Newman, 1990; Chisholm,1998). At some level, each of these reasons for not collaborating is the very reason a commons degrades in quality.

However, when the individually oriented firms are confronted with problems or opportunities arising from their membership in a TS, they can choose to go it alone or collaborate with other members of the TS to address the issue or opportunity. When the issues are social and ecological "meta-problems," multiparty collaboration is one strategy for developing sustainable solutions (Gray, 1989; Huxham, 1996; Huxham & Vangen, 1996). Multiparty collaboration is defined as " ... a process through which parties who see different aspects of a problem can constructively explore their differences and search for solutions that go beyond their own limited vision of what is possible" (Gray, 1989, p. 5).

Cummings proposed that developing a TS required a new and specific type of planned change based on the nature of the TS and the meta-problem being addressed. TD is a unique form of planned change aimed at creating and improving TS effectiveness (Cummings, 1984; Gray, 1989; Harrigan & Newman, 1990; Boje & Hillon, 2008). Whereas collaboration scholars describe how and why organizations work together, TD is concerned with intentional intervention. One or more individuals or organizations try to get the TS to operate more effectively than it would without intervention. The TD process has four phases.

Identification involves understanding the existing and potential membership of the TS. It is generally carried out by one or a few organizations interested in exploring the possibility of creating a more effective network. Cummings suggests that an organization's motivation to interact and the subsequent levels of effort to engage in TS problem solving will be a function of resource dependency (Pfeffer & Salancik, 1978), their commitment to problem solving in the domain, and any mandates requiring participation, such as regulatory compliance. Because networks are intended to perform specific tasks, a practical criterion for membership is how much organizations can contribute. Identifying potential members also should take into account the political realities of the situation (Gricar, 1981; Williams, 1980; Gray & Hay, 1986). Potential members can be identified and judged in terms of the skills, knowledge, and resources that they bring to bear on improving sustainability outcomes.

An important difficulty at this stage can be insufficient leadership and cohesion among participants to choose potential members. In these situations, someone may need to play a more activist role in creating the network (Cummings, 1984). They may need to bring structure to a group of autonomous organizations that do not see the need to join together or may not know how to form relationships. In several cases of network development, change agents helped members create a special leadership group of committed members who were able to develop enough cohesion among members to carry out the identification stage.

Convention is concerned with bringing stakeholders together to assess whether formalizing the network is desirable and feasible. This face-to-face meeting enables potential members to explore mutually their motivations for joining and their perceptions of the joint task. They work to establish sufficient levels of motivation and task consensus to form the network.

Like the identification stage, this phase of network creation generally requires considerable direction and facilitation. Existing stakeholders may not have the legitimacy or skills to perform the convening function. As a result, academics, researchers, or consultants can serve as conveners if they are perceived as legitimate and credible by the attending organizations. This necessitates that change agents be seen by members as working on behalf of the total system, rather than as being aligned with particular organizations or views. Under these conditions, network members are more likely to share information with them and to listen to their inputs. Such neutrality can enhance change agents' ability to mediate conflicts among members. Because participating organizations tend to have diverse motives and views and limited means for resolving differences, change agents may need to structure and manage interactions to facilitate airing of differences and arriving at consensus about forming the network. They may need to help organizations work through differences and reconcile self-interests with those of the larger network.

Organization involves intentionally formalizing structures and mechanisms that promote communication and interaction among stakeholders and that direct collaboration toward resource restoration. It includes the organizations to be involved in the network and the roles each will play; the communication and relationships among them; and the control system that will guide decision making and provide a mechanism for monitoring performance. These "referent organizations" (Trist, 1983) are controlled by stakeholders involved in the domain and concerned with development, not operations. That is, referent organizations represent a regulatory function or a part of the infrastructure that oversees projects, resources, and information sharing. Referent organizations conceptualize the problems for TS activity, direct individual organization and TS direction setting, and develop collectively shared understandings while leaving operations and implementation to member organizations.

Despite considerable agreement on the concept, there is very little research on these forms (Pasquero, 1991). For example, members may create a coordinating council to manage the network and a powerful leader to head it. They might choose to create a new organization or association that formalizes exchanges among members by developing rules, policies, and formal operating procedures. Referent organizations can be an existing organization in the TS or an organization created for this purpose by the domain. For example, Gap, Inc. is a member of the apparel industry yet because of their position and capabilities, they will take on a coordinating role to address issues such as freedom of association, child labor, or unsafe environmental practices (Worley, Feyerherm, & Knudsen, 2010). Alternatively, referent organizations can be independent organizations created to take purposive action on behalf of the collective as in the case of the United Nations.

Evaluation involves assessing how the network is performing. Members need feedback so they can identify problems and begin to resolve them. This generally includes information about performance outcomes and member satisfactions, as well as indicators of how well members are interacting jointly. Change agents can periodically interview or survey member organizations about various outcomes and features of the network and feed that data back to network leaders. Such information enables network leaders to make necessary operational modifications and adjustments. It may signal the need to return to previous stages in the process to make necessary corrections.

Despite its wide acknowledgment among researchers and practitioners, there have been no formal tests of Cummings' (1984) TD process. For example, Clarke (2005) used the TD framework to understand the convention phase and found that social network analysis provided important insights into changes in network perceptions. While he did not look at the entire process of TD, the data supported the conclusion that the intra-phase dynamics were likely to be much more complex than indicated in Cummings four-phase model.

Most of the research on collaboration, trans-organization development, and interorganizational relationships has focused on the challenges facing organizations that want to collaborate and on how to overcome or address those challenges. Pasquero's (1991) summary of this literature suggested that critical success factors in interorganizational relations included (a) following a well-defined sequence of stages with early stages focused on "domain definition" or agreeing on problem boundaries and trust building; (b) ensuring participant legitimacy and inclusiveness; (c) recognizing interdependence (Logsdon,1991); (d) finding members with similar motivations regarding communitarian values and utilitarian benefits; and (e) having the capacity to implement the partnership's decisions whatever the distribution of power (p. 42). These factors map well to the TD process.

Huxham and her colleagues have spent considerable effort understanding how and when trust can be formed and the consequences of trust on collaboration effectiveness and identity (Vangen & Huxham, 2003; Zhang & Huxham, 2009). Similarly, because stakeholders have vested interests in the domain and differ in perspective, information, power, and resources, conflicts are predominant and have received considerable attention (Prins, 2010; Cropper, Ebers, Huxham, & Smith Ring, 2008; Schruijer & Vansina, 2008; Vansina, Taillieu, & Schruijer, 1998).

A Note on Methodology

The Cuyahoga River Valley case study is a longitudinal, qualitative field study. The second author has been involved with the case since its inception and is identified as the OD consultant in the case description. Data collection began during a supervised organization design project as the early phases of the case were happening. Since then, four waves of interviews have been conducted. Formal interviews were conducted by both authors as part of a case study written for an OD text book in 2007, in preparation for a case presentation in October 2008, as part of a symposium in August 2009, and in preparation for this chapter in September 2010.

Interviews were conducted in person and by phone with key stakeholders in the case. Each round of interviews consisted of five to seven discussions with individuals or groups, and three stakeholders have been involved in every round. Transcripts of the interviews were compiled into a case description and shared with the members of the TS for verification and confirmation.

RESTORING THE CUYAHOGA VALLEY

History and Context

Deriving its name from the Iroquois word meaning crooked, the Cuyahoga (or "Crooked") River Valley emerged in the early 1800s as a critical trade center thanks to a Lake Erie port and superhighways of canals and railroads that transported everything from cotton and coal, to coffee and window glass. The region soon became a nexus for steel mills, oil refineries, and tire manufacturers that increased industrial waste and turned the lower Cuyahoga River into a "flowing dump." After catching on fire for the *third* time in 1969, the Cuyahoga River became the impetus of the 1972 Clean Water Act. In 1998, the region's centrality to economic activity and a long process of healing helped to establish the river's designation as one of 14 American Heritage Rivers although it remains one of the EPA's areas of concern.

Eventually, the region's economic health also declined. Whether associated with environmental degradation, economic shifts, or technological changes, area jobs, population, and personal income declined at a rate above that of the rest of the country. As a result, individual communities and municipalities compete with each other over the businesses, development funds, and residents that they hope will jumpstart their economies, and assume "the place" – the all-encompassing natural environment – will continue to provide support without cost. Meanwhile, a growing number of initiatives and organizations have advocated regional approaches to address shared economic challenges, leverage regional assets, and market northeast Ohio as a great place for new businesses, leisure travelers, and conventions.

In November 2000, a series of articles in the Cleveland Plain Dealer entitled "The Forgotten Valley" traced the history of the Cuyahoga River Valley with its "natural beauty and full-throated industry" and challenged the community to recognize and embrace the valley as a place for "enjoyment, exploration, reinvestment, and renewal." Cuyahoga County commissioner Timothy McCormick took up the challenge, designated funding for the Cuyahoga Valley Initiative (CVI), and charged the Cuyahoga County Planning Commission (CCPC) to direct its efforts.

The Emergence of a Framework for Collaboration

The CCPC director, Paul Alsenas, and his staff initially viewed the CVI as a "planning exercise" to create codes, guidelines, and other tools to direct development in the Cuyahoga River Valley, and engaged a national team to assist them in the task. The team soon determined that regeneration of the Valley would require more than a set of codes and guidelines, and adopted sustainability as a framework to guide and inform the Valley's transformation. The vision included a set of six organizing goals:

> *Working River*: Innovative watershed management will maintain a state-of-the-art working river that serves industry and recreation.
>
> *Healthy Valley*: The valley community will restore the urban watershed to become an environmental treasure for the region.
>
> *Destination*: The valley will become a popular recreation and tourist destination where residents and visitors enjoy the valley's cultural, historical, and ecological amenities.
>
> *Art and Design*: The valley will be a place of experimentation and creativity and new design paradigms.
>
> *Business Innovation*: The valley will become known for environmental friendly economic development and business practices.
>
> *Community Capacity*: Communities will combine their diverse assets and talents with global best practices to increase individual and community wealth, encourage the development of existing and new businesses, and bring about environmental health.

Identification

As work on the vision and framework advanced and more and more business, municipal, and NGO stakeholders became aware of or involved in the CVI, its definition and scope continued to shift. Although the original focus was Cuyahoga County, the CCPC team realized that the CVI should be a regional rather than a county initiative. It also became evident to Alsenas and his team that the valley's transformation would require more capacity than the CCPC could commit. Collaboration and cooperation among many different stakeholders with many different agendas over a long time period was required to accomplish the CVI vision. CCPC's ability to direct CVI implementation was constrained by their constitution as a government agency, by the resources available for funding, by the available people, and to some extent, by its legitimacy. The CCPC could develop a framework and guidelines for development projects, but such a stance did not tap into the creativity and energy of individuals, businesses, and civil NGOs.

With these realizations, Alsenas engaged an organization design and development consultant to explore the type of organization required to take on the work of the initiative. The consultant team interviewed more than 80 representatives from valley municipalities, community and economic development organizations, county government, regional authorities, local universities, valley related nonprofit organizations, real estate developers, and valley businesses and landowners. Through the effort, the consultant concluded:

- The Cuyahoga Valley was seen as an asset for the northeast Ohio region. People saw a place of "connection and joining," a natural and non-threatening "venue for regionalism," and a way to leverage the region's sustainability efforts and other agendas, such as improving racial inclusion and income equity, attracting and growing businesses, reducing government fragmentation and inefficiency, reducing sprawl, and improving regional connectivity. However, if the CVI was to advance its vision, the effort had to expand beyond Cuyahoga County to include Summit County. This meant that the CVI framework would have to "scale" to an area including 25 local governments, three special government districts, numerous state of Ohio Departments, over 40 nonprofit organizations, and thousands of private businesses and residents whose work and property management practices influence the Cuyahoga Valley.
- The CVI was not widely understood, was at times confused with other projects and initiatives in the Valley, and was considered suspicious by some, often because of its association with Cuyahoga County government. For those with knowledge of the CVI, it appeared to be an adequate, if not inspiring, framework for its regeneration. People were generally optimistic and intrigued with its approach and were eager to see results.
- To accomplish its objectives, the CVI needed organizational capacity beyond that currently present in the community. It needed an entity able to work with the agendas of a wide variety of organizations and be positioned to provide overall coordination and a cohesive context for the organizations working in the valley. It would need to facilitate new kinds of collaborations to benefit both the valley and its members. However, many participants warned the county to "think long and hard" before recommending a new organization in a region already saturated with nonprofits and governmental entities competing for an insufficient and shrinking pool of resources. The formation of any new organization would be scrutinized by the community; consequently, its initiation would need to be perceived as essential, legitimate, and nonredundant.

Convening the TS

With these conclusions, the consultant worked with the CCPC to secure a grant from The Gund Foundation to convene members of the TS in exploring how this additional capacity could be delivered. The consultant and Alsenas' team formed an ad hoc design team of "usual and unusual suspects" whose job was to develop and present a set of organizational design recommendations to the county. The consultant and CCPC sought broad and systemic thinkers, civic champions, innovators, and leaders; they looked for individuals who were not afraid to represent their perspectives but also willing to listen to others. Fourteen individuals representing different organizations and initiatives throughout Cuyahoga and Summit Counties, the consultant, and the CCPC composed the final design team.

Over a period of five months, the design team met about every three weeks for half-day sessions that were held in different locations throughout the valley. These meetings resulted in the design team grasping the complexity and scale of the valley and its ability and potential to support a diversity of ecological, economic, and social activities. They realized how many organizations – large and small from different sectors – were already working to advance their agendas and affect the valley. They also wrestled with questions about the essential "DNA" of an organization whose function was the transformation of such a place. They talked about the valley as a whole system and wondered where attention and energy should be focused to catalyze and accelerate transformation and regeneration, achieve results, and create value. The design team's epiphany, as they struggled to define the physical boundaries of the valley and to prioritize the places where work should be focused, was that *the primary point of leverage for affecting change in the valley was not a project or a physical place, it was the people and the human network they formed.* With this insight, the group's focus shifted to looking at the valley as a networked system of people and organizations. That is, while some type of orchestrating capacity was still necessary, the design team tried to describe and design the entire TS, including how the different stakeholders could and should contribute.

The Design for Transformation

The result of this thinking was a design for transformation – a way of organizing resources and capacities to accelerate development and

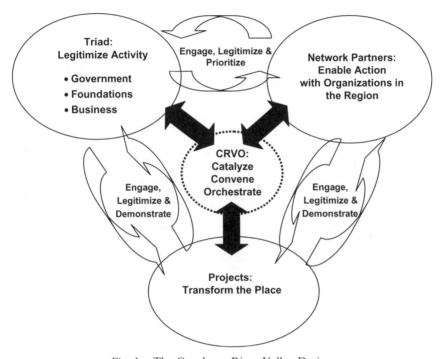

Fig. 1. The Cuyahoga River Valley Design.

regeneration in the valley. It was comprised of four interdependent organizational forms (Fig. 1).

- A Triad of Civic Leadership
- Network Partners
- Projects and Project Teams
- The Cuyahoga River Valley Organization (CRVO)

The Triad referred to a proposed civic collaboration of three key stakeholders – government, business, and foundations within the two counties. Its purpose was to:

- Legitimize and fund the transformation of the valley as a top regional priority
- Authorize and fund a leader, catalyst, and orchestrator of valley transformation

- Ensure the leader's autonomy and neutrality in service of regional transformation

Network Partners referred to organizations and individuals committed to transformation in the valley. Many were already working on a wide variety of interests in the valley, and while well-intended, these stakeholders were often fragmented and adversarial, driven by a wide range of agendas that competed for the same pool of resources. For example, a major initiative long vying for attention in the valley has been the extension and completion of the Ohio and Erie Canal Towpath Trail or "towpath," one of Ohio's longest and most scenic biking and hiking trails. A desire to complete the towpath has brought together many organizations including numerous NGOs, the Cleveland Metroparks, the CCPC, private developers, and CSX Railroad. Unfortunately, these key stakeholders are not necessarily in agreement about the objectives and criteria for success. Some organizations define success as simply completing the towpath. For others, success implies an inherent experience of aesthetic quality. For still others, success means that the towpaths will be completed with little or no impact on them at all.

Valley Projects are where the rubber meets the road – where the valley transformation will take shape. Many valley projects and initiatives were already underway engaging numerous organizations. Projects should address the most pressing needs of the valley, have impact at scale, and help build the valley network.

The CRVO was to serve as the valley's champion for transformation and regeneration and orchestrate the larger network. The CRVO would provide vision, leadership, context, and coordination. CRVO was the only organizational form that would require the incorporation of a new entity to engage in three primary activities:

- Promote the valley as a living lab, providing opportunities for learning and research
- Generate a unified identity and brand for the valley to unite the valley communities under a common vision
- Assemble the assets of the valley and take them to scale to achieve sustainable results

The design team believed that all four forms were essential to valley transformation and regeneration. They worked hard to specify the membership, roles, and responsibilities of the different design components and especially the CRVO knowing that the purpose and value of the CRVO as an integral part of a larger organizational system had to be clear and compelling to stakeholders. Ironically, while the ultimate success of the CRVO would rely on robust relationships with the other organizational forms, the design team realized that CRVO would be needed to catalyze and encourage the emergence and formation of these other organizational forms.

An Operating Process

Once the design recommendations describing the roles and organizations necessary to operate the TS were substantially complete, the design team was officially disbanded. However, the consultant and the CCPC team continued to develop the model by designing a process for working together to promote integrated economic, environmental, and social benefit. Even though northeast Ohioans were expressing a growing interest in regionalism, there were very few examples of collaborative regional initiatives and fewer, if any, at the CVI's scale and level of complexity. They outlined a preliminary set of principles and practices for engagement in the valley (Table 1). Combined, the principles and practices encouraged individuals to suspend disbelief, "slow down to speed up," and to spend time building a foundation for intelligent and aligned action. In addition, divergent groups were asked to set aside individual and corporate agendas and be curious about the agendas of others in the interest of mutual benefit. The intention was to encourage the integration of divergent views without paralyzing action. In essence, the CRVO would be asking individuals and organizations to take action, trust an exploratory process, and collaborate with others for mutual value in a region historically characterized as risk averse, fragmented, and distrustful.

As attention shifted to implementation, the consultant and CCPC focused on CRVO's launch. Initial recommendations of the design team suggested that the CRVO start small. They emphasized that CRVO's initial work was to continue the CVI process with valley stakeholders, build awareness about the role of the valley in building a vital northeast Ohio, recruit champions, build the network and encourage valley projects that could demonstrate CVI principles and practices, and support on the ground change in the valley. However, the CCPC was concerned that starting too small with insufficient institutional capacity could undermine CRVO's impact.

A debate arose about how and where to start. For some, there was a desire to take an entrepreneurial approach – to learn in action, start small, and remain stealth-like. For others, there was concern that a poor,

Table 1. The Cuyahoga Valley River Principles and Practices.

Guiding Principles	Operating Practices
• Serve the needs of the valley • Work to reveal the assets and opportunities within the valley • Work to build a network of people and organizations committed to a sustainable valley • Elevate the principles of ecological design and human needs to be commensurate with economic objectives – seek "triple bottom line" impacts • Accomplish results while building capacity to accomplish results • Refuse to be obsessed with avoiding mistakes • Refuse to fix blame and not tolerating others who do so • Acknowledge and study mistakes to establish a pattern of learning • Offer incentives and awards for risk-taking and innovation including praise for daring efforts that fail • Judge a new idea by first considering what could work	• Suspend disbelief • Show respect and humility • Be curious • Be willing to admit ignorance • Appreciate what "exists" and what "can be" • Learn in action • Trust your intuition • Codevelop solutions • Create mutual value • Start small • Be patient • Hold the whole and the individual • Seek to understand the Cuyahoga River Valley as a regional asset

insufficient start could derail a fledgling organization, recognizing that the scope and complexity of the challenges facing the valley would require significant resources to have any true impact. Ultimately, design recommendations included a large, more robust organization with a significant operational budget. This design was shared with former design team members and presented to the Gund Foundation and the County Commissioners. Several design team members joined both presentations. At best, the presentation met with a neutral response. In the end, the process stalled and was sidelined due to the economic downturn and a countywide corruption scandal.

Recent Events

By mid-2010, three years after the design, principles, and practices for transforming the valley had been crafted, neither the Triad nor the CRVO had formed. Today, the CVI remains an initiative inside the CCPC and the

CRVO is not a focus. When asked about whether a CRVO was needed, one stakeholder declared

> I'm afraid that if an organization was set up, it would get chewed up ... it has to bubble up ... If you came out and said here's a new organization and here's the board – everybody would be laughing. It's the people with the land and the money who call the shots. It's still the right idea, but it has to emerge and it needs to operate that way ...

There was also some concern about whether the CVI process had engaged the right people to date. Were there any advantages to shifting the focus from "those that get it or are willing to try" to intentionally including some of the loose cannons and small businesses that make up 80% of the industrial valley economy? "The idea of engaging the stakeholders and understanding their needs ... this is a place where I really see opportunity."

As for the Triad, it will also ultimately require the blessing and support of three sectors – government, business, and foundations – that do not have a strong history of working together. Reflecting perhaps the general business perspective, a local entrepreneur and venture capital executive believed that funding and strong action were necessary.

> The ideal situation is someone with power, such as a foundation or even the county, to say "we want to take this deeper." The concept/entity [CRVO] needs to say, 'We are not here to tell you what to do but to help you do what you want so that we are all working together and the valley is at the center.' The bottom line is, it has to be funded ... people will listen to that kind of group and they won't have to deal with jurisdictional issues.

The foundation community however was reluctant to play the "father role" and the county lacked resources to ensure major funding.

While many cited frustration and disappointment about the CVI/CRVO's perceived "inaction," others felt that social change required some "steeping" time and that new conversations were beginning to happen. The valley's transformation required a lot of people to think differently and these shifts were starting to take place. In time, the organization would emerge. "We're not stuck ... it's a constant process ... the design is there and we are working on it. At the same, every day there's an adjustment that you have to account for and modify your actions."

Despite the lack of a formal CRVO or Triad, the 2008–2009 recession, and a major voter-led reconstitution of the County's governance system, many of the CVI objectives were moving forward. A small number of original members of the design team – a local retired business executive and venture capitalist, Alsenas and his team, and the local OD consultant – were still working to advance the CVI principles and practices, operating tacitly as a de facto CRVO. Between projects initiated by the different network partners, the County, and other independent municipalities or private individuals, the valley had a variety of projects underway, and many of them had to operate with the approval of the county planning commission and the guidelines established early in the process.

For example, the "green bulkhead project" was run by Cuyahoga County as a rudimentary collaboration among the Cuyahoga River Remedial Action Plan and representatives from business, government, and environmental stakeholders. Along the navigable banks of the Cuyahoga River, steel bulkheads exist that while friendly to ships make it difficult for native fish to make the swim upstream to spawning grounds. As part of an overall plan to repair the shoreline, the Cuyahoga habitat underwater basket (CHUB) is hung alongside parts of the bulkheads that are not used for commerce. The basket contains native plants that grow well in the current conditions and provide fish a place to rest before continuing the swim.

To some, the green bulkheads project represents a whole shoreline restoration initiative promising to decrease maintenance costs, maintain navigability, and increase natural plant and fish species. They see it as a win–win process that has drawn a lot of local, regional, and national attention. Others are more skeptical and see the CHUB as a narrowly focused habitat solution that has not involved the whole river system and consequently has not created a sufficient solution to the real bulkhead problems. Would a CRVO have brought value to the Green Bulkhead project, would it have ensured a more systemic approach?

DISCUSSION

The newspaper article represented a call to action that tapped into the region's historical and emotional commitment to the valley. In an attempt to reverse the tragedy, the CVI was created and the CCPC responded by defining and then expanding the vision of the CVI. Their attempts to date to bridge organizations and community interests in service of the valley and the regional economy have been both successful and inadequate. This section discusses the CVI case in light of our understanding of the dynamics of TSs, determines what additional research is necessary, and makes suggestions for future practice. The CVI case provides a great opportunity to understand how collaboration and TD concepts can be used to address economic, social, and ecological sustainability.

The Process of Trans-Organization Development

Cummings' (1984) TD process provides a reasonable framework to describe and guide the intentional development of a TS and the restoration of an economic, social, and ecological system. Once the CCPC staff realized that writing policy and land use guidelines for development projects was insufficient to regenerate the region, they embarked on a process to increase the valley's capacity to deliver on CVI objectives. Their activities closely follow the phases of identification, convention, and organization.

The identification phase led to a deeper understanding of stakeholder motivations for participating as well as their relationships to issues in the valley. The data from the interviews resulted in a clear appreciation of the challenge and the full range of stakeholders that would need to be involved to affect a solution. The enthusiasm to engage in these conversations led Alsenas' team to believe that convention was a feasible and productive next step.

The focus of the convention phase was to determine what capacity was necessary to coordinate TS activities. However, they were creating an organized, thorough, and comprehensive way of thinking about how *someone else* could restore the valley's economic, social, and environmental health. The design team members had real epiphanies about the valley and the role that the different stakeholders were playing in degrading the resource and constraining economic growth, but they were not designing a way for them to address these issues. They developed a deep understanding of what it would take to reverse the tragedy and there was momentum to organize and create CRVO even though data from the TS specifically warned against creating a new organization.

The output of the convention process was a blueprint for the organization phase. The design, principles, and practices described roles and responsibilities for the Triad, the members of the TS (network partners), projects to restore the valley, and an organization to orchestrate activities (CRVO). There was a strong belief that the design and the process represented a strategy for restoring the valley's health, reversing the commons tragedy, and supporting the economic development of the region. But as the case describes, neither the design nor the principles and practices were fully implemented. Many of the pieces are in place and operating, but not as envisioned by the design team.

This longitudinal study completed the initial TD cycle by evaluating the process to date. True to the CVI's objective of using the valley as a laboratory, the participants in the CVI have openly shared their experiences and insights so that others can learn from their work. In addition, feedback to the system has sparked additional activity. There are active discussions about how to move forward.

The TD phases are an adequate, if high level, representation of the activities necessary to move *underorganized* TSs forward. However, in support of Clarke's (2005) conclusion, the intra-phase dynamics appear to be much more complex, nonlinear, perhaps even cyclical, and much more determinant of successful progress through the TD process. Like traditional organization development, just following a process does not appear sufficient to bring about the outcomes desired by some TS members and the CVI organizers. The TD process phases must be supplemented with specific tools, concepts, and frameworks to ensure that TS outcomes are improved. In the CVI case, the concepts of negotiated order and referent organization are particularly useful in explaining the CVI's progress (or lack thereof).

The Role of a Negotiated Order in TD

The negotiated order concept helps to explain the nature and focus of the conversations during the identification and convention phases as well as the efficacy of those phases in contributing to valley outcomes. In the CVI case, a negotiated order or domain of common concern has never existed at the scale of the valley as a whole. The identification and convention phases were attempts to understand the valley's ecology as a whole, including its economic, social, and environmental operations, and manifest a shared understanding and a negotiated order. However, both the scale of the valley and the use of a triple bottom line framework as a basis for study and action contributed to a level of complexity that many people had a very hard time wrapping their heads around. There appears to be a variety of reasons for this.

First, Nathan and Mitroff (1991) and McCann (1983) suggest that addressing a problem shared by two or more organizations requires that they be able to grasp the problem's full scope. This is particularly challenging with a large-scale TS like the valley where there are a multitude of organizations and motivations. Similarly, the sustainability framework poses a multidimensional "problem" that is viewed through numerous lenses by different organizations and sectors.

The design team was able to grasp the essence of the problem's full scope and their thinking was informed by the broader set of valley stakeholders;

however, the broader set of stakeholder did not go through the same process as the design team and therefore did not gain their own grasp of its full scope. The design team "got" the epiphany, but the rest of the valley didn't. This may be similar to a large-scale organization change effort where a senior management team goes away for an off-site meeting and spends three days reflecting on the business and gaining deep insight into the nature of the problem and solutions to address it. Following the meeting, memos are sent out to an unsuspecting organization membership who has no insight into the epiphanies and yet are told what the answers are. The design team understood the problem and the early work of the CRVO was to continue the diffusion process to communicate this insight to the other stakeholders in the valley. The design team was not a critical mass for a problem of this scale and when the formation of a CRVO stalled, so did the TD process.

The data from the CVI case suggests that in complex large-scale systems, the process of transitioning from identification to convention and from convention to organization may be more cyclical as domain formation and negotiated order are established at different levels of the TS. Unless the understanding is shared at the same level and scope of the problem, the various stakeholders have no basis for understanding how their individual interests will be considered or how the larger TS effectiveness outcomes will be influenced. The challenge is that this process of engaging and developing understanding with a large number and wide variety of stakeholders can only happen over time – just like with the design team of the CVI. And in a large-scale TS that is *underorganized*, it requires dedicated organizational capacity which is typically missing from the system. Without understanding, there seems little reason for anyone to support the formation of a legitimate referent organization that can guide TS activities. An uninvolved stakeholder's resistance to the process would easily be forgiven with a quick glance at the proposed design and processes. On its face, it asks parties to set aside their own goals, to think about the whole, and to go slow.

Second, a negotiated order at scale never existed because the valley projects with a CVI focus were often defined in a way where one aspect of the triple bottom line was subservient to another (usually environment as subservient to economics). Part of the problem with the tragedy of the commons and central to Gray's (1989) definition of collaboration is that each stakeholder sees the "problem" from slightly different perspectives and attempts to address the problem from that perspective. With the exception of the design team, each major stakeholder brought a predominant lens – environmental, economic, and to lesser degree social – and there were many sub-lenses within each of the predominate lenses. For example, within the environmental lens, there were sub-lenses for water quality, ecologically sound planning and development practices, and habitat preservation. The result was a loosely coordinated and too narrowly focused set of activities that had their own momentum and identity. The people working on the towpath think that's the most important project and the people working on the green bulkhead baskets think that's the most important project. Creating a negotiated order for the CVI – or any multi-stakeholder collaboration for that matter – may need a project that demonstrates how an integrated view works.

Third, the case research on collaboration suggests that organizational crises are often inherent in the emergence of a negotiated order – or make the apparent need for negotiated order more urgent. The history of the valley supports this observation. Only after the river caught fire for the third time did coordinated action take place. Similarly, Nathan and Mitroff's (1991) study of the negotiated order among stakeholders was in response to product tampering crises. Crises can help stakeholders "appreciate the degree to which their fates are correlated" (Boje, 1982).

A negotiated order never existed because for the CVI, there was no crisis driving a need for collaborative action at the scale of the Cuyahoga River Valley as a whole. Cummings (1984) and Pfeiffer and Salancik (1978) suggest that an organization's commitment to problem solving is a function of resource dependency. Today, few organizations in the Cuyahoga River Valley are directly dependent on the river as a key input. Thus, most organization's commitment to problem solving is based on altruism rather than mandate. One potential reason the negotiated order did not form was the lack of any meaningful and relevant motivation. In a short-term focus world, working on the Valley is a nice or good thing to do, not a requirement for today's success and survival. Any stakeholder's level of effort is tied to their personal motivation despite the likely detrimental long-term implications. Such is the essence of the tragedy of the commons.

The Role of Referent Organizations in TD

The organizing phase of the TD process is crucial. It is the point when the TS commits to coordinated action. Exactly how that coordination takes place is the responsibility of a referent organization, and the clear implication of CVI case is that changes in TS effectiveness are dependent on an improved method of coordination.

Alsenas and the CCPC initially tried to act as the referent organization. Their planning and development guidelines served part of the regulatory function identified by Trist (1983) and others. It allowed others to do the work of transformation but it could not continue as one because it could not orchestrate the resource allocation and project identification functions. Searching for that additional capacity was the task of the design team.

The results of the CVI case suggest a reciprocal relationship between negotiated order and referent organizations. Trist (1983) and others suggest that the formation of a negotiated order is a complex conceptual process that integrates judgments of reality and judgments of value. "It is most important that the identity of the domain is not mistaken through errors in the appreciative process, otherwise all subsequent social shaping becomes mismatched with what is required to deal with the meta-problem" (Trist, 1983, p. 274). That is, if the negotiated order doesn't exist, is wrong, or flawed in some important way, the coordinated action of the TS to address the problem will be suboptimal. Any referent organization that forms will be handicapped by the flawed negotiated order.

Without a sufficient and intentional process for creating a negotiated order at scale, the necessary context for any kind of a referent organization to emerge and engage effectively does not happen. The design team's conversation and understanding of the valley was a process that effectively generated a negotiated order for them and led to their support for a referent organization – CRVO. But without a parallel process to generate a negotiated order for the TS at large there was no parallel support for CRVO. While the design team started the process of forming a negotiated order, the CRVO was needed to continue it. Instead, the CCPC director and his staff, the OD consultant, and one other design team member began to act as an ad hoc CRVO or referent organization but without the TS-wide mandate and legitimacy. Such an ad hoc referent organization can only support the locally agreed to negotiated orders that accompany any particular project the CCPC staff is aware of or has interactions with.

Suggestions for Practice

To be fair, a tremendous amount of goodwill has been generated, there are a number of people committed to the valley and its restoration, and there are important projects being implemented. The CVI is far from dead. It is not, however, operating as a "regional priority" across counties, municipalities, and businesses. Progress is taking place at a much more fragmented and incremental pace. In addition, the 2008–2009 recession quickly dried up any discretionary resources the stakeholders had to support CVI activity and the voter approved county reorganization in the face of widespread corruption represents an enormous distraction. Finally, several "big" initiatives are competing for attention and resources. Many political leaders and citizens are looking for "home-run" solutions that can dismiss the value of small, coordinated steps. A "wait for the silver bullet" approach prevents action and stymies progress.

However, we do not know nearly enough about how to bring concerted action in support of reversing the tragedy of the commons. The CVI case experience provides us with at least three practice suggestions: work out negotiated order at multiple levels, address funding, and pay attention to interdependency.

In general, the identification and convention phases resulted in a negotiated order and framework that provided a context for making sense of the valley as a whole. However, to be a leverage point for change in a system this complex, the negotiated order must get worked out at multiple levels of the system. An important learning is to recognize that negotiated order serves a different purpose at different levels and with different stakeholders but must get worked out in all facets of the system. While the team did an effective job of defining a negotiated order at the valley level and proposing a constellation of organizations to support and guide work in the valley, what was (and continues to be) missing in the TD process is an accepted negotiated order at all levels of the valley. Any good negotiated order must get translated to the natural subsystems of the valley. The design, principles, and practices did not effectively unbundle the valley in a way that allowed others to acknowledge and accept their role. In other words, they did not articulate the features and benefits of the valley in layman's terms and in a way that was immediately compelling and urgent.

One way this might occur is through one or more large group interventions (Weisbord, 1989; Bunker & Alban, 2006). Large group interventions attempt to bring the "whole system into the room" to increase the understanding and appreciation of the relationships among the stakeholders. Through a sequence of plenary sessions and small-group problem solving debates, stakeholders develop not only a clearer picture of the problem and its solution, but an understanding of their role and a stronger commitment to action. Such a process might help to establish a pervasive negotiated order and momentum for a referent organization.

A second important learning and implication for practice from the CVI case is that the CRVO's birthing was an important non-event. While there was disagreement over how to launch the main referent organization – slow and stealthy versus fast and flashy – both groups agreed that CRVO had to be funded and resourced properly. The launch plan that was developed and presented to the County reflected a large organization with an equally large operating budget. Bigger made it harder to approve funding and in fact bigger was not what was needed. What was really needed was dedicated organizational capacity to continue the convention and organization stages of the TD cycle. TD is a cycle, not a linear process. Perhaps the first part of the organization stage is to conceive of the capacity necessary and then return to the convention stage to support an emerging set of agreements among TS members. Without that recognition, there can be no shared domain, no negotiated order, and no ability to legitimize a referent organization. The second part of the organization phase may need to address funding of the referent organization. Solving the tragedy of the commons requires coordinated action and that requires resources from the stakeholders in the form of time, people, assets, or cash. Individuals and organizations working to develop TSs in service of sustainability need to understand and address this key issue, which leads to our third practical lesson.

Finally, it is unlikely that a stakeholder will commit resources to the restoration of the commons if it is not dependent on the commons for success. Interdependence, both among the stakeholders in a TS and between the TS and the resource must be real and felt. Theory and practice suggest that organizational crises often make the need for a negotiated order more urgent and apparent. A crisis may highlight the extent to which their fates are correlated and motivate a collaborative approach (Boje, 1982). To many, the CVI was an abstraction and that limited its ability to connect to people with urgency on the ground. By modeling the TS itself or how others might address valley rejuvenation, the drivers of action – the interdependencies of the TS members with the resource – were not leveraged. Future collaborations intended to address the tragedy of the commons should ensure that negotiated order and the role of the referent organization incorporates interdependency, otherwise there is little reason to collaborate with others or act differently.

CONCLUSIONS

The CVI case represents one of the first complete descriptions of Cummings (1984) process of TD applied to sustainability issues. The CVI demonstrated the processes of identification and convention, and the organization phase was clearly considered and is still in process. The CCPC and a variety of independent groups have evaluated the effort and are feeding back their observations and recommendations for input into another cycle of activity.

The case also provides additional data about the difficulty of creating a negotiated order. The evidence suggests that a shared, multilevel view of the issue is necessary for TS development. Finally, the case suggests that there may be a strong link between negotiated order and the creation of a referent organization. In the absence of negotiated order at scale and a legitimate referent organization, a small cadre of individuals, with the county planning offices serving as a proxy for the CRVO, act "as if" they are CRVO as different forces play out.

Sustainability is one of the critical meta-problems of our time, and there are an increasing number of people committed to addressing it. By its nature, it will require coordinated action by governments, businesses, NGOs, and individuals. The TD process is a legitimate means to achieve such coordination but the process must be supplemented with concepts and tools that explain and drive successful movement through the phases. Gaining traction within a phase requires an understanding of motivation and commitment that goes beyond homily and altruism. To solve the tragedy of the commons, a critical mass of TS members must be involved and their commitment to problem solving gained through an understanding of negotiated order and their interdependency with others. It is one thing to appreciate that a domain opportunity exists, it is quite another to get resources committed to it that overcome lack of interdependence.

REFERENCES

Ackoff, R. (1981). The art and science of mess management. *Interfaces, 11*(1), 20–26.

Boje, D. (1982). *Towards a theory and praxis of transorganizational development: Stakeholder networks and their habitats.* Working Paper no. 79-6. Behavioral and organizational science study center, Graduate School of Management, University of California at Los Angeles, CA, February.

Boje, D., & Hillon, M. (2008). Transorganizational development. In: T. Cummings (Ed.), *Handbook of organization development* (pp. 651–663). Thousand Oaks, CA: Sage Publications.

Bornstein, D. (2007). *How to change the world: Social entrepreneurs and the power of new ideas.* Oxford, UK: Oxford University Press.

Brown, L. D. (1980). Planned change in underorganized systems. In: T. Cummings (Ed.), *Systems theory for organization development.* Chichester, UK: Wiley.

Bunker, B., & Alban, B. (2006). *The handbook of large group methods: Creating systemic change in organizations and communities.* San Francisco: Jossey-Bass.

Chevalier, M., Bailey, L., & Burns, T. (1974). Toward a framework for large-scale problem management. *Human Relations, 27*(1), 43–69.

Chisholm, R. (1998). *Developing network organizations: Learning from practice and theory.* Reading, MA: Addison-Wesley.

Clarke, N. (2005). Transorganization development for network building. *The Journal of Applied Behavioral Science, 41*(1), 30–47.

Cropper, S., Ebers, M., Huxham, C., & Smith Ring, P. (2008). *The Oxford handbook of interorganizational relations.* Oxford, UK: Oxford University Press.

Cummings, T. (1984). Transorganization development. In: B. Staw & L. Cummings (Eds), *Research in organization behavior* (pp. 367–422). Greenwich, CT: JAI Press.

Daniels, B. (2007). Emerging commons, tragic institutions. *Environmental Law, 37*, 515–571.

Emery, F., & Trist, E. (1973). *Towards a social ecology: Contextual appreciation of the future in the present.* New York: Plenum Press.

Gray, B. (1985). Conditions facilitating interorganizational collaboration. *Human Relations, 38*, 911–936.

Gray, B. (1989). *Collaborating: Finding common ground for multiparty problems.* San Francisco: Jossey-Bass.

Gray, B., & Hay, T. (1986). Political limits to interorganizational consensus and change. *Journal of Applied Behavioral Science, 22*, 95–112.

Gricar, B. (1981). The legitimacy of consultants and stakeholders in interorganizational problems. Paper presented at annual meeting of the Academy of Management, San Diego, CA, August.

Gricar, B. G. (1981). Fostering collaboration among organizations. In: H. Meltzer & W. R. Nord (Eds), *Making organizations human and productive* (pp. 403–420). New York: Wiley.

Harrigan, K., & Newman, W. (1990). Bases of interorganization co-operation: Propensity, power, persistence. *Journal of Management Studies, 27*, 417–434.

Huxham, C. (1993). Collaborative capacity: An intra-organizational perspective on collaborative advantage. *Public Money & Management, 13*(3), 21–28.

Huxham, C. (1996). *Creating collaborative advantage.* London: Sage Publications.

Huxham, C., & Vangen, S. (1996). Working together key themes in the management of relationships between public and non-profit organizations. *The International Journal of Public Sector Management, 9*(7), 5–17.

Huxham, C., & Vangen, S. (2003). Researching organizational practice through action research: Case studies and design choices. *Organizational Research Methods, 6*(3), 383–403.

Katz, D., & Kahn, R. (1978). *The social psychology of organizations.* Hoboken, NJ: Wiley.

Logsdon, J. (1991). Interests and interdependence in the formation of social problem-solving collaborations. *Journal of Applied Behavioral Science, 27*(1), 23–37.

McCann, J. (1983). Design guidelines for social problem-solving interventions. *The Journal of Applied Behavioral Science, 19*(2), 177–189.

Nathan, M., & Mitroff, I. (1991). The use of negotiated order theory as a tool for analysis and development of an inter-organizational field. *Journal of Applied Behavioral Science, 27*(2), 163–180.

Pasquero, J. (1991). Supraorganizational collaboration: The Canadian environmental experiment. *The Journal of Applied Behavioral Science, 27*(1), 38–65.

Pfeffer, J., & Salancik, G. (1978). *The external control of organizations: A resource dependence perspective*. New York: Harper & Row.

Prins, S. (2010). From competition to collaboration critical challenges and dynamics in multiparty collaboration. *The Journal of Applied Behavioral Science, 46*(3), 281–312.

Schruijer, S., & Vansina, L. (2008). Working across organizational boundaries: Understanding and working with intergroup dynamics. In: L. Vansina & M. Vansina-Cobbaert (Eds), *Psychodynamics for consultants and managers* (pp. 390–410). Chichester, UK: Wiley-Blackwell.

Thompson, J. (1967). *Organizations in action*. New York: McGraw-Hill.

Trist, E. (1983). Referent organizations and the development of inter-organizational domains. *Human Relations, 36*(3), 269–285.

Vangen, S., & Huxham, C. (2003). Nurturing collaborative relations: Building trust in interorganizational collaboration. *Journal of Applied Behavioral Science, 39*(1), 5–31.

Vansina, L., Taillieu, T., & Schruijer, S. (1998). Managing multiparty issues: Learning from experience. In: R. Woodman & W. Pasmore (Eds), *Research in organization change and development* (pp. 159–181). Greenwich, CT: JAI Press.

Weick, K. (2001). *Making sense of the organization*. Malden, MA: Blackwell.

Weisbord, M. (1989). *Productive workplaces: Organizing and managing for dignity, meaning and community*. San Francisco: Jossey-Bass.

Williams, T. (1980). The search conference in active adaptive planning. *Journal of Applied Behavioral Science, 16*, 470–483.

Worley, C., Feyerherm, A., & Knudsen, D. (2010). Building a collaboration capability for sustainability: How Gap Inc. is creating and leveraging a strategic asset. *Organizational Dynamics, 39*(4), 325–334.

Zhang, Y., & Huxham, C. (2009). Identity construction and trust building in developing international collaborations. *The Journal of Applied Behavioral Science, 45*(2), 186–211.

CHAPTER 8

ORGANIZING FOR SUSTAINABLE EFFECTIVENESS: REPRISE AND WAY FORWARD

Abraham B. (Rami) Shani and
Susan Albers Mohrman

ABSTRACT

The chapters in this first volume of the book series "Organizing for Sustainable Effectiveness" captured a rich set of cases in which sustainable effectiveness was the central focus. Each chapter illuminated the development of a distinct sustainable system, and had a special focus on reporting theoretically informed and rigorously explored knowledge to guide purposeful design and learning approaches. Collectively the chapters highlighted the processes, organization and design, system regulation, and continuous learning approaches in complex organizational and multiorganizational systems that enabled simultaneous focus on and advancing of economic, social, and ecological outcomes. In this concluding chapter, we capture, via a comparative investigation, some of the learning from the cases about the development of new capabilities, design orientations, and learning mechanisms, and we chart directions for further research and managerial actions.

Organizing for Sustainability
Organizing for Sustainable Effectiveness, Volume 1, 215–237
Copyright © 2011 by Emerald Group Publishing Limited
ISSN: 2045-0605/doi:10.1108/S2045-0605(2011)0000001013

INTRODUCTION

The idea for this book series began when a group of practitioners and academics came together in October 2008, at the University of Southern California for a two-day workshop to share learning and struggles about sustainability. The energy generated was contagious. The people in the room reflected on initiatives, including most recounted in this volume, that were leading to more sustainable outcomes. There was a sense of optimism that with hard work and collaboration organizations can lead the transformation required for sustainable economies, societies, and natural ecologies. We concluded that a large amount of knowledge about sustainability and sustainable development has been published during the past decade and is starting to be applied, including knowledge about the science of sustainability, the content of sustainability initiatives, and increasingly about how to more closely link the economic, environmental, and social purposes and operating logics of the firm. Discussion at the conference gravitated to a thornier task – making this focus fundamental to organizing rather than a set of initiatives.

Despite rich case examples, guidance on how to organize for the triple bottom line is limited. Until recently, the management literature has been curiously silent about this need and focus. Taking a complex adaptive system perspective, we believe that solutions to deal with the stresses on the ecosystems upon which the human species depends will come from hard work and adaptive self-organizing among actors as they develop new understandings about what will enable them to function sustainably through time. Formal political or hierarchical mandates may prod actors to align with the purpose of creating sustainable social systems, but progress is only possible if actors behave fundamentally differently. The urgency to establish more sustainable ways of functioning requires purposeful and accelerated learning and dissemination of knowledge to inform new forms of practice.

The intent of the conference and of this resultant volume is to take stock of and advance theoretical and practical knowledge about organizing for sustainable effectiveness. We set out to build a collaborative community to discover and understand the challenges to and the achievements of practice through the examination of rich case examples, while simultaneously exploring and trying to extend the power of theoretically based academic research to illuminate and contribute to the development of new and more sustainable forms of organization.

It was clear from the presentations at the 2008 conference that the development of new capabilities to address triple bottom line outcomes requires a change in organizational logic and requires new rules of interaction, new organizational, and interorganizational designs, and new ways of learning, leading, and changing organizations. The premise of our collective work is that systems can build on their inherent capabilities to learn and to act collectively in order to adapt. Never has it been more important for academics to aspire to relevance, to work collaboratively with practitioners, and to contribute to the generation of knowledge to support organizational designs and transitions. We propose that by working together to collaboratively explore how to organize for sustainability, academics and practitioners can accelerate knowledge generation and progress.

The broad theoretical underpinnings, purposes, and framing for this volume were laid out in some detail in Chapter 1. We used an adaptive complex systems perspective to frame challenges and approaches to sustainable effectiveness. We argued that complexity is related to global interconnectedness and rapid change that yield organizational, societal, ecological, and economic landscapes that are difficult to predict and navigate, and impossible to control. Individuals, organizations, families, communities, and governments deal with only one certainty: that the actions they take and the decisions they make today must prepare them for an uncertain future. As such, achieving sustainable effectiveness requires agility informed by frameworks of thought and action in which actors see themselves as contributing to, operating within, and dependent on the larger systems of which they are part. Sustainability is an inherently future-oriented concept, and achieving it demands that we take future scenarios into account while acting in the present. Sustainable effectiveness of each actor depends on the overall sustainability of complex ecosystems – of the natural environments, markets, and societies that define the contexts in which we function.

In this final chapter, we reflect on the rich material in this volume and discuss learning about sustainability, sustainable effectiveness, and organizing for sustainable effectiveness – and their implications for theory and practice. It is clear from these case examples that adopting a sustainability orientation and enacting new ways of operating in complex systems is a challenging task, but one with great potential to improve the quality and viability of human systems and long-term business success.

CASE FOCUSES AND THEORETICAL PERSPECTIVES: A SYNOPSIS

The chapters in this volume, as can be seen from Table 1, are case studies of sustainability approaches in diverse industries, regions, and nations. They provide rich empirical data about organizations that are individually or collectively working to build a more sustainable future. The Unilever case captured a 10-year transformation to build corporate social responsibility and sustainable operations into the company's identity and its entire value stream. The Gap Corporation's journey to become more sustainable began with the development of multistakeholder collaborative approaches to improve human rights in its global supply chain, and collaboration for sustainable effectiveness has subsequently been expanded into the core operations of the company. The Skaraborg County sustainability story describes a 10-year journey that built participative learning mechanisms to

Table 1. The Focuses of the Cases.

Chapter	Focus of the Case
2. Unilever	Unilever's 10-year transformation to build corporate responsibility and sustainable operations into its identity and its entire value stream
3. Gap, Inc.	Gap Corporation's journey to become more sustainable that began with the development of collaborative approaches to improve human rights its global supply chain
4. Skaraborg Hospital Group	Skaraborg County's 10-year sustainability journey to achieve interorganizational integration to provide a higher quality of healthcare, greater personnel satisfaction, and a better use of the system's social, economic, and material resources in the West Skaraborg Healthcare System in Sweden
5. Housing Authority	The Cleveland Municipal Housing Authority's gravitation to collaboration as a core methodology to increase the sustainability of the public housing system, and the new forms of leadership that developed
6. Port Of Los Angeles	A complex, multiyear, multisectoral initiative that has fundamentally changed the capabilities of the Port of Los Angeles to address what had previously been treated as environmental and social externalities from the Port's operation
7. Cuyahoga Valley Initiative	The unfolding of the Cuyahoga River Valley Organization – a coordinating organization in Northeast Ohio to achieve synergy among a multitude of hitherto disconnected initiatives to address the sustainability of the region

achieve greater integration of healthcare in multiple organizational systems in order to provide higher quality of healthcare, greater personnel satisfaction, and a better use of the system's social, economic, and material resources. The Cleveland Municipal Housing Authority developed collaboration as a core methodology to increase the sustainability of the public housing system through the involvement of a broad variety of stakeholders, and in so doing saw new forms of leadership develop. The Port of Los Angeles (POLA) has been the hub of a set of complex, ongoing, multiyear, multisectoral initiatives that have fundamentally changed the capacity of the system to address what had previously been treated as environmental and social externalities from the Port's operation. The last case captures the unfolding of the Cuyahoga River Valley Organization (CRVO) – a voluntary coordinating organization that was set up by the Cuyahoga County Planning Commission in Northeast Ohio to try to achieve synergy among the many disparate activities that were underway to try to reverse the waning economic, social, and environmental fortunes of the region.

The diversity of these cases and of the participants in each suggests that achieving sustainable effectiveness requires action by many kinds of actors and stakeholders at many levels of aggregation. Any single agent or actor has limited capacity to address this challenge. As in any complex system, system-level outcomes emerge from the interactions among actors in the system, but are not a simple linear aggregation of the actions and accomplishments of those actors. The six cases in this volume involved large multinational corporations, NGOs, industry collaboratives, value chains, public sector services, community advisory groups, customers, and partnerships between public and private sectors and among diverse yet interdependent regional actors and stakeholders. It is clear that the relationships, coordinated activities, and organizing mechanisms have to be as diverse as the range of participants and the varying domains and scopes of the sustainability challenges that are faced.

Some of the chapters have been written collaboratively by academics and practitioners. Even those written solely by academics build heavily on the perspectives of the case participants, as gleaned from systematic interviews and in some cases from participant observation. The authors delivered faithfully on our request that they view these cases through theoretical lenses that they thought yielded a useful way of understanding and learning from what went on in the case setting. Diverse theoretical perspectives have been employed to examine and learn from the variety of case settings.

Table 2 captures the theoretical lenses and key organizing concepts that the authors used in each chapter. These include complex adaptive systems

Table 2.   Key Theoretical Perspectives and Analytical Concepts.

	Key Theoretical Perspective	Key Analytical Concepts
Unilever	System transformation, corporate identity, and complex adaptive systems	• Sustainability and corporate social responsibility • Developmental stages of corporate responsibility • Top-down versus communal leadership • "Game changing" change • Employee and customer engagement • Mission and identity
Gap, Inc.	Institutionalization theory and multilevel collaboration	• Institutionalization phases and processes • Human rights • Sustainability and the global supply chain • Organizing and institutionalizing sustainability • Indicators of institutionalization • Levers for institutionalization of sustainability
Skaraborg Hospital Group	Participation theory, learning mechanisms, and multiorganizational transformation	• Sustainable healthcare system • Development coalition management • Democratic dialogue conference • Transformation, planned, and emergent change • Learning mechanisms: structural, procedural, and cognitive. Learning mechanism tapestry
Housing Authority	Leadership theory and collaboration methodology	• Public sector organization • Emergent partnership • Complexity of collaborative engagement • Leadership and sustainability • Complexity leadership, adaptive leadership, and generative leadership
Port of Los Angeles	Systems theory and learning theory	• Sustainable organizational culture and ecology • Learning organization and learning culture • Action learning and complex forcefield • Collaborative generation of knowledge and tools • Sustainability assessment

Table 2. (*Continued*)

	Key Theoretical Perspective	Key Analytical Concepts
Cuyahoga Valley Initiative	Trans-organizational development theory and multistakeholder sustainability network	• Trans-organization development planned change phases and process • Collaboration and multistakeholder collaboration network • Negotiated order • Referent organization

theory, which is a broad framing theory that provides a perspective on the multiple levels, the variety of actors and subsystems, and the range of simultaneous dynamics that must be addressed. Theories of leadership, change, learning, institutionalization, participation, and interorganizational collaboration are employed, and provide a sample of the various dynamics that may be simultaneously in operation and that may provide levers and intervention points to change the system and deal with the complexity.

Table 2 also lists key concepts that are explored in each chapter and in so doing shows the broad range of phenomena that can be intertwined with a focus on becoming sustainably effective. The domains of focus include environmental sustainability, human rights, corporate social responsibility, developmental stages of corporate responsibility, planned and emergent change, democratic dialogues, collaboration, sustainable supply chains and a sustainable healthcare system, culture, adaptive leadership and development coalitions, learning mechanisms, and design for sustainability – a laundry list to be sure, but also an indication of the scope of the problems that are inherent in transitioning to a sustainable way of operating.

The breadth of the theoretical perspectives and analytical concepts that were included in this volume suggest that many perspectives can and indeed are needed to shed insight on the complex nature of sustainability, sustainable development, and sustainable effectiveness. These contribute to the broader learning discourse through which practical organizing solutions are designed and research-based guidance is provided. Through these multiple perspectives, we come to appreciate not only the diversity of the phenomena being examined but also the complexity of the dynamics in these social systems that are striving for greater sustainability. Ideally, testing theory in the context of the cases also provides insight about where our theories must expand and evolve if we are to provide knowledge relevant to the problem at hand.

WHAT WE HAVE LEARNED: PERSPECTIVE
OF THEORY AND PRACTICE

Sustainability is by definition a future-oriented, system-level concept. An actor in the system cannot be sustainably effective if the system of which it is a part is not sustainable through time. We are operating in a global economy in which our theories and practices have been established to fit a competitive market place – one in which single entities are taught how to survive at the expense of others, and to exploit knowledge and resources for competitive advantage. Particularly in the past decades, effectiveness has come to be defined primarily and in many people's minds solely by short-term economic outcomes. Many organizations work hard to make sure that they prosper by pushing the "externalities" off to others – the costs of pollution and toxicity, the costs of the infrastructure upon which they depend, the social costs of moving jobs and closing plants. Given this context, it is no wonder that making a transition to focus on sustainable triple bottom line effectiveness – to expand focus beyond achieving a string of positive quarterly earnings – is a tremendously difficult and long journey, and that the knowledge base is sparse.

In this series of cases, we have focused on systems where at least some of the participants have come to understand the shortsightedness of current practice, and to accept it as their responsibility to take action to achieve a new trajectory that heads to greater sustainability both for their own organization and for the larger system of which it is a part. Yet all feel they are at the beginning of the journey, that progress is fragile, and that they have at best picked the low hanging fruit. And all feel that there is much to be learned, invented, and designed in order to continue to make progress and to embed sustainable functioning in all that they do.

We have learned from these cases that humanity's capability for intentional, purpose-related activity does indeed provide the possibility that new patterns of interaction can be purposefully established and new outcomes can be achieved. Gap, Inc., for example, is working with plants, NGOs, and other industry members, including competitors, to achieve basic human rights for workers in garment factories in Asia (Chap. 3). A remarkable collection of organizations with little to individually gain have voluntarily come together with the POLA to deal with the problems of pollution, toxicity, and the related health problems in a densely populated area of Los Angeles. They have made and continue to make significant measurable progress and this collaboration has catalyzed innovative approaches that are now being used far beyond POLA (Chap. 6). Cases such as these make us realize that it is possible to focus on new purposes that have to do with the system beyond your own boundaries – with maintaining a healthy context in which to operate. By reading about these efforts, we start to get a handle on the complexity of these initiatives and the conditions and organizing approaches that have contributed to success in the first steps of this journey to sustainable effectiveness.

There is not a common definition of sustainability in use in these cases, nor often even within a company or among the organizations in collaborative initiatives. Some companies look at what they are doing through the lens of corporate responsibility or social responsibility, while others focus squarely on environmental sustainability and counteracting the impact of greenhouse gas emission. Yet most have come over time to focus on the full triple bottom line. The genesis of the sustainability focus also differs. It may have been triggered by an event, such as a well-publicized human rights violation, an NGO-led boycott of a company's products, or a new regulation or governmental mandate that can't be achieved through business as usual. Some companies come from a core values perspective, accepting responsibility for working to ensure that we do not deplete the resources required by subsequent generations. Others are pragmatic. They have come to understand that we are entering an era of shortage of available resources and growth in demand, and that there are business imperatives and opportunities associated with that reality. Despite this variation in definition, focus, and genesis of concern, we see some common elements in how they are going about trying to become sustainably effective. These are listed and described below.

Change in Fundamental Understandings and Purpose

Seeing one's fate as deeply intertwined with the health and well-being of the social and natural environmental contexts requires a shift in understanding that can lead to a shift in purpose. Little is known about how to change purpose in social systems. Unilever's journey is described in Chapter 2. Managers within Unilever came to the realization that the company's products and operations have an impact on the health of consumers and on the availability of natural resources such as seafood and palm trees. This made apparent the tight dependency of Unilever's success on its social and natural environments. The company combined several catalyzing approaches that led to a shift in orientation of many managers and employees: (1) the formulation of a new mission stated as contributing to the vitality of its consumers, communities, and the natural environment; (2) the direct developmental exposure of large numbers of managers to the problems and realities of the forests and oceans and communities upon which the company depends; and (3) widespread collective reflection on the purpose of the firm and how it could best embed the new mission in its core operating processes of building brands, developing, manufacturing, and delivering products to consumers.

The Cleveland Metropolitan Housing Authority (CMHA) leadership team (Chap. 5) chose to respond to the anticipation of an inevitable decline of public funding for low-cost housing by creating a sense of urgency around delivering greater value to society with the resources available to them – going beyond the provision of safe, clean, and functional housing to find ways to stretch resources to contribute to the development of the educational, work skills, citizenship, and leadership capabilities of residents. The introduction of energy-efficient changes to the housing complexes was an opportunity to get involvement and understanding among staff and residents of the need to consume fewer resources and yield more value in everything that they did. This broadening of purpose and alteration in mental models became pervasive and led to an altered portfolio of activities and benefits and contribution by residents.

Change in Boundaries of the Organization

Every case example involved partnerships or even more complex multi-stakeholder collaborations with other entities. This reflects the notion grounded in ecology studies that when ecosystems become stressed their various elements start developing synergistic and symbiotic relationships in order to survive (Astley, 1985). In the sustainability cases, these are not transactional relationships such as in vendor supplier situations, but rather they involve laterally coordinated activity to accomplish outcomes that go beyond the interests of the two parties. Changes in the way organizations and populations relate to one another may emerge as early movers try out new approaches. For example, the chemical industry was among the first where several companies in the industry joined together to establish sustainability standards as a result of NGO pressures and public pressure (Hoffman, 1999, 2010). Others have learned from that industry that such an approach can foster success throughout the ecosystem, and in the past decade we have seen many examples of industry collaboratives and partnerships with NGOs to address thorny issues where collaboration is necessary for success but interests are in conflict and emotions are high.

CMHA learned the power of partnerships through trial and error, having had one unsuccessful energy efficiency program and then deciding to take a partnership approach to working with Siemens in order to achieve and ensure that both the technical and social aspects of energy efficiency were addressed and to achieve lasting impact. CMHA then applied the partnership approach to other initiatives aimed at enhancing the outcomes of the housing authority for its many stakeholders.

In the first five cases in the book, we see many examples of partnership where, by identifying a larger societal focus, the participating organizations simultaneously contribute to their own valued outcomes as well as those of their partners and the larger society. As can be learned from the CRVO case (Chap. 7), the success of such complex collaborations is hardly guaranteed, even with extensive up-front work to try to build agreement about purpose and desired outcomes. Voluntary, noncontractual partnerships are becoming increasingly prevalent as organizations strive to promote sustainability. Although transorganizational theory provides some leverage on understanding the conditions for success, Worley points out in the CRVO case that we are far from understanding the features of such collaboration that lead to successful outcomes.

Combining Planned and Emergent Change

Change in complex systems cannot be mandated from the top but rather relies on the self-organizing activities of actors within. Such self-organization is more likely to occur when the system's components are self-generative, when knowledge flows between them, resulting in greater capability and the creation of new knowledge, and when there is a "requisite variety" of knowledge (Ashby, 1956, p. 64) to address the problems of interest (Monge & Contractor, 2003). These conditions were carefully created by the design of the learning mechanisms tapestry in the Skaraborg Health System (Chap. 4), where diverse networks set up for innovation and improvement were connected for knowledge sharing to the performing units of the organization in order to promote implementable innovation and improvement.

Any transition to become a more sustainably effective system can only be partially planned. Unilever's CEO, Patrick Cescau, got input from the organization and along with the Board of Directors gave legitimacy to the vitality mission as a core element of Unilever's strategy. A tremendous amount of self-organized activity within the organization was catalyzed, sending the system out of equilibrium, and leading to even more change from within (Mirvis & Manga, 2010). Very little of the sustainability change in the corporation has been centrally planned and implemented. Rather, it has relied on spontaneous energies and initiatives from employees and self-organization in business units and teams.

As at Unilever, both planned change and emergent change were in operation in all the cases. In Skaraborg, for example, the improvement networks and the multistakeholder democratic dialogue sessions were designed by the management team, which was itself an informal council of the leaders of three different organizations. The activities of the networks then took on a life of their own, with each involving various working groups dispersed throughout the three organizations. In the POLA (Chap. 6), formal advisory groups and working groups were set up to carry out projects and yield solutions. In addition, an informal multicompany learning network was convened that operated largely through self-forming interest groups that carved out projects of interest to a subset of the members of the network. The POLA chapter discusses the complementarity of these two ways of operating.

There is a very large literature on planned change, and a growing literature that looks at emergent change. Very little research has focused on the interplay between the two approaches, nor considered how to intentionally intervene in a system to set in play dynamics that will change the organization in a less controlled but potentially more fundamental and sustainable manner than change planned and led from the top.

Participation

A key indicator of a company's social sustainability is its impact on its own employees. Sustainable effectiveness demands a highly involving, high-performance workplace (Russo, 2010; Schroeder & Robinson, 2010) in which employees are treated as stakeholders of the corporation and engaged in socially responsible jobs (Googins, Mirvis, & Rochlin, 2007). If this were not the case, it would be very difficult for a company to have credibility in an espoused purpose of enhancing and not depleting societal and environmental resources.

Studies of efforts in the 1980s and 1990s to establish high-involvement/ high-performance work systems based on the broad distribution of resources, responsibility, and benefits found that these systems were a departure from the engrained assumptions of hierarchical control and work designs based on narrow job descriptions and unskilled workers. These transitions relied heavily on people throughout the organization clearly defining new workplace values and learning a new way to operate. Highly participative processes were used to put in place the design features to support these values (Mohrman & Cummings, 1989; Pasmore, 1988). Strong leaders can create a context with clear strategies, mission, and values, but putting in place the work systems to make these a reality can only occur through widespread self-organization (Mohrman, 1998) and learning. This does not happen if the organization does not foster participation and influence throughout the organization.

Both the Skaraborg Health Care System (Chap. 4) and Unilever (Chap. 2) had a very participative and open process for generating and implementing ideas to accomplish the sustainability strategy. In the case of Skaraborg, participation was the fundamental cornerstone of the transition, and the external researchers brought a deep grounding in the design of participative mechanisms. Two other cases, Gap, Inc. (Chap. 3) and the POLA (Chap. 6), started out with initiatives that relied heavily on cross-organizational action, and only now in the second stage of their transition are they focusing on broader participation throughout the organization. The sense in both cases was that the leaders felt they would not be able to maintain progress and focus if people throughout the organization did not start operating in a new and more highly involving and connected manner.

New Leadership Behavior

These cases point out three fundamental changes in leadership for sustainable effectiveness. First, leaders in these transitions have to become facile and comfortable enabling rather than controlling. Second, leadership extends beyond the bounds of the organization and is shared. Third, leadership can become disassociated from formal managerial roles in the organization, and may be carried out by people throughout the organization and beyond, and in initiatives and actions where leaders step up to the plate with no particular hierarchical authority. These new approaches fit with the increasing complexity in the world and with the inability to fully plan and control, given the speed of change and amount of uncertainty inherent in the problems that organizations are trying to solve.

The changes in leadership are captured by Ann Feyerherm and Sally Breyley Parker in the CMHA case (Chap. 5), and fit nicely with the complexity leadership theory (Uhl-Bien, Marion, & McKelvey, 2007; Uhl-Bien & Marion, 2008) that they apply in analyzing the case. This theory does not suggest that administrative and managerial control of the ongoing work processes of the organization go away. Rather, all organizations must find a way to articulate the needs of the system for predictable and effective performance with its needs to innovate, adapt to changes in its environment, and take advantage of opportunities. Innovation, environmental adaptation, and opportunities can be strategically encouraged from the top, but an organizational transformation demands such behavior throughout the organization. Achieving sustainable effectiveness is only possible if people throughout the organization are following a new meta-rule: do your work in ways that contribute to the sustainable effectiveness of the organization. This meta-rule leads to a critical mass of behavior changes that lead to new performance capabilities in the organization. Mirvis, in describing the Unilever case (Chap. 2), calls this catalytic leadership. The leader takes actions that catalyze the energies and self-organizing capacity of the system.

Learning

The need for learning is a theme that runs through all the cases, and we see many mechanisms used for this purpose. CRVO (Chap. 7) conducted workshops. Unilever (Chap. 2) sent managers on field trips to learn about the impact of the company on society and the environment. CMHA (Chap. 5) brought in experts from outside to work with staff and residents and expand their knowledge as part of on-going projects. Gap Inc. (Chap. 3) worked with NGOs to set up educational systems in the rural communities where their supplier plants functioned. POLA (Chap. 7) used multi-stakeholder learning networks. Skaraborg (Chap. 4) held workshops and brought in researchers who provided facilitation and expertise. Establishing a tapestry of learning mechanisms (Docherty & Shani, 2008) was the primary path to participation in the Skaraborg case, and can be considered its major strategy for developing sustainable effectiveness. Its foundational assumption is that sustainable effectiveness depends on the self-organizing and renewal capabilities that are built into the way the organization functions.

Sustainability efforts emerge over time and constitute a new capability, enabling the system to continually generate enhanced outcomes and more sustainable effectiveness. Adaptation to continually changing social, economic, and environmental contexts will be a major challenge for organizations in the future, and being able to learn and rapidly adopt new approaches demands an embedded learning capability. The development of this new capability, from a design perspective, requires the systematic exploration of different types and tapestries of learning mechanisms and decisions about the most appropriate tapestry that is likely to yield the desired sustainability outcomes.

Institutionalization

We do not know whether the changes described in these cases will be sustained. The important issue of institutionalization of change is explicitly examined by Chris Worley as he chronicles Gap Inc.'s journey (Chap. 3) and finds indications that the multistakeholder collaborative approach first used to improve human rights in the plants is now being built into the structure of the organization and being employed at other places along the value stream. He argues collaboration is becoming a capability of the organization. Such capabilities as collaboration, collective learning, knowledge generation, value stream integration, and social change have been enhanced in many of the organizations in these cases.

New roles and structures, such as Community Advisory Boards, Development Coalitions, Industry Consortia, and Sustainability leadership roles have been established to enable cross-organizational partnering or to govern and lead a company's transition. Gap, Inc. has restructured to elevate and better integrate Sustainability and Corporate Responsibility with the other functions of the organization. Corporate Responsibility, for example, is now organizationally linked to Talent Management and has become a core element of developing managers in the company. In Skaraborg (Chap. 4), the Development Coalition Management Team continues to function and to set up teams to work aggressively to integrate healthcare in the region despite the fact that the Swedish initiative to integrate healthcare has formally ended. It continues to examine the balanced scorecard for the region even though the three parts of the system are different organizations with different formal governance systems. Yet it is concerned about overload, as employees increasingly are finding it difficult to sustain the level of effort required to do their core jobs and be part of improvement projects.

What is to keep the flurry of initiatives and announced transitions that have emerged in the past decade from atrophying and sustainability from becoming last decade's concern? Will enough fundamental change occur to feel confident that new ways of thinking and acting have been institutionalized, and that organizations have moved from an initiative stage to a period when organizing and managing for sustainable effectiveness is a core capability? Will the learning and experimentation needed to generate solutions as humanity continues to face a burgeoning global population and economy continue?

We need to reach a future where the new meta-rule that guides actions and decisions is "operate in a sustainable manner." It is imperative that we understand what is required for institutionalization of attention to the triple bottom line. In future research, we need to keep our eye on the approaches that are being used to embed this in the logics and designs of organizations.

DIRECTIONS FOR FUTURE RESEARCH AND PRACTICE

Capturing the learning from the cases sets the stage for a discussion about direction for future research and practice about organizing for sustainable effectiveness. Owing to the emergent nature of the domain, its broad scope and systemic nature, and the variability inherent in the evolution of new practices in any ecosystem, we do not strive to provide a comprehensive path. Our objective is to identify a few areas that we view as critical for both research and practice.

Interdisciplinary Research Orientation

The complexity of sustainability and sustainable effectiveness, coupled with the realization that current theoretical knowledge needs to be revisited and expanded, point to the need for interdisciplinary, multiactor, and multilevel perspectives. One theoretical perspective is insufficient to guide research and practice. Understanding sustainability and the transition to a more sustainable way of operating requires both hard science and social scientific perspectives. The changes that are emerging as the agents in our complex systems struggle to adapt are the application of scientific and engineering knowledge and the reconfiguration of social systems to repurpose them toward social and environmental outcomes. Evolutionary and network approaches to understanding organizations are very helpful in dealing with such a domain. Within complex systems, a myriad of complex dynamics influence the behavior of actors. Thus, we must examine the system from many theoretical perspectives, often simultaneously. For example, examining the CMHA case in Chapter 5 through the lenses of leadership theory and partnership and alliance theories provided a more robust understanding of how the system was becoming more sustainable than would have been possible with only one lens.

Disciplines tend to develop as distinct communities of practice and to develop theories and knowledge-based ways of thinking that become isolated from one another (Daft & Lewin, 2008). They may advocate specific levels of analysis and tend to develop distinct approaches to inquiry, languages, and problem-statements that are not complementary to each other. Our cases show that when continuous dialogue between researchers from different disciplines takes place over time as the research projects get formulated, carried out, and analyzed, a true interdisciplinary perspective can emerge. In the Skaraborg healthcare case (Chap. 4), for example, the engineering-based six sigma approach that views organizations as a set of processes, the balanced scorecard approach that has its roots in management control theory, and participation approaches based on the field of organizational development were equally important contributors to system renewal, and are equally important in teasing out the dynamics when trying to learn from the case. While no one of those theoretically based action models was sufficient to move the system, the combination was powerful. From this, we can learn a lot about the limits and boundaries of various theoretical perspectives.

Achieving an interdisciplinary perspective requires a major commitment by all the parties involved to learn enough about each other's perspectives to find the theoretical and empirical intersection, to develop ways to talk across their diverse thought worlds and languages, and to work through methodological, intellectual, and interpersonal tension. Such integration is facilitated by the desire to solve a common problem that cannot be fully understood, let alone solved, through one theoretical lens that artificially narrows the focus on inquiry (Van de Ven & Johnson, 2006; Mohrman & Wagner, 2008).

It is clear that acceleration of learning about sustainable effectiveness will require such interdisciplinary alliances, just as it requires multistakeholder, cross-functional and interorganizational collaboration, and coordinated practice. In this area, it would behoove us to study the phenomenon of interdisciplinary collaboration to generate knowledge that is useful in solving problems, even as we study collaboration across different actors to change practice.

Framing Research Across Actors, Cultures, Nations, and Governments

Patterns of activities that impact sustainability are embedded in different levels, actors, systems, culture, and regions. This complexity is magnified with the view of sustainability as a synergistic triple bottom line of environment, economic, and social outcomes. This is the complexity faced every day by organizations as they strive to be successful, and even more so as they chart new directions in the quest for sustainable effectiveness. If researchers are to generate knowledge relevant to this journey, we can ill afford to ignore this complexity in favor of narrow focuses with tested research methodologies. The complex context suggests the need to apply context based and longitudinal scientific frameworks and methods (Pettigrew, Woodman, & Cameron, 2001). We learn much more about the approaches used in the cases reported in this book by understanding the contexts in which they are applied than we could if we took them out of context and only looked at relationships between arbitrary operationalizations of constructs and measurements of phenomena and outcomes. By considering the dynamics of the context that operate on the actors we are studying, we learn the limits and boundaries of our theories and how they themselves are embedded in complex systems contexts. Without understanding of context, for example, it would be hard to understand why the learning and collaboration approaches used in the POLA (Chap. 6) and in the CRVO (Chap. 7) resulted in the first case in huge progress and redirection of an extremely loosely coupled system of stakeholders who came together in temporary systems, while the latter found it much more difficult to catalyze coordinated activity.

We advocate that research on sustainability and sustainable effectiveness should explore the contexts, content, and processes of sustainability, examining them at multiple levels of analysis, and depicting the interconnecting dynamics over time (Docherty, Kira, & Shani, 2009). Additionally, we believe it is important to continue to refine our capabilities to do theory-based and multiple theory-based research in complex systems. The combination of the chosen levels of context, the processes, and the interaction field brought into theoretically guided analyses is likely to generate new insights into the phenomenon of sustainability and new theoretical advances in general.

Actionable Knowledge Creation and Collaborative Research Orientation

Developing actionable knowledge is imperative when it comes to the area of sustainability and sustainable effectiveness. Actionable knowledge is knowledge that can simultaneously serve the needs of science and of social systems (Argyris, 2003). This relates to the notion of useful research – knowledge that advances theory and practice, and that is used by organizations (Lawler et al., 1985, 1999; Mohrman & Lawler, 2011) – and to the concept of engaged research to address real problems that are faced in our world (Van de Ven & Johnson, 2006; Van de Ven, 2007). The issues of sustainability are of such critical social, economic, and ecological importance that we believe that the development of actionable knowledge must be the sustainability research agenda, and relevant actors must increasingly be brought in to participate in the research process to enhance the likelihood of generation of problem relevant knowledge and of implementation.

We began this project with the notion that because the organizational aspects of achieving sustainable effectiveness constitute a relatively new domain of practice and of scientific investigation, collaborative research in the form of rich, theory-driven case studies of companies and systems with considerable experience in this area would be a good place to start to generate the desired actionable knowledge. Collaborative research is: "an effort by two or more parties, at least one of whom is a member of an organization or system under study and at least one of whom is an external researcher, to work together in learning about how the behavior of managers, management methods, or organizational arrangements affect outcomes in the system or systems under study, using methods that are scientifically based and intended to reduce the likelihood of drawing false conclusions from the data collected, with the intent of both im-proving performance of the system and adding to the broader body of knowledge in the field of management" (Pasmore, Woodman, & Simmons, 2008, p. 20).

Creating rich case studies of complex social action is an intrusive process that depends on the willingness of the participants in the setting to expose their actions, strategies, and outcomes to scrutiny and to engage in reflection. At the heart of this collaborative research is "joint inquiry" in the pursuit of answers to questions of mutual interest through dialogue, experimentation, the review of knowledge, or other means (Shani, Mohrman, Pasmore, Stymne, & Adler, 2008). Practitioners engage in the inquiry in order to get a better understanding of a certain issue or phenomenon by means of input of scientifically valid knowledge from researchers. Similarly, scientists engage in the inquiry in order to get a better understanding of a certain issue or phenomenon by combining their theoretically based knowledge with the knowledge of practice. If two parties don't share a fundamental interest in learning, there can be no collaborative research.

Although this volume is centered around rich case studies, collaborative research can use any methodology. We anticipate that as more is learned about sustainable ways of organizing, comparative case studies, theory testing research, action research, and evaluation research will become common. If new forms of organizing become prevalent, many important new theoretical and practical avenues of investigation should become evident. We believe this is an ideal domain in which to experiment with and learn about new forms of knowledge generating collaborations that lead to actionable knowledge.

The Measurement Challenge

We have argued in this manuscript that achieving sustainable effectiveness requires agility informed by frameworks of thought and action in which actors see themselves as contributing to, operating within, and dependent on the larger systems of which they are part. Sustainable effectiveness of each actor depends on the overall sustainability of complex ecosystems – of the natural environments, markets, and societies that define the contexts in which we function. Systems need feedback about outcomes and process in order to regulate themselves in their quest to achieve their purposes. A key to sustainable effectiveness is measurement that includes economic/performance, environmental, and social indicators. Given variation in context, substance, and purpose, the indicators for each system and each actor are likely to vary.

The importance of measurement became clear in a number of the cases. In the Skaraborg case (Chap. 4), the articulation of key performance indicators that constituted the balanced scorecard embedded the assessment of hitherto abstract concepts of improvement and development in specific measurement terms that allowed the system to see its progress against its valued outcomes. In the POLA case (Chap. 7), measurable outcomes of emissions and health status mandated by the Mayor of Los Angeles served as the target for a whole series of multistakeholder activities, including the development of measurement systems for the environmental footprint of the shipping industry. Sustainability initiatives are yielding new measurement schema suited to nonfinancial outcomes. These measurement systems become part of the logic of the organization and impact the way people think and make decisions, and how they monitor progress against purpose. We are at the front end, particularly of measures of social sustainability (Cerf & Savage, 2009), and are just beginning to conceptualize how to deal with three simultaneous outcomes. Further research into the measurement of sustainable effectiveness and how they are best used by organizations to advance sustainability of the organization and its context will help accelerate progress in this area.

CONCLUSION

This first volume of "Organizing for Sustainable Effectiveness" set out to capture current thinking and practice as viewed by scholars and practitioners. It shares insights about the organizing imperatives associated with achieving sustainable effectiveness. The complex adaptive system perspective was used as a broad theoretical perspective to frame the context and domain in which organizations are pursuing sustainable effectiveness. The different authors brought various theoretical lenses to bear in examining the systems that they have studied. Each of these lenses detects important elements of the transition to sustainable effectiveness. And each finds areas where our knowledge is lacking and more investigation will be useful.

In this final chapter, we have highlighted some of the cross-case patterns and learning. By examining outliers – systems that are experimenting and learning – our intent has been to yield actionable knowledge. We have purposefully focused on organizing challenges, based on our belief that sustainably effective organizations will use new approaches to organize their resources and connect to their contexts. This approach and focus will continue in future volumes, as we expand the network of scholars and practitioners in order to further understand and better address the complex problems that are threatening businesses, humanity, and the earth.

REFERENCES

Argyris, C. (2003). Actionable knowledge. In: T. Tsoukas & C. Knudsen (Eds), *The Oxford handbook of organization theory* (pp. 423–452). Oxford: Oxford University Press.

Ashby, W. R. (1956). *An introduction to cybernetics*. New York: Wiley.

Astley, W. G. (1985). The two ecologies: Population and community perspectives on organizational evolution. *Administrative Science Quarterly, 30*, 224–241.

Cerf, D., & Savage, A. (2009). Financial management to support sustainability. In: P. Docherty, M. Kira & A. B. Shani (Eds), *Creating sustainable work systems* (pp. 147–164). London: Routledge.

Daft, R. L., & Lewin, A. Y. (2008). Perspective – Rigor and relevance in organization studies: Idea migration and academic journal evolution. *Organization Science, 19*(1), 177–183.

Docherty, P., Kira, M., & Shani, A. B. (Eds). (2009). *Creating sustainable work systems*. New York: Routledge.

Docherty, P., & Shani, A. B. (2008). Learning mechanisms as means and ends in collaborative management research. In: A. B. Shani, S. A. Mohrman, W. A. Pasmore, B. A. Stymne & N. Adler (Eds), *Handbook of collaborative management research* (pp. 163–182). Thousand Oaks, CA: Sage.

Googins, B. K., Mirvis, P. H., & Rochlin, S. A. (2007). *Beyond good company: Next generation corporate citizenship*. New York: Palgrave MacMillan.

Hoffman, A. J. (1999). Institutional evolution and change: Environmentalism and the U.S. chemical industry. *Academy of Management Journal, 42*(4), 351–371.

Hoffman, A. J. (2010). Climate change as a cultural and behavioral issue: Addressing barriers and implementing solutions. *Organizational Dynamics, 39*(4), 295–305.

Lawler, E. E., III., Mohrman, A. M., Jr., Mohrman, S. A., Ledford, G. E., Jr., Cummings, T. G., & Associates. (1985). *Doing research that is useful for theory and practice*. San Francisco: Jossey-Bass.

Lawler, E. E., III., Mohrman, A. M., Jr., Mohrman, S. A., Ledford, G. E., Jr., Cummings, T. G., & Associates. (1999). *Doing research that is useful for theory and practice*. San Francisco: Jossey-Bass.

Mirvis, P. H., & Manga, J. (2010). Integrating corporate citizenship: Leading from the middle. In: N. Craig Smith, C. B. Bhattacharya, D. Vogel & D. Levine (Eds), *Global challenges in responsible business* (pp. 78–106). Cambridge, UK: Cambridge University Press.

Mohrman, S. A. (1998). Top management viewed from below: A learning perspective on transformation. In: J. A. Conger, G. M. Spreitzer & E. E. Lawler (Eds), *The leader's change handbook: An essential guide to setting direction and taking action* (pp. 271–300). San Francisco: Jossey-Bass.

Mohrman, S. A., & Cummings, T. G. (1989). *Self-designing organizations: Learning how to create high performance*. Reading, MA: Addison-Wesley.

Mohrman, S. A., & Lawler, E. E., III. (2011). Research for theory and practice: Framing the challenge. In: S. A. Mohrman & E. E. Lawler, III (Eds), *Useful research: Advancing theory and practice* (pp. 9–35). San Francisco: Berrett-Koehler.

Mohrman, S. A., & Wagner, C. (2008). *The dynamics of knowledge creation: Phase one assessment of the role and contribution of the department of energy's nanoscale science research centers*. Submitted to the U.S. Department of Energy/Office of Science through Contract No. DE-AC02-04ER30321, September, 2008.

Monge, P. R., & Contractor, N. S. (2003). *Theories of communication networks.* Oxford, UK: Oxford University Press.

Pasmore, W. A. (1988). *Designing effective organizations: The socio-technical systems perspective.* New York: Wiley.

Pasmore, W. A., Woodman, R. W., & Simmons, A. L. (2008). Towards a more rigorous, reflective and relevant science of collaborative management research. In: A. B. Shani, S. A. Mohrman, W. A. Pasmore, B. A. Stymne & N. Adler (Eds), *Handbook of collaborative management research* (pp. 567–582). Thousand Oaks, CA: Sage.

Pettigrew, A. M., Woodman, R. W., & Cameron, K. S. (2001). Studying organizational change and development: Challenges for future research. *Academy of Management Journal, 44,* 697–713.

Russo, M. V. (2010). *Companies on a mission: Entrepreneurial strategies for growing sustainably, responsibly, and profitably.* Stanford, CA: Stanford Business Books.

Schroeder, D. E., & Robinson, A. G. (2010). Creating sustainable competitive advantage through green excellence. *Organization Dynamics, 39*(4), 345–352.

Shani, A. B., Mohrman, S. A., Pasmore, W. A., Stymne, B., & Adler, N. (Eds). (2008). *Handbook of collaborative management research.* Thousand Oaks, CA: Sage.

Uhl-Bien, M., & Marion, R. (2008). *Complexity leadership.* Charlotte, NC: Information Age Publishing.

Uhl-Bien, M., Marion, R., & McKelvey, B. (2007). Complexity leadership theory: Shifting leadership from the industrial age to the knowledge era. *The Leadership Quarterly, 18,* 298–318.

Van de Ven, A. H. (2007). *Engaged scholarship: A guide for organizational and social research.* Oxford, UK: Oxford University Press.

Van de Ven, A. H., & Johnson, P. E. (2006). Knowledge for theory and practice. *Academy of Management Review, 31,* 802–821.

ABOUT THE CONTRIBUTORS

Hilary Bradbury-Huang is professor in the Management Division of Oregon Health & Science University (OHSU). Her research, scholarly activism, and teaching focus on the human and organizational dimensions of creating healthy communities. At OHSU she teaches in the healthcare MBA and physician leadership development programs. She also develops the action research approach to community based participatory research for health.

Hilary is editor-in-chief of *Action Research Journal*. She co-edited the best-selling *Handbook of Action Research* (Sage, 2001, 2008) with Peter Reason. Her journal articles have appeared in *Leadership Quarterly, Organization Science, Sloan Management Review*, and the *Journal of Management Inquiry*, among others. Previously Hilary was research associate professor at University of Southern California and director of Sustainable Business Research at the Center for Sustainable Cities. Before that she was associate professor of organizational behavior at Case Western Reserve University (during which time the department was ranked by *the Financial Times* as the No. 1 Organization Behavior department in the world). Hilary's current scholarship focuses on executive leadership in a context of complex stakeholder demands. Her most recent course development for MBA students is a course on the science and practice of mindfulness for healthcare management. She lives with her family in Portland, OR.

Peter Docherty is professor in organizational and quality development at the Division of Quality Sciences and the Centre for Healthcare Improvement at the Chalmers University of Technology in Gothenburg, Sweden. He received his Ph.D. in psychology from London University (UK) in 1971 and his D.Sc. in business administration from the Stockholm School of Economics in 1976. His main research interests concern individual, collective, and organizational learning and the management and development of sustainable organizations. Recent edited and co-authored works are *Creating Sustainable Work Systems* (2002, 2009), *Learning by Design – Building Sustainable Organizations* (2003), *Home and Away: Learning in and Learning from Organizational Networks in Europe* (2004), and *Productive Reflection at Work: Learning for Changing Organizations* (2006).

Ann E. Feyerherm is the chair of the Applied Behavior Science and Organization Theory and Management Department. Before earning her doctorate, Dr. Feyerherm spent 11 years as a manager of organization development at Procter & Gamble, where she was involved in employee relations, organization design, and corporate downsizing. As a consultant, she has worked with Healthways, Honeywell, Monsanto, Frito-Lay, Two Chefs on a Roll and Boeing on projects such as improving multifunctional teams, creating learning organizations, negotiating effectively, leadership development, and managing change. Dr. Feyerherm conducted research on the role of leadership in negotiating regulatory policy. She is particularly interested in mediation and negotiation of environmental issues and in interorganizational collaboration across government, business, and environmental communities. In addition, she is interested in increasing human capacity through strength-based approaches. Her work has been published in the *Leadership Quarterly*, *The Graziadio Business Report*, and several book chapters. She regularly presents at the Academy of Management and Western Academy of Management. Dr. Feyerherm currently serves in a five-year leadership position of the Organization Development and Change Division of the Academy of Management.

Svante Lifvergren, M.D., currently works as development director in the Strategic Management Committee at the Hospital Group of Skaraborg (SkaS), where he is also a resident consultant physician with more than 20 years of clinical experience. He is also one of the managers of CHI, Centre for Healthcare Improvement. CHI is located at the Chalmers University of Technology, and the Centre focuses on improvement, research, and education pertaining to sustainable healthcare development.

Philip Mirvis is an organizational psychologist whose studies and private practice concerns large-scale organizational change, the character of the workforce and workplace, and business leadership in society. An advisor to businesses and NGOs in five continents, he has authored 10 books on his studies including *The Cynical Americans* (social trends), *Building the Competitive Workforce* (human capital), *To the Desert and Back* (a business transformation case), and *Beyond Good Company: Next Generation Corporate Citizenship* (with Bradley Googins and Steve Rochlin). Mitchell Marks and Mirvis have recently authored their second edition of *Joining Forces* (on mergers and acquisitions). Mirvis has a B.A. from Yale University and a Ph.D. in organizational psychology from the University of Michigan.

Susan Albers Mohrman is senior research scientist at the Center for Effective Organizations in the Marshall School of Business at the University of Southern California. Her research is in the areas of organization design and effectiveness. She is the author or co-author of many books, including *Achieving Strategic Excellence: An Assessment of Human Resource Organizations* (Stanford University Press, 2006) and *Useful Research: Advancing Theory and Practice* (Berrett-Koehler, 2011). Dr. Mohrman has been actively involved as a consultant and/or researcher to a wide variety of organizations instituting innovative management systems and organizational designs. She received her Ph.D. in organizational behavior from Northwestern University.

Sally Breyley Parker is president and founder of Currere, Inc., an organizational development and design firm that is helping build the human and social capital for vital and sustainable organizations, communities, and regions. She and her firm have contributed expertise in collaboration, trans-organizational design, and leadership development to a variety of sustainability initiatives. These include Sustainable Cleveland 2019, the Cuyahoga River Valley (the regeneration of a multicounty river valley), and numerous collaborations supporting the transformation of pre-K through 12 urban public education in Cleveland, OH. She and her family live in Shaker Heights, OH.

Jan Green Rebstock has over 11 years of experience managing environmental policy and permitting issues for complex public infrastructure and development projects. Jan is currently environmental project manager at the Port of Los Angeles, where she has successfully completed the environmental review process for the Port's LA Waterfront Program, a series of waterfront redevelopment projects covering over 500 acres that showcase the Port's commitment to sustainability and total over $1.5 billion in construction costs. Both environmental impact reports for the waterfront projects have received Outstanding Environmental Analysis awards from the Association of Environmental Professionals. Jan is currently managing the environmental review process for expanding the Port's second largest cargo container terminal and the development of a marine science research center and green technology business park. As the Port's Sustainability Liaison, she is responsible for coordinating sustainability initiatives and annual reporting.

Jan is doctoral student at the University of Southern California pursuing a degree in policy, planning, and development with a focus on sustainability. Her research interests include sustainable business models, organizational change, and green technologies. She lives with her husband Matthew in West Hollywood, CA.

Abraham B. (Rami) Shani is professor of organization behavior and management at the Orfalea College of Business, California Polytechnic State University and research professor at the School of Management, Politecnico di Milano, Milan, Italy. He received his Ph.D. in organizational behavior from Case Western Reserve University in 1981. His main research interest concerns work and organization design, organizational change and development, collaborative research methodologies, learning in and by organizations, and sustainable work systems. In addition to his published articles, chapters, and presentations, he is the author, co-author, or editor of *Creating Sustainable Work Systems* (2002, 2009), *Behavior in Organizations* (9th edition, 2009), *The Handbook of Collaborative Management Research* (2008), *Learning By Design: Building Sustainable Organizations* (2003), *Collaborative Research in Organizations: Foundations for Learning, Change and Theoretical Development* (2004), and *Research in Organization Change and Development* (2009, 2010 – an annual research series co-edited with W. Pasmore and R. Woodman, Emerald).

Christopher G. Worley (Ph.D., University of Southern California) is senior research scientist at the Center for Effective Organizations (USC's Marshall School of Business) and professor of management in Pepperdine University's Master of Science in Organization (MSOD) program. Dr. Worley's most recent books, co-authored with Ed Lawler, are *Management Reset* and *Built to Change*. He also authored *Integrated Strategic Change* and with Tom Cummings has co-authored five editions of *Organization Development and Change*, the leading textbook on organization development. His articles on agility and strategic organization design have appeared in the *Journal of Applied Behavioral Science*, *Journal of Organization Behavior*, *Sloan Management Review*, and *Organizational Dynamics*. He and his family live in San Juan Capistrano, CA.

INDEX